Francis A. Drexel
LIBRARY

Books For College Libraries
Third Edition

Core Collection

Beyond Ideology

Dante Germino

Rockefeller Foundation Field Staff Member,

Visiting Professor of Political Science,

University of the Philippines

BEYOND IDEOLOGY

THE REVIVAL OF
POLITICAL THEORY

JA71
.G37

96960

Harper & Row

Publishers

New York, Evanston, and London

To Virginia

CONTENTS

PREFACE ix

Part I: The Nature of Political Theory

ONE THE ALLEGED DECLINE OF POLITICAL
THEORY 1

TWO POLITICAL THEORY AS A TRADITION OF
INQUIRY 17

Part II: The Assault upon Political Theory

THREE THE IDEOLOGICAL REDUCTIONISM OF TRACY,
COMTE, AND MARX 45

FOUR POSITIVISM, THE NEW POLITICAL SCIENCE, AND
THE DECLINE OF POLITICAL THEORY 67

Part III: The Saving Remnant: the Survival of the Theoretical Perspective in the Age of Ideology and Positivism

FIVE PHILOSOPHICAL CURRENTS OF RESISTANCE TO
THE POSITIVIST ASCENDANCY 89

SIX THE PARTIAL SURVIVAL OF POLITICAL THEORY
IN THE ELITIST SCHOOL 109

Part IV: The Revival of Political Theory

SEVEN THE CONTEMPORARY REVIVAL OF POLITICAL
THEORY: OAKESHOTT, ARENDT, JOUVENEL,
AND STRAUSS 131

EIGHT   ERIC VOEGELIN'S CONTRIBUTION TO
CONTEMPORARY THEORY   161

Part V: Political Theory and the Open Society

NINE   BEHAVIORALISM AND THE IDEA OF THE CLOSED
SOCIETY   187

TEN   POLITICAL THEORY AND THE OPEN SOCIETY   214

APPENDIX   BIBLIOGRAPHICAL NOTES   239

INDEX   247

PREFACE

The plan for this book was conceived in 1960–1961, when a grant under the Rockefeller Foundation's Political and Legal Philosophy Program and a leave from Wellesley College made possible a year of research and reflection in London and Munich. I am deeply grateful to these institutions for this opportunity. Chapter Eight, with minor revisions and additions, previously appeared in *The Review of Politics* (Vol. 26, No. 3, July, 1964, 378–402); it is included herein with permission of the editors. An early attempt to state the general argument of this volume may be found in my article "The Revival of Political Theory" (*The Journal of Politics*, Vol. 25, August, 1963, 437–460). Most of the book was written during the academic year 1965–1966, my first year in the land of beauty and grace that is the Philippines.

Leon Bramson, John H. Hallowell, John R. Rodman, and Kenneth W. Thompson read the manuscript at an earlier stage and offered detailed and invaluable suggestions. Together with Alfred E. Prettyman, Executive Editor at Harper & Row, these friends have encouraged me more than I can say. It has not been possible for me, however, to incorporate all of their suggestions, and any errors of fact and mistakes in judgment which remain are entirely my own.

The able clerical assistance of Miss Pilar P. Basilio and Miss Ching A. Castro is gratefully acknowledged.

This book is dedicated to my wife.

DANTE GERMINO

Quezon City, Philippines
June, 1967

Beyond Ideology

PART I ⚜ THE NATURE
OF POLITICAL THEORY

ONE: ᏬHE ALLEGED DECLINE
OF POLITICAL THEORY

Political theory, according to numerous observers, is in a bad way.
Alfred Cobban and David Easton have written of its "decline."[1] Peter
Laslett and Robert A. Dahl have proclaimed its "death."[2] These are
not unrepresentative judgments; within the political science profession
as a whole, these views are frequently echoed. One political scientist
has even referred, rather infelicitously, to political theory as being "in
the doghouse."[3]

It is not out of any desire to engage in vain and fruitless polemics
that I challenge the validity of these assertions. Were this only a
matter of terminological niceties in a given scholarly profession, one
would be content to let the matter drop and go on with his work.
"For more comfort it were for us," as Richard Hooker has written
in the Preface of his *Laws of Ecclesiastical Polity*, not "in such dis-
membered sort" to spend our days "in a tedious persecuting of weari-
some contentions."

[1] For Alfred Cobban, see his article "The Decline of Political Theory," *Political Science Quarterly*, LXVIII (September, 1953), 321-337, and his book *In
Search of Humanity* (New York, Braziller, 1960), pp. 20-29, 229-245. Easton's
views are principally contained in his volume *The Political System* (New
York, Knopf, 1953), chap. 10.

[2] Peter Laslett, Introduction to *Philosophy, Politics and Society*, first series
(New York, Barnes & Noble, 1957); Robert A. Dahl, "Political Theory,"
World Politics, XI (October, 1958), 89-102.

[3] Neal Riemer, *The Revival of Democratic Theory* (New York, Appleton-
Century-Crofts, 1962), p. 1.

Rather, it is out of the conviction that the revival of political theory is one of the momentous intellectual and cultural developments of our time, and that blindness in the face of this occurrence is indicative of a profound intellectual crisis, that I have written this volume.

"Political theory" is employed in this volume with reference to a tradition of inquiry extending at least from Plato to Hegel. My argument may be summarized as follows:

1. The paradigmatic or master thinkers in this tradition possess certain traits which at once join them together and set them apart from publicists, utopians, and ideologists.

2. This tradition, although dangerously eclipsed during the past 150 years by inimical intellectual forces and political movements, is in our time undergoing a noteworthy resurgence.

3. This resurgence deserves the support of all thoughtful people who are today concerned with the preservation of the open society. The specific meaning of the term "open society," as herein conceived, will be explored as the work proceeds.

The myopia of many present-day political scientists respecting the revival of political theory going on in their midst is rooted in a fundamental misunderstanding about what political theory has been in the past. More often than not, the works of Plato, Aristotle, Aquinas, Rousseau, Hegel and others are regarded as more "normative" than "empirical," and political science is sharply distinguished from "political philosophy," or from political theory in the traditional sense. Thus, Harold D. Lasswell and Abraham Kaplan, operating on the basis of the neopositivist separation of "factual" and "valuational" propositions, come to the following conclusions about some of the masterpieces of political theory:

> A rough classification of a sample of 300 sentences from each of the following yielded these proportions of political philosophy (demand statements and valuations) to political science (statements of fact and empirical hypotheses): Aristotle's Politics, 25 to 75; Rousseau's Social Contract, 45 to 55 . . . Machiavelli's Prince, by contrast, consisted entirely (in the sample) of statements of political science in the present sense.[4]

---

[4] Harold D. Lasswell and Abraham Kaplan, *Power and Society* (London, Routledge, 1952), p. 118. It would be difficult to say whether this statement betrays a deeper misunderstanding of Aristotle and Rousseau or of Machiavelli. In any event, it fails to reveal even the vaguest awareness of what these political theorists set out to do.

The great treatises, we are told, are a mixed bag, a confusion of factual statements and value judgments. Only in the twentieth century does a self-conscious and "purified" empirical political science become possible. Lasswell and Kaplan's view of traditional political theory (the supposedly scientific Machiavelli excepted) as containing numerous propositions "hopelessly removed from empirical control" is frequently encountered in the literature of contemporary political and social science. On occasion, the entire tradition of Western ethical, theological, and political speculation is dismissed as sheer superstition and soothsaying—as "soul stuff" in the memorable words of Arthur Fisher Bentley, one of the fathers of contemporary American behavioralist political science. To quote from a more recent text of the "behavioral persuasion":

> There are, of course, many ways in which one may attempt to "explain" human behavior. For example, it used to be thought, and some people still believe, that the behavior of individuals is determined by the activity of spirits. "Evil" people (that is, those people who violate the generally accepted standards of how people should behave in the society) are considered to be under the influence of "evil" spirits; "good" people (that is, those who follow the generally accepted standards of how people should behave in the society) are considered to be under the influence of "good" spirits. Much religious thought has been devoted to the study of various kinds of spirits and the consequences for human behavior which result from being under the influence of one type of spirit as opposed to another. . . .
>
> This kind of explanation of human behavior we shall call normative theory. It relates to the kinds of questions about what man "should" or "ought" to do in order to lead the "good" life. Normative theorists include religious leaders, theologians, certain kinds of philosophers (for example, Confucius, Plato, Aristotle, Rousseau, and Mill), moralists, and others who attempt to determine the "proper" behavior for man that will lead to the "good" life and perhaps, in some religions, a "heavenly" life after death.[5]

Without exaggeration it can be said that something akin to the above conception of political theory is held by a sizeable minority of contemporary political and social scientists. These men are so confident that they are riding the crest of a wave and that a new scientific era

[5] Lewis W. Froman, Jr., *People and Politics* (Englewood Cliffs, N.J., Prentice-Hall, 1962), p. 16.

of history is about to unfold, that they fully expect the virtually total disappearance of traditional political theory in respectable intellectual circles. The history of political speculation runs the gamut "from lore to science," as Harry Elmer Barnes once put it. The "lore" of Plato and Hegel is being replaced by the "science" of Lasswell and Simon. In the eyes of extreme behavioralists, therefore, the "decline" of political theory is to be greeted with rejoicing as evidence of momentous intellectual progress for the human species.

Not all chroniclers of the presumed decline or demise of traditional political theory greet the news with enthusiasm. There are thoughtful observers such as Easton, Dwight Waldo, and Cobban who continue to insist that the construction of political theories in the grand manner of our prepositivist past is an undertaking not to be despised. Cobban fears that the decline of political theory will dry up the springs of reform in society and that democracy will go begging for champions to "justify" her. Easton insists that the formulation of "moral theory" must remain an important task of the political theorist, although it should increasingly take second place to the construction of "causal theory," which offers general conceptual schemes and specific hypotheses for eventual testing through "empirical" observation. The "adoption of a correct conception of moral relativism," says Easton, need not lead political theorists to forswear the promulgation of moral ideals for society. The political theorist must not shrink from indulging his creative imagination to lay out his "total scheme of preferences" about how society should be organized, and indeed should reconstruct a political system *de novo* and in his own image.[6] Easton's view finds support in the writings of Dwight Waldo, who also agrees that moral theory, although unscientific and only the expression of a personal scheme of preferences by an articulate individual, is nonetheless urgently needed at the present time. "Political theorists should undertake 'imaginative moral architecture,' and indulge their creative imaginations in utopia-building. . . . Whose function is it, if not the political theorist's, to project ways of organizing the political aspects of our lives?"[7]

As the ensuing pages will attempt to demonstrate, the difficulty

[6] Cobban, *The Political System*, *op. cit.*, pp. 230, 254, 261.

[7] Dwight Waldo, " 'Values' in the Political Science Curriculum," in Roland Young, ed., *Approaches to the Study of Politics* (Evanston, Ill., Northwestern University Press, 1958), pp. 96-111, at p. 111.

with the Cobban-Easton-Waldo school of thought is that it has confused normative political theory with political doctrine and utopia
construction. These men then proceed to look around them and to
find, with a few exceptions to be noted later, that the period since
1945 has been deficient in the production of doctrinal tracts which
claim to justify extant political systems as well as in utopias demand-
ing root and branch institutional change. They then conclude that
political theory is dead or in decline. The noteworthy resurgence of
interest in the history of political thought that has occurred in many
places in recent years is dismissed by the same authors as "historicism,"
or living off the presumably exhausted intellectual capital of the past
by writing histories of what previous political thinkers have taught.
This is held to be a sterile exercise, an escape from the job of "doing"
political theory which would be adequate for today.

The contention of this book is that political theory is in truth
nothing other than the critical science of politics, that political theory
is political science in the full sense of the term, that this critical
political science takes as its starting point the empirical fact of the
existing human person in the totality of his experience as a creature
in society, and that we are now living in a period—let us call it, with
Romano Guardini, the "post-modern" period—that has been in many
ways conducive to and which is witnessing the recrudescence of authentic political theory. This body of contemporary political theory
is at once a continuation and a new departure with reference to the
political theory of the past.

Today political theory is all too often misconceived as opinion,
subjective preference, or utopia, when as a matter of fact the great
political theorists of the past saw themselves as going beyond opinion
to arrive at a critical *understanding* of man's role in society. At the
very origin of this tradition of inquiry, Plato made the distinction
between *doxa* (opinion) and *epistēmē* (knowledge) and called what
he was doing in the *Republic, Statesman,* and *Laws epistēmē politikē*
(political knowledge or science). It is only with the nineteenth century and the subsequent neopositivist dispensation that the dichotomy
has arisen between political science in the narrow sense dealing with
observable "facts" of political behavior, and political theory or "philosophy" or ideology treating of subjective, unverifiable "value-judgments"
and preferences. There is a third way of approaching politics, and
this is the way of the great political theorists from Plato to Hegel.

Political theory is neither reductionist, behavioral science nor opinionated ideology; it is the critical study of the principles of right order in human social existence. As such, it claims to be "science," but not a science which confines itself to propositions capable of sensory verification. Political theory insists that a science of man in society must be rooted in the inwardness of human experience and that the basic principles of order can be tested or verified by meditatively reenacting the experience to which the propositions refer. Human experience has many levels, and it is no less real or factual for being inner experience instead of external observation or sensory response to a physical stimulus. Political theory insists with Heraclitus that an authentic political science must complement the "much-knowing" of our senses with the "deep-knowing" of our minds.

Political theory, used here in the Platonic manner as interchangeable with political science, is, or strives to be, knowledge as distinct from opinion (*doxa*), but both its scope and its methods differ extensively from the way those of the physical and biological sciences are often regarded.[8] Max Scheler has distinguished between sciences which have man at the periphery of their concern and sciences which place him at the center. Political science falls emphatically in the second category. Man in the fullness of his experience is the proper focus of the political scientist's attention, and whole areas of that experience—labelled 'ethical,' 'metaphysical,' or 'theological,'—may not arbitrarily be banished from the realm of science on the ground that they do not yield hypotheses testable by the precise canons of neopositivist methodology. The methods of science are determined by the subject matter to be investigated, and not the reverse; if the empirical fact of the existing human person cannot be investigated by means of the sensory observation of phenomenal regularities alone, then it must mean that these methods in themselves are inadequate and require supplementation by inward seeing through the "eye of the mind." Political theory is an experiential, as opposed to an exclusively experimental, science.

[8] Floyd W. Matson, in his illuminating study *The Broken Image: Man, Science and Society* (New York, Braziller, 1964), has argued persuasively that many social scientists have a profound misunderstanding of the contemporary methods and orientation of the natural sciences, claiming their notions of science are based on Newtonian concepts which, since Heisenberg, Einstein and numerous others, have been decisively superseded.

The Meaning of Theory

Political *theory* is the most appropriate term to employ in designating that intellectual tradition which affirms the possibility of transcending the sphere of immediate practical concerns and "viewing" man's societal existence from a critical perspective. The term "political theory" recommends itself as the most faithful rendition of the classical *epistēmē politikē*. Let us note carefully that originally political theory and political science were synonymous with each other. *Theōria* (theory) was the activity of searching out intellectually the principles that comprised *epistēmē* (science). Science was simply the reporting of the results of the theoretical probings of the mind. Plato and Aristotle (and the great masters of political theory after them) were incapable of thinking in terms of the contemporary distinction between an "empirical" political science concerned with "facts" and a subjective political theory concerned with "values." Political theory *was* political science in the full sense, and there could be no science without theory. Just as we may speak of theory as either the activity of theorizing or the recorded results of the theorizing, so political theory may legitimately and accurately be used as synonymous with political science.

Because there is today vast confusion over the meaning of theory and because there have been extensive assaults (to be discussed in succeeding chapters) on the validity and possibility of the theoretic enterprise as such, it will be useful to engage in a brief excursus on the meaning of this term. During the past century in particular, the very notion of theoretical knowledge, of knowledge for its own sake, has been in danger of being lost as knowledge increasingly tended to be regarded as know-how. Bacon's slogan that "knowledge is power" was taken with grim seriousness in many quarters. The "unity of theory and practice" which Karl Marx advocated came more and more to the fore, and the joys of contemplation were regarded with suspicion, contempt, or incomprehension by a culture becoming increasingly manipulative and technocratic. There were forces of the mind and spirit which resisted this trend, however, and particularly in the very recent period we have witnessed a rediscovery of the reality and relevance of dimensions of experience other than the immediately practical and productive. The contemporary revival of political theory in the West is a part of a general resurgence of the life of the spirit against the pressures of merely material interests and calculating rationality. The elemental truth that there is more to human existence than getting and spending, dominating and controlling, is being rediscovered in many quarters today.

Philologists tell us that from its earliest usage, *theōria* was associated with the activity of seeing, beholding, or "taking in." For the Greeks, to go on a *theōria* originally meant to undertake a "visit of inspection" to neighboring *poleis* in order to take in or witness their games and festivals. Given the pervasive influence which religion had in Greek life, these spectacles were also sacred in character. The verb *theōrein*, then, meant to behold or observe something in the sense of physically "seeing" it. The *theōros*, or theorist, was the man whose role it was to be a spectator or onlooker. Cicero, in the *Tusculan Disputations* (V,3,8), retained this archaic meaning when he compared the *theōros* to a spectator at the Olympic games.

With the development of philosophy in Greece, *theōria* took on an additional, more profound meaning: it was applied to the act of knowing, or inward seeing, through the eye of the mind. *Theōria*, Plato informs us in the *Republic*, is what the philosopher is engaged in when he experiences the *periagogē*, or conversion, and, escaping the prison of the cave, beholds the *agathon*, or the Good.[9] With Aristotle we have the introduction of the distinction between theoretical, practical, and productive knowledge. Theoretical knowledge is knowledge for its own sake rather than for some utilitarian end, and

[9] θεωρία stood initially for the "action of the θεωρός or of the θεωροί." The *theōroi* were magistrates assigned to witness or contemplate with reverence the celebration of a festival or religious ceremony of another *polis*, or to announce the holding of such ceremony. The root of the word may be θεᾶ or "spectacle" which is etymologically derived from the verb δραν (to see). Some authorities, e.g., Plutarch, think that its root may have been θεός (God). Typically, the magistrates were led by an archtheorist. These terms were used as late as the fourth century B.C. in connection with the Panhellenic games. From this visual, physical meaning of beholding and seeing, the term *theōria* became applied to the act of knowing, or seeing with the eye of the mind—for the Greeks, knowing was a concrete act and seeing and knowing were closely related. The spirit of reverent contemplation is carried over in the attitude of the Greek philosopher toward reality. In this latter sense the concept of the βίος θεωρητικός was developed in contradistinction to the βίος πρακτικός. See Articles "Teori" and "Teoria" in *Enciclopedia Italiana*, XXXIII, 534.

the *bios theōretikos*, or theoretic life, because it is most akin to the divine, is the highest form of human existence. Although the question is complicated as to whether Plato and Aristotle would have admitted *epistēmē politikē*, or political knowledge, into the citadel of theoretic science exactly understood, their teaching about political matters has an affinity with the archaic meaning of *theōria* in at least two respects. First of all, an act of observing, or seeing something real takes place when one theorizes; theory is not mere empty speculation, a projection of the writer's emotive preferences. A sector of real experience is isolated and observed. Second, the political theorist is in a decisive sense detached from the immediate political struggle: he has a different vantage point or perspective from that of the combatants in the political arena. The theorist is searching for truth rather than struggling for the victory of a party or a cause. He makes the decision to place his intellectual integrity above his popularity and to report what he sees rather than what he thinks his constituency wants to hear. His is, in many instances, a lonely road, for as Martin Heidegger has well said, *"Erklären heisst beleidigen"* ("to clarify is to offend"). Alfred Cobban to the contrary, the theorist is anything but a partisan, a "party man."[10] Turning his back on distortions, oversimplifications, sloganeering, and demagoguery, the political theorist speaks out with honesty on the perennial problems confronting man in his existence in society. What Matthew Arnold wrote of the literary critic applies also to the political theorist: "I say the critic must keep out of the region of immediate practice in the political, social, humanitarian sphere, if he wants to make a beginning for that more free speculative treatment of things, which may perhaps one day make its benefits felt even in this sphere, but in a natural and thence irresistible manner."[11] And Goethe was also

[10] See Cobban "The Decline of Political Theory," *op. cit.*, for an argument on the nature of political theory far removed from the one presented here. Cobban's error is to confuse the political theorist and the publicist. The great political theorists of the past allegedly "wrote with a practical purpose in mind. Their object was to influence actual political behavior. They wrote to condemn or support existing institutions, to justify a political system or persuade their fellow citizens to change it. . . . The political theorist, in his way, was a party man. . . ." (p. 330).

[11] Matthew Arnold, "The Function of Criticism at the Present Times," *Essays, Literary and Critical* (London, 1954), p. 17.

uttering something true about the political theorist when he decried the poet's giving himself up to a party: "As soon as he does this, he is lost as a poet [and] must bid farewell to his free spirit, his wide, unprejudiced view and draw over his ears instead the cap of limitation. . . ."[12]

In recent years, Alfred Schuetz has written a significant article about the characteristics of the theoretical attitude from the perspective of Husserl's phenomenological philosophy. According to Schuetz's analysis, the theorist performs an *epoché*, or suspension of experience, and puts the following aspects of everyday experience in "brackets": (1) his subjectivity or bias, (2) the practical orientation of the everyday "world of working" and (3) the "fundamental anxiety" about the fate of his projects. "Scientific theorizing," he wrote, "does not serve any practical purpose. Its aim is not to master the world but to observe and possibly to understand it." The results of science *may* be used in an effort to master the world, but "theorizing is one thing, dealing with the world of working is another."[13]

Elaborating these points, Schuetz concluded that the attitude of the disinterested observer is the "prerequisite for all theorizing. It consists in the abandoning of the system of relevances which prevails within the practical sphere of the natural attitude." It may even be said that the theorist performs a " 'leap' into the disinterested attitude" and thereby becomes "free from the fundamental anxiety and free from all the hopes and fears arising from it."[14] This fundamental anxiety may be the spur to theorizing, but once the leap is made into the realm of *theōria* this anxiety is put in brackets.

There must be certain clarifications and emendations of Schuetz's conclusions before we will be entitled to appropriate them for political theory proper. The detachment or "distinterested" attitude which Schuetz quite properly stresses as essential for the theorist is particularly difficult to achieve in ethical and political studies and must be understood to have a special meaning for them. Detachment certainly does not mean inhuman indifference, ethical neutrality, absence of

---

[12] Quoted in Reinhold Aris, *History of Political Thought in Germany from 1789 to 1815* (New York, Russell, 1965).

[13] Alfred Schuetz, "On Multiple Realities," *Philosophy and Phenomenological Research*, V (September, 1944), 533-575 at 564.

[14] *Ibid.*, 565.

political passion, or moral eunuchism. Nor does it imply an escapist flight from the problems of the world. All the giants in the history of political theory appear to have held strong views regarding the burning public issues of their day. Indeed, their strong interest in these issues may be said to have brought them to reflect on politics in the first place. In the course of such reflection, however, they were led to transcend the arena of partisan combat, to renounce or at least place in a secondary position the goal of pursuing public office and the implementation of a specific program in order to consider the general principles of right order in the psyche and in society. In the process, their thought moves to a different level, the level of elucidating principles of action valid for men as men.

The political theorist is or strives to be a philosopher, and a philosopher, as Plato saw so clearly, is a lover of wisdom and truth. This means, of course, that the theorist's attitude of disinterest scarcely extends to the realm of truth. The theorist is profoundly interested in and committed to knowledge and truth. As Jacques Maritain has expressed the matter: "Philosophy is essentially a disinterested activity, directed toward truth loved for its own sake, not utilitarian activity over things."[15] It is precisely his interest in and attachment to a truth that transcends all practical considerations that drives the political theorist to adopt wherever and to whatever degree possible a disinterested and detached relationship vis-à-vis the contending interests and forces in the world of *praxis*. Of course, common sense and a minimal ethical awareness, to say nothing of his commitment to truth and the possibility of independent inquiry, would impel him overtly to oppose any attempt by a totalitarian system to conquer the world. In that sense, the political theorist takes sides. The novel attempts by twentieth-century totalitarian movements to destroy systematically the dignity of the person have today made it essential for the theorist to oppose such regimes on principle and if possible to win them over to a recognition of that dignity through persuasion and reason. In all such endeavors (see Chapter Ten) the theorist walks a tightrope. He

---

[15] Jacques Maritain, *On the Use of Philosophy: Three Essays* (Princeton, Princeton University Press, 1961), p. 8. See also Robert E. Cushman, *Therapeia: Plato's Conception of Philosophy* (Chapel Hill, N.C., University of North Carolina Press, 1958), pp. 296 ff. for an acute and perceptive account of Plato's understanding of the philosopher as a man motivated by *eros* toward the transcendent *agathon*.

must avoid the peril of parochialism and irrationality particularly in the period known as the "cold war." He must contend *for* the dignity of the person and the freedom of the spirit, but not against the legitimate national interests of societies doctrinally opposed to his own.

Detachment for the political theorist does not imply neutrality to the contending forces in his immediate environment. Nor does it mean inhabiting a so-called ivory tower utterly removed from the practical world of politics wherein he can devote himself to constructing purely abstract models and concepts. It is not that the political theorist-scientist becomes disembodied, removing himself altogether from the world of human beings: it is rather that he sees that world from a new perspective and has a new scheme of priorities and relevances for his research and for his life. Political theory is not an escape mechanism, but an arduous calling.

The political theorist is concerned with the practical effect of his teaching, but not in the sense of looking to its implementation in this or that structural reform. He is concerned with substance rather than with structure. Such influence as he may have is, more often than not, subtle, indirect, and unrecognized beyond the purview of a limited circle of readers and students. There is always the risk that his voice may not be heard at all, at least not in his own time. The satisfactions accruing to the theorist will be correspondingly less tangible and immediate than those enjoyed by the successful practising politician or the best-selling publicist.

A Japanese political scientist, Masao Marayuma, has pointed out that the "spirit of abstinence" necessary to any critical science (or theory) of politics is won only after inner struggle and discipline, for "abstinence is meaningful only where desire is present. The keener the inner struggle against desire, the greater the moral value of abstinence."[16] Once one embarks on the scientific analysis of political reality, "all his political . . . likes and dislikes must be subordinated to the cognitive process. So long as he is not inspired with the spirit of abstinence, the only difference between his theoretical *magnum opus* and a party pamphlet will be the number of pages." Professor Marayuma also makes clear that objectivity in political analysis must

[16] Masao Marayuma, from a lecture on "Politics as a Science in Japan," in *Thought and Behavior in Modern Japanese Politics* (London, Oxford, 1963), p. 240.

never be allowed to take the form of a "whatever-wins-is-right type of opportunism."[17]

Objectivity in political theory comes not from the vain attempt to avoid evaluation and thereby appear impartial but through the adoption of critical standards and criteria of evaluation that are not transitory and parochial but are based on an experientially sound anthropology. The theorist's objectivity is reflected in the quality and validity of his critical standards. Authentic political theory, then, eschews both pseudo-objective descriptivism and opinionated ideology.

The Levels of Political Thought

Anyone who spends much time studying the history of political thought is immediately struck by the "unevenness" of the thinkers who come under review. Some figures deserve far more careful attention than others, and this fact cannot be accounted for exclusively on the basis of their influence, style, productivity, and "originality." For a certain class of writers is preoccupied with a wider range of problems and considers political man in a fashion different from the others. These men speak to us across the ages precisely because they investigate in a sustained way the perennial problems of societal order. Other men, although also reflecting in more than a perfunctory and commonplace way on the perennial questions of social existence, are so involved in the disputes prevailing in a particular historical period that they appear dated to us. They write tracts instead of treatises and, taking first principles for granted, devote themselves to the furthering of a given practical objective. Their writings are often fragmentary, excluding from their ken all material not directly related to the practical question at hand.

This distinction between two classes of writers on politics—let us call them theorists and publicists—seems quite obvious but has to be reiterated today when the tendency in some quarters is to reduce all political thinkers to the same level (that of ideology), ignoring gross differences in the quality of their thought. Great emphasis is then laid upon their class interests and personality structures. While the data offered by the "sociology of knowledge" are of obvious relevance in explaining the thinking of some propagandists for mass

[17] *Ibid.*, p. 235. Max Weber, in his famous essay on "Objectivity in the Social Sciences" had similar things to say about the role of the social scientist.

movements, they are of scant significance in helping us understand a Plato or a Hegel. Nor are all writers merely or even chiefly reflections of a given "climate of opinion"; some of them help to produce or change that climate.

There is legitimate debate over precisely where to draw the line between the two classes of political thinkers whom we have discussed, i.e., between those who have made the leap to the perspective of theory and those who remain for the most part tied to the demands and urgencies of the immediate practical situation. It is always possible to demonstrate the existence of some degree of theoretical reflection in the most practically minded publicist as well as at least some involvement with immediate, transient issues in the work of the most profound theorist. Yet surely our powers of discrimination would appear to have deserted us entirely were we to fail to recognize that between an Aristotle and a Phaleas of Chalcedon, a Thomas Aquinas and a Giles of Rome, a Machiavelli and a Botero, a Hobbes and a Filmer, a Rousseau and a Condorcet, a Hegel and a Joseph de Maistre, a great gulf exists. This is the gulf between political theory and political doctrine, and the two types of reflection on politics diverge fundamentally in orientation, scope, emphasis, tone, and terminological sophistication.

Although judgment varies among scholars about whom to include as inhabiting the mansions of theory, agreement is quite general that the list should contain at least the names of Plato, Aristotle, Machiavelli, Hobbes, Rousseau, and Hegel. Many would want to widen it to take in Augustine, Aquinas, Richard Hooker, Montesquieu, and T. H. Green; some would add the names of Bodin, Locke, and others. Regardless of the exact composition of the list (in addition to the recognized masters), it is obvious that a tradition of inquiry exists which reflects on politics in a manner and idiom altogether different from that employed at the level of the political struggle.

Conclusion: The Plan of This Volume

The thesis of this volume is that the "decline of political theory" in our time is a myth. The myopia prevalent among numerous social scientists with respect to the current revival of political theory by Voegelin, Jouvenel, Oakeshott, Arendt, Maritain, Reinhold Niebuhr, and others, is apparently attributable chiefly to a profound misconception of the nature and function of political theory itself. If political theory be understood as synonymous with doctrines or "isms"—and to some authors and teachers even Communism and Fascism are political theories[18]—then of course in the West the period since 1945 has indeed been one of the decline in the manufacture and elaboration of such doctrines. We have entered a period in the history of political thought that is "beyond ideology." A new critical freedom has been gained which is most propitious for the recovery of political theory or political science in the authentic meaning of these terms.

Nonetheless, strong currents of resistance remain indifferent or opposed to the success of this venture which has as its goal the restoration of man, as human being, to the place previously occupied by isms dealing in abstractions and illusions. The process of demythologization of our political vocabulary is a painful one because it is difficult to give up familiar slogans and shibboleths, especially when they claim the prestige of science. Things would be simpler in a closed society dominated by isms, and political theory complicates matters by exposing the oversimplifications, false promises, and experiential inadequacies of such doctrines. But to treat a complex and multidimensional reality as if it were simple and unidimensional is the work not of wisdom but of manipulative *hybris*. Unless the theoretical attitude to politics is recovered and becomes again an active force in the intellectual life of the West, then this civilization instead of contributing to the enhancement of human life may well, by virtue of its vast influence, lead mankind into a dark night of the spirit. Such an outcome is in no sense inevitable, however, and the following pages will chronicle numerous reasons if not for optimism, at least for hope that it will be avoided.

In order to see the contemporary revival of political theory in perspective, it will be necessary to trace the fortunes of theory in the previous age of ideology. Broadly speaking, the period from the French Revolution to World War II was one which witnessed the ascendancy of ideology and the near eclipse of political theory. During this time, increasing numbers of scholars whose function it might have been to elaborate a critical theory of politics have retreated into the neopositivist cul-de-sac. Some have persisted in the face of strenuous efforts

[18] See, for example, the all too typical anthology for use in political science courses by Carl Cohen, *Communism, Fascism, and Democracy: The Theoretical Foundations* (New York, Random House, 1961).

at methodological purification to make positivism itself an ideology. As today we move with the representatives of political theory beyond ideology, so also must we move beyond positivism. This volume will attempt to place the contemporary revival of political theory in the context of its resistance and opposition to both positivism and ideology.

Before getting on with this task, however, it will be necessary in the following chapter to describe more fully the character of political theory as it was conceived by the great masters of the past. If today we are confused about the meaning of political theory—and contradictory meanings abound in the current literature of political science —we have a way out of such confusion. It is scarcely necessary to stipulate arbitrarily our definition, for we have already before us a rich tradition of inquiry waiting to be interrogated. Although his analysis is mistaken in various respects, Alfred Cobban made at least one valid observation when he wrote that, fortunately, "we have not to *invent* political theory; that was invented long ago. If there is a right way of considering its problems, I think we should be modest enough to believe that it might possibly be the way of all the greater political thinkers of the past. . . ."[19]

The nature of political theory is embodied in its history. Strictly speaking, in the philosophical sense political theory has no "essence" because it does not have independent ontological status. As it has developed historically in the western civilizational area,[20] it is the human

[19] Cobban, "The Decline of Political Theory," *op. cit.*, 330. Cobban's error is that he fails to make the necessary fundamental distinction between different levels of political thought, so that publicists like Bentham and Laski (can Laski be one of the "greater political thinkers of the past?") are lumped with Plato and Rousseau. The failure to make elementary and obvious distinctions of rank is evident in numerous books and articles published in recent times. How often one sees political thinkers of vastly different rank, e.g., Plato and Drucker, coupled in such a way that they sound equivalent philosophically.

[20] It would take us too far afield to deal with the obvious objection that political theory is itself parochial or culture-bound rather than being universally valid if it is a product of only one specific civilization, that of the West. On principle, I agree with the conclusions reached by M. Hauriou and Eric Voegelin [see the latter's *Order and History*, vol. 1 (Baton Rouge, Louisiana State University Press, 1956)]. It is not in this instance a limitation to be bound to the culture which has developed the most fully differentiated concepts and symbols for understanding the problem of order in society. Such

activity which, through the elaboration of critically refined concepts, attempts to represent and point to realities which bear upon the problem of order in society. Accordingly, it is to that history that we turn in the following chapter.

TWO: POLITICAL THEORY AS A TRADITION OF INQUIRY

The great masters of political theory from Plato to Hegel display an impressive unity in the style of their thought. Their writings reveal certain formal characteristics common to them all which set them off from publicists and latter-day ideologists. These traits will be enumerated and discussed in the final section of this chapter. With regard to the substance or content of their teaching, there are of course divergences, in some instances seemingly profound ones, between individual thinkers. This is scarcely surprising because a tradition is not a grey, monolithic uniformity but a growing and developing entity which admits of variety within a common framework. A tradition is a unity of diversity. Inevitably, there will be some variation in the symbols and concepts employed and the weight given certain aspects of experience. But, concerning the substance of their teaching, the great representatives of political theory do not leave us with a bewildering chaos of answers to the key questions confronting man in his societal existence. Broadly speaking, and without oversimplification or distortion, it can be said that there exist within the single tradition of political theory two subtraditions. Following Jacques Maritain's fruitful distinction, these may be denominated the sub-

---

a position in no way implies chauvinism, ethno-centricism, blindness to the right of other civilizations to preserve their heritage, or lack of appreciation for the intellectual and spiritual achievements of those civilizations. In China, India, and the civilization molded by Islam, the break-through from a closed to an open society was also achieved. One of the principal tasks of contemporary political theory in the West is to enrich its perspective with greater knowledge of the contribution of the non-Western higher religions to the science of order.

traditions of "theocentric humanism" and "anthropocentric humanism." Although to present the content and implications of these
theoretical currents in an adequate fashion would require a massive
and detailed history of political theory, it is possible for our present
purposes to indicate briefly the character of each subtradition.

Theocentric Humanism

The keynote of theocentric humanism is sounded by Plato in
Laws 716: "God is the measure of all things." This dictum, which
is hardly an arbitrary pronouncement but has as its basis the entire
exploration of the experience of the philosopher in numerous dialogues,
is explicitly juxtaposed by Plato to the sophist Protagoras' teaching
that "man is the measure of all things—of things being as they are
and of things not being what they are not." The philosopher, the
highest, most fully developed human type, is a "theomorph," or a
man who measures himself by divine Being. The philosopher is the
man who takes God for his measure and who aspires, within the
limitations of his humanity, to be "like God." In the splendid language of the *Republic,* so well captured in Cornford's translation,
the philosopher

> contemplates a world of unchanging and harmonious order, where
> reason governs and nothing can do or suffer wrong; and, like
> one who imitates an admired companion, he cannot fail to fashion
> himself in its likeness. So the philosopher, in constant com-
> panionship with the divine order of the world, will reproduce
> that order in his soul and, so far as man may, become god-
> like. . . ."[1]

In fashioning the model of the philosopher, Plato was aided not
only by the intellectual tradition going back to Xenophanes, Parmenides, and Heraclitus, but also by the concrete example of Socrates.
The martyrdom of Socrates was the critical event in the development
of philosophical truth as opposed to the truth of the *polis* myth. The
opening of the psyche toward attunement with the transcendental
ground of being achieved by Socrates in his own life was a victory
for mankind at large. In the *Euthyphro* one witnesses the epoch-

[1] *Republic,* 500 (Cornford translation, New York, Oxford University Press,
p. 209).

making confrontation between Socrates, the representative of the open morality of the spirit, and Euthyphro, who defended the closed morality of the civil religion. The clash of opposing moralities, based on different spiritual experiences, is repeated in the *Gorgias*, except that this time the encounter is between Socrates and the "enlightened" sophistic intellectual who takes advantage of and enhances the moral decadence which has begun with the loss of belief in the traditional pieties. The conflict between philosopher and sophist is a major theme of the *Republic*. Immured in the deep recesses of the cave, the sophist consciously seeks to attune himself with the *doxa* (opinion) of society. The sophist becomes superbly expert in interpreting the succession of shadows on the wall of the cave, mistaking appearance for reality.

In his allegory of the cave, Plato portrays philosophy as an existential conversion from a perverted mode of existence, as liberation from the prison of closed existence. When the philosopher accomplishes the *periagogē*, or turning around, he beholds the vision of the *agathon*. He inwardly "sees" the highest good, or the *ens realissimum*. The *agathon* is "beyond being" and is the source of all particular goods. It lights the inner world of spirit as the sun lights the visible world. The Good is neither sensual pleasure, nor wealth, nor honor, nor power. The Good is God. The chief end of man, insofar as it lies within his capacity, is to know and to do The Good. Man's humanity is defined with reference to his capacity to participate through his partial and finite reason in the divine reason. The soul, or psyche, is the medium by which man experiences transcendence. The Good must be experienced rather than "learned" as a piece of information or "defined" as an abstract concept. To follow The Good is to follow the highest ("most godly") element in the soul—the *logos*, or the rational element.

Plato's anthropology establishes a scale of character types extending from the philosopher at the apex through the intermediary strata (comprising men of "true opinion") to the tyrant at the base. The tyrant has betrayed his essential humanity by following that which is most bestial in his nature. He turns out to be, thanks to Plato's fascination with numbers, "729 times as unhappy" as the just man or philosopher.[2] A pathology of corruption is expounded in the parables of the timocratic, oligarchical, democratic, and tyrannical character

[2] *Ibid.*, 587.

types. Recognition is thereby made of the fact that most men live underdeveloped lives and that the "remnant who . . . consort with philosophy will be small indeed."[3] While all are called, few choose to enter the ranks of philosophic or theomorphic men.

Corresponding to his scale of character types is Plato's scale of types of polity. The model of the best regime (explicated in the *Republic*) is an extrapolation from the psyche of the most fully developed human type, the philosopher. Just as reason rules the spirited and appetitive elements of the individual philosopher's psyche, so in the best regime the philosophic character types rule the spirited and appetitive parts of the total population. Similarly, the various defective regimes (timocracy, oligarchy, democracy, and tyranny) are reflections of the relative disorder in the psyches of their ruling and ascendant strata. To Plato, institutions do not grow out of "rock and stone" but out of the human beings who collectively constitute them.

Plato's political theory, in addition to indicating a hierarchy of character types and the polities corresponding to them, grappled with the problem of the dilution of the paradigm. As a political realist,[4] Plato was well aware that the *aristē politeia* (best regime) was, save by some divine chance, impossible of achievement within history for the simple reason that philosophers, who are in essence lovers of wisdom rather than power, will not engineer a *coup d'état*. Nor will they be invited to rule, because the vast majority of the populace either rejects the philosophers' claim to authority outright or only partially acknowledges it from the distance of imperfect understanding. All of this means that the paradigm cannot be applied directly and without alteration or dilution to existential reality.

The problem which Plato confronts in the *Laws* is how to inject a measure of philosophical truth into a society run by nonphilosophers. The regime set forth in the *Laws* is a "second-best" polity or "best practicable" regime. The best that the philosopher can hope for in practical terms is to rule indirectly through a detailed set of *nomoi* (laws and customs) which he himself has devised and which incorporates as much of the truth of philosophical existence as relatively favorable historical circumstances will permit. From the open society of the *aristē politeia* (which nonetheless remains the paradigm in the

---

[3] *Ibid.*, 495.

[4] He was also, of course, and in a different sense, a philosophical realist.

absolute sense) we descend to the partially open society of the *Laws*. The second-best *polis* of the *Laws* is a "mixed regime" in that wealth, age, birth, and numbers (a concession to democracy) join wisdom as criteria determining the participation in political rule. The members of the Nocturnal Council, and most august body in the society, experience the universe as Cosmos (order) rather than as Chaos, but this understanding is not gained directly through the inward seeing of philosophy but indirectly through the philosopher's authority as reflected in the laws and through the study of the visible order of the heavens. In contrast to the *Republic*, which omits many matters of basic importance, the *Laws* is extremely lengthy and detailed[5] because Plato conceived the realization of the regime therein described as a live possibility.

Although Plato did not hold his paradigmatic society to be realizable, he obviously thought the elaboration of such a model society to be of central concern to political theory or political science. The sketch of the best regime was not a pointless exercise of the imagination. First of all, the model society could and did serve as the critical standard by which the relative defectiveness of existing regimes was evaluated. The paradigm at once served the function of preventing the deification of any existing regime (all regimes being judged as imperfect to some degree with reference to the paradigm) and, thanks to the realistic awareness of the paradigm as at best an impossible possibility (to borrow a felicitous phrase from Reinhold Niebuhr), of avoiding the indiscriminate and hyperperfectionist rejection of existing regimes through failure to appreciate the degree of order which many of them contained.

A second consideration of Plato's in elaborating the paradigm was that an understanding of the principles of right order in society will aid us in achieving right order in our own individual psyches, and, if this achievement becomes a reality in the lives of enough people, the effect will be to change the society imperceptibly and indirectly. Individuals may choose to found the paradigmatic society "in themselves";[6] they can become statesmen or rulers in their own commonwealths. Therefore, in the larger sense it is no matter whether

---

[5] The *Laws* is by far the longest of Plato's dialogues and would presumably have been of even greater bulk had Plato lived to finish it. His pupil, Philip of Opus, made certain additions which may be assumed to be in keeping with the master's intentions.

[6] *Republic*, 591 (Cornford, pp. 319-320).

the polity outlined in the *Republic* is instituted or not because inevitably those who heed the call of philosophical existence will leaven the mass of the society in which they participate. The interior reorientation of the psyche (called *metanoia*, or "change of heart") experienced by the philosopher will have a profound effect on his own life as well as on the lives of those who are touched by his vision. These individuals will be led to impose demands on themselves and to leave the comfort and mediocrity of the cave, of existence in spiritual torpor. They can, therefore, never be content simply to adjust to the prevailing norms of society but, as representatives of a truth transcending society, must always live in "loving strife"[7] with their environment, as goads and gadflies, like Plato's mentor, Socrates, although hopefully without having to pay his ultimate penalty.

It will not be necessary in a detailed way to go into the Aristotelian political theory here, because in its essentials it was in agreement with that of Plato. The fact that the two great philosophers are in agreement is often overlooked by writers who give undue emphasis to Aristotle's criticism of the *Republic* in Book II of the *Politics*. Aristotle's intentions in this attack, which is studded with obvious and perhaps deliberate errors, can not be gleaned with certainty, but the most plausible explanation is that Aristotle, fearing that Plato had endangered the entire purpose of the paradigm by espousing communism for the philosophic guardians, wanted to make a fresh start for political theory by constructing a paradigm freed from the institutional excrescences of the *Republic*. He may well have concluded that Plato had unnecessarily left himself open to misinterpretation by men who would fail to understand that the *Republic* was a dialogue on the formation of the philosophic character type in an environment congenial to his development rather than a tract on social salvation through institutional tinkering. Accordingly, Aristotle, in Books VII and VIII of the *Politics*, presents what might be called a purified paradigm, which imitates Plato in putting education in character formation at its center but which departs from him in eliminating communism.

In his writings, principally the *Ethics*, *Politics*, and *Rhetoric*, Aristotle ranges over the entire field of *epistēmē politikē*, leaving like Plato, an imperishable legacy. His anthropology as expounded in the

---

[7] The phrase is Gabriel Marcel's, but it seems completely appropriate to describe the relationship of the Platonic Socrates to his own society.

Ethics serves even today as a point of departure for critical political theory. Here we find the masterful portrait of the *spoudaios,* or "mature man," and the experiential justification for his authority on metaphysical and ethical questions. In leading the life of contemplation, man encounters the fullness of his humanity in the *nous,* or intellect, and achieves a realization that "the intellect more than anything else *is* man." As J. A. K. Thompson renders the passage which more than any other expresses the substance of Aristotle's theocentric humanism:

> Yes, but such a life [the bios theoretikos] will be too high for human attainment. It will not be lived by us in our merely human capacity but in virtue of something divine within us, and so far as this divine particle is superior to man's composite nature, to that extent will its activity be superior to that of the other forms of excellence [aretai]. If the intellect is divine compared with man, the life of the intellect must be divine compared with the life of a human creature. And we ought not to listen to those who counsel us O man, think as man should and O mortal, remember your mortality. Rather ought we, so far as in us lies, to put on immortality and to leave nothing unattempted in the effort to live in conformity with the highest thing within us. Small in bulk it may be, yet in power and preciousness it transcends all the rest. We may in fact believe that this of the true self of the individual being the sovran and better part of him. It would be strange, then, if a man should choose to live not his own life but another's. Moreover, the rule, as I stated it a little before, will apply here—the rule that what is best and pleasantest for each creature is that which intimately belongs to it. Applying it, we shall conclude that the life of the intellect is the best and pleasantest for man, because the intellect more than anything else is the man. Thus it will be the happiest life as well.[8]

The theme of man as theomorph, of authentic human existence as openness toward the transcendental ground of being, is also central and fundamental to Stoic philosophy. To Zeno, the founder of Stoicism, the universe is the work of the divine *logos* (reason), and man is preeminently the creature who is capable of participating in and attuning himself with this *logos.* In Stoicism one detects very clearly the anticipation of Aquinas' dictum that natural law is the participa-

[8] *Nicomachean Ethics,* Book X, Thompson trans. (London, Penguin Books, 1953), p. 305.

tion of the rational creature in the eternal law of God. To Stoicism, the end of man is *homologoumenōs zēn*, or "life in attunement with the *logos*." Human existence is communal existence; one does not live alone but participates in a larger whole not of his own making. All parts of the universe are linked in one all-embracing Order. The Epicurean conception of the universe as a chaos of colliding atoms is rejected in favor of the experience of reality as Order. Men are partners with all being and brothers of each other by virtue of their common father, God, the divine *logos*, the *spermatikos logos* (seminal reason). The true and ultimate community of men is the *cosmopolis* of the *logos*, the universal commonwealth binding men together by a kinship of the spirit—through *homonoia* or "like-mindedness" that results from taking the divine *nous* (intellect) as measure—rather than by racial, ethnic, or class ties. Membership in the universal community of the spirit does not annul loyalty to the concrete-parochial communities in which men find themselves. But these communities may make only relative claims upon the person: they are themselves measured by a higher law, the law of nature, which transcends any statutes they can lay down. As Marcus Aurelius was to put it in the period of late Stoicism: "Every man has two countries: Rome and the universe."[9]

The Western tradition of theocentric humanism has three principal sources: classical philosophy, Judaism, and Christianity. In Judaism and Christianity revelation takes its place with reason as the medium through which man apprehends and is apprehended by the world-transcendent God. If philosophy is the reaching out of the psyche toward the invisible God, then revelation is the descent of the divine into history. Through the revelatory event, the divinity makes itself visible in a new and decisive way. While the structure of human existence does not change as the result of the divine descent into time, the interpretation of that existence changes profoundly for those who accept the truth of revelation and open themselves to the *metanoia* which it demands. Anyone who contemplates with seriousness the revelatory encounters of Moses with the burning bush or Elijah with the still small voice or who reads thoughtfully the celebration of the joys of existence under the God who although beyond the heaven of heavens made a covenant with Abraham and revealed him-

[9] See M. Pohlenz, *Die Stoa*, 2 vols., for the best treatment of Stoic philosophy.

self to Moses on Sinai cannot fail to perceive that existence is bathed in a new light. The human person in existence under God discovers himself as little lower than the angels and as made capable through the freedom of the spirit of soaring aloft with eagle's wings, as the Psalmist sings.

For Christianity, the divine *logos*, who in the beginning was with God and who was God and through whom the world came into being, "became flesh and lived among us."[10] "While all things were in quiet silence and night was in the midst of her course," the almighty Word "leapt down from heaven."[11] The fact of the Incarnation had stupendous and unparalleled consequences for the interpretation of history and these were treated by the greatest of the early Christian theologians, St. Augustine. History as the Sheol of civilizational cycles was overcome in favor of the view of history as the linear succession of unique events. Furthermore, the Incarnation was seen as the axial point of history; the Word became flesh only once and world history prior to this supreme revelatory event was *preparatio evangelica* while everything coming after it was anticlimatic and a "waiting for the end," the *eschaton*, which would be fulfilled beyond time. There would be no transfiguration of historical existence itself, no thousand-year reign of the saints on earth. Christ was experienced as present in his Church, which was in essence the continuation of the Incarnation and the font of sacramental grace. Both Augustine and Thomas Aquinas felt called upon to reject as "ridiculous fancies" the chiliastic interpretations of the book of Revelation espoused by the gnostic movements of their times.[12]

The reality of the Church in both its visible and invisible aspects made concrete and explicit the latent tendencies in Greek philosophy and Stoicism to disengage the order of truth from the order of power. The pronouncement of Pope Gelasius I, "Two there are, the royal power and the authority of the Holy Roman Pontiff," made the Two Realms principle of Matthew 22 a living institutional reality. The paradigmatic society for the Christian world was the single, universal Christian Commonwealth with its two distinct, yet parallel and interrelated orders, the *regnum* and the *sacerdotium*. The temporal power

[10] John 1:1-14.

[11] Wisdom 18:14-15.

[12] Augustine, *De Civitate Dei*, XX, chap. 7; Aquinas, *Summa Theologica*, I-II, Q.106, art. 4.

structure was not rejected but was seen as possessing its own dignity. However, it was placed on a proximate and secondary level to the Church's which ministered to man's *summum bonum*.

With regard to the question of the *summum bonum*, of such decisive significance to political theory conceived as the study of right order in human existence, Augustine, Aquinas, and Richard Hooker made noteworthy elaborations from the viewpoint of Christian revelation on the work already begun by Plato and Aristotle. This trio of Christian thinkers accepted the analysis of Greek philosophy as far as it went: they agreed that human existence is disordered when men follow such illusory ends as pleasure, power, glory, honor, or wealth as if any of these were in reality the chief end of man. And they agreed that the *vita contemplativa* was the highest human life, although its joys derived from the context of earthly existence were in themselves only a preparation for fulfillment beyond time in the *visio Dei*. To the natural perfection of man attainable by human reason, Aquinas and Hooker were to add the supernatural perfection through grace and revelation. For Christianity, not the *bios theoretikos* within time but eternal life beyond time is the true *summum bonum* for man. Reason and nature required perfection through revelation and grace. Thus, a further differentiation of the concepts of Greek philosophy was achieved by Christianity and resulted in a further development of the anthropology of theocentric humanism.

Richard Hooker, writing in the sixteenth century, sums up two thousand years of development of the theocentric humanist tradition in Western political thought in this magisterial paragraph in the *Laws of Ecclesiastical Polity*:

> Man doth seek a triple perfection: first a sensual, consisting in those things which very life itself requireth . . .; then an intellectual, consisting in those things which none underneath man is either capable of or acquainted with; lastly a spiritual and divine, consisting in those things whereunto we tend by supernatural means here, but cannot here attain unto them. . . . For man doth not seem to rest satisfied, either with fruition of that whereunto his life is preserved, or with performance of such actions as advance him most deservedly in estimation; but doth further covet . . . that which exceedeth the reach of sense; yet somewhat above the capacity of reason, somewhat divine and heavenly. . . . If the soul of man did serve only to give him

being in this life, then things appertaining unto this life would content him, as we see they do with other creatures. . . . With us it is otherwise. For although the beauties, riches, honours, sciences, virtues, and perfections of all men living, were in present possession of one; yet somewhat beyond and above all this there would still be sought and earnestly thirsted for. So that Nature even in this life doth plainly claim and call for a more divine perfection than either of these two that have been mentioned. (Of the Laws of Ecclesiastical Polity, I, XI, 4).[13]

Anthropocentric Humanism

Anthropocentric humanism is that tendency in political thought which takes man as the "measure of all things" (Protagoras) without explicitly considering the problem of his attunement with the transcendental ground of being. Thus, man in his intramundane existence becomes the basis for the model society. There is a corresponding shrinking of the experiential horizon, with transcendence being put aside in favor of concentration on the dimension of immanent existence. The *summum bonum* tends to become temporalized and is seen as worldly glory or peace or freedom. With Hobbes, indeed, we encounter a profound analysis of the *summum malum*, or highest evil, whose avoidance becomes the chief human task.

Transcendence and immanence are indispensable concepts for any ontological discourse. Transcendence refers to the source of existing things which of its nature must be over and beyond—or transcending—all existing things. Immanent or inner-worldly reality is all that is created, comes into being, and passes away; the material or physical world as experienced by the senses but also including inward consciousness of immediate, temporal existence. "Transcendence within immanence," a phrase employed a number of times in this volume, with reference to Croce, Oakeshott, and others, is not a true transcendence but results from the recognition of different "levels" to world-immanent existence, different modes of reflecting on and orienting oneself to that existence without making the decisive breakthrough to seeing all inner-worldly activity in relation to the transcendental ground. Transcendence within immanence may be designated "horizontal transcendence" as opposed to "vertical" or "authentic" transcendence.

[13] Richard Hooker, *Of the Laws of Ecclesiastical Polity*, I, 11, 4.

These distinctions should not be treated as exact "definitions," but as realities to be experienced. The apprehension of the transcendental ground of being as radically other than world-immanent reality is scarcely a private or idiosyncratic experience, however. Rather it follows ineluctably from the "experience of existence" (see the discussion of Voegelin in Chapter 8), the experience of creatureliness, of finitude.

It is significant that at the crucial point in the *Republic* when Plato sought to explicate the meaning of the experience of transcendence he did not offer a set of definitions but turned to allegory, thereby succeeding in doing all that language can do to illumine the transcendence-immanence distinction. The cave symbolizes world-immanent reality, while the sun in the upper world represents the *ens realissium*, the source of that reality, the ultimate ground of being. One can criticize, as Aristotle did, the Platonic doctrine of forms as an inadequate exposition of the problem, but the allegory of the cave more than compensates for the woodenness and clumsiness of the doctrine of forms with the suppleness and sensitivity of its imagery.

Modern political theory partakes in general of the anthropocentric subtradition within the broad stream of Western humanism. Modern political theory is prevented from deteriorating into dogmatic and messianic immanentism by its derivation from the tradition of theocentric humanism we have just described. While appearing to revolt, at least in part, against theocentric humanism, modern anthropocentric humanism retains a kinship and affinity with it by virtue of its achievement of a kind of inner-worldly or horizontal transcendence. The worlds of theory and practice, of essence and existence, of eternity and time are not merged but remain distinct in the works of the great modern theorists. Although the gradual process of the immanent-izing of symbols that occurs throughout the modern period is related in an indirect and complex way to the emergence of messianic political doctrines coming to the fore beginning with the French Revolution, nonetheless the differences between theorists such as Hobbes and Hegel and ideologists such as Comte and Marx are profound indeed.

Although many writers assert the contrary, it is false to view Machiavelli's *Prince* and *Discourses*, Hobbes's *Leviathan*, Rousseau's *Social Contract*, and Hegel's *Philosophy of Right* as either calls to revolution or defenses of the status quo. Along with their predecessors who comprised the theocentric subtradition, the modern greats fall under Karl Marx's indictment: they are men who sought in the first instance to *interpret* the world rather than to change it (or to keep it from changing, as the case may be). Their thinking is intractable for immediate practical purposes—this becomes obvious when one examines attempts to turn Hobbes or Hegel into precursors of Fascism or to make Rousseau the father of the French Revolution. All of these men are outsiders with respect to the mass movements which appear in the modern period. They are not partisans of a cause but seekers after truth. This fact did not in itself ensure that partisan causes would not attempt to claim them (as the Jacobins did Rousseau and the Italian Fascists, Hegel, for example) for precursors, but they cannot be held primarily responsible for the emergence of an intellectual climate in which the understanding of the distinction between political theory and ideology was in danger of being lost altogether.

The ordering principles of the theocentric tradition remain, at least in part, embedded in the analyses of the moderns, but their source beyond man is obscured. Thus, reliance is placed upon an order engendered within the human community itself rather than flowing into it from a divine origin. Machiavelli's and Rousseau's founder-legislators, Hobbes' sovereign, and Hegel's world-historical individuals become the sources of order. They establish the legal framework of the modern nation-state, and order is maintained by horizontal forces (Machiavelli's felicitous factional struggle in a republican regime, Hobbes's rational bargain to dispense with private violence, Rousseau's immanent consensus animating a well-ordered community, or Hegel's rational synthesis of the universal and particular will).

From the perspective of theocentric humanism, modern anthropocentric humanism in political theory is "secular," although by this appellation it must not be assumed that the modern greats were in any way blind to the role which religion has in societal life. Machiavelli, Hobbes, and Rousseau all maintained that an ordered society would perforce possess an official civil theology, and that the religious convictions of the citizenry have a profound effect on a society's temporal well-being. Machiavelli and Hobbes were content to use Christianity, with certain reinterpretations, as such a civil religion. Rousseau would have preferred in the paradigmatic situation to substitute a simplified deism on the grounds that Christianity, with its principle of double loyalty, inevitably fosters *incivisme*, or an "uncivic spirit." Although none of the above three thinkers explicitly denied the claims of theistic religion to absolute truth, there is in the writings of all of them a noticeable shift of emphasis from the question of the truth of religion to that of its utility for temporal political purposes. For Hegel, although the separation of Church and State is hailed as a major accomplishment of modern constitutionalism, the State takes on some of the qualities formerly associated with the Church. "The State is Spirit (*Geist*) *which is present in the world.*"[14] It is not an exaggeration to say with Alois Dempf that to Hegel "the State is the Church":[15] the weight of his analysis is on the world-immanent aspects of religion.

Although there are important differences in content between the theocentric humanism of classical and Christian political theory and the anthropocentric humanism of the modern greats, they join in opposing the third type of humanism in Western political thought, viz., messianic humanism. Messianic humanism, in truth an antihumanism seeking to turn man into something other than he is or can become, is that current of thought of which St. Simon, Comte, Marx, Proudhon, and Bakunin are typical representatives. It became an especially powerful intellectual force in the nineteenth century, and its protagonists unknowingly paved the way for twentieth-century totalitarian ideologies. When theocentric and anthropocentric humanism—the two great subtraditions of the one tradition of Western political theory—are compared with messianic humanism, then the extent of their agreement becomes more apparent.

For both the theocentric and anthropocentric humanists, man remains *man*, a finite creature of limited capabilities. The anthropologies of Machiavelli and Hobbes are so darkly realistic, that they often seem out of focus in their pessimism. Men are "more prone to evil than to good" (Machiavelli); "every man is enemy to every other man" (Hobbes). Even civil society for Hobbes is at best a sublimated state of war of all against all. Rousseau and Hegel are more appreciative of the cooperative or communal potentialities in man's

[14] Hegel, *Grundlinien der Philosophie des Rechts* (Hamburg, Hoffmeister ed., 1955), p. 221. See the whole of #270 (pp. 220-233) for his discussion of Church and State.

[15] For Hegel, "science is objective spirit, the State is the Church, personality is the State, and the objective spirit is personality." Alois Dempf, *Sacrum Imperium*, 2nd ed., (Darmstadt, Wissenschaftliche Buchgemeinschaft, 1954), p. 402.

nature; however, they scarcely deny the reality of the agonistic passions as an ever-present danger to the maintenance of an ordered society.

Both theocentric and anthropocentric humanists were in agreement that it was impermissible to indulge in millennarian fantasies about a qualitative transformation of existence in which, after an apocalyptic struggle between the children of darkness and the children of light, all worldly woes and anxieties would be dissipated and a reign of perpetual and untroubled bliss would ensue. Such fantasies were indeed entertained and mistaken for realities by the messianic humanists, the adherents of what Eric Voegelin has termed metastatic faith. The *metastasis* of messianic humanism is a very different matter from the *metanoia* of theocentric humanism. *Metastasis* is belief in the change *of* existence; *metanoia* is a change of attitude or orientation by man *toward* existence. The proponents of metastatic faith look to the establishment of a new world populated by new men—with "new" in both instances being taken to mean a condition qualitatively different from that which preceded it. Thus, messianic humanism is the doctrine which maintains that man can be something other than he is, and that, indeed, by his own efforts he is capable of becoming a god. Instead of creature, he will become creator; instead of being limited, he will proclaim his limitlessness. The brave new world of the messianic humanist imagination will be a marvelous improvement over the work of the Creator, which the book of Genesis symbolically portrays.

The master assumption of messianic humanism is that reality can be molded to conform to the infinite will of man. A "second reality" can be constructed by an elite of gnostic supermen. To employ Camus's phrase, the messianic humanists are in rebellion, not just against this or that existential evil, but against existence itself. They reject root and branch the fact of man's inevitable dependence on an order which he did not create and to which he must conform. The *libido dominandi* (lust for power) reflected in the writings of the messianic humanists is the same disease of the spirit which characterizes the totalitarian ideologies of our time. Although the messianic humanists of the nineteenth century may not properly be accused of having been totalitarian themselves (to do so would be anachronistic because totalitarianism is a twentieth-century invention), it is nonetheless true to say that such men as St. Simon, Comte, Fourier,

Proudhon, Marx, Mazzini, and Bakunin created the intellectual climate in which the totalitarian regimes of our time could develop and flourish.

Political theory, whether ancient or modern, is aware that the world is as it is and not some other way. The task of political theory is to describe the *conditio humana* and not engage in the fallacious attempt to transform it into something which on principle it cannot be. Political theorists, then, in contrast to the partisans of messianic humanism, are realists, and seek to evolve adequate concepts for portraying political man as he is, in all his greatness and decadence, glory and infamy, good and evil.

As in statesmanship, so in political theory, the fragile bark of realism sails between the Scylla of utopianism and the Charybdis of cynical despair. Although the theorist rejects utopian black magic, he does not counsel the abandonment of standards and adaptation to every existing situation, no matter how corrupt. The theorist recognizes that social existence has a certain amplitude of possibility and is capable of taking place on various levels. Within the limitations of existence itself there is room for maneuver, for change *within* existence without deluding oneself into thinking it amounts to a change *of* existence. Thus, the paradigm—again emphatically distinguished from a utopia—remains at the core of even the most "realistic" modern political theories. The elaboration of paradigmatic society remains a central preoccupation even for Machiavelli, who never loses hope in the possibility of establishing in his own time well-ordered republics whose institutions would give expression to the aspirations of both the numerous poor and the wealthy *gentiluomini* and whose laws should foster a rebirth of public spiritedness throughout the citizenry. With Hobbes we have the construction of the model society of the *Leviathan*. In the *Contrat Social*, Rousseau elaborates a model of the optimal body politic in which freedom is realized through participation in the making of laws and the conscious sharing and constant reaffirmation of communal consensus. The *amour de soi-même* of precivilizational man is raised to a new level in the small, face-to-face paradigmatic society and the *amour propre* encouraged by a corrupt and alienated society is overcome. Like Rousseau, Hegel sets forth the "principles of political right" that govern an ordered society; the modern constitutional state as the dialectical unity of family and civil society is presented as Idea, which is to say as concrete, actualized reality.

And yet all of these authors were aware that their models of the paradigmatic society, which they derive from their understanding of man as he is, were anything but blueprints to be applied indiscriminately to any and every historical situation. They recognized that they were elucidating critical standards to employ in evaluating the relative defectiveness of all existing modes and orders. At least one of the modern greats, Rousseau, went on to consider thoroughly the problem of diluting the paradigm and constructing a model in closer conformity to historical circumstances then prevailing. The polity described in the *Contrat Social* was intended for a small society uncorrupted by cosmopolitan *mores*, and in all Europe its author found only the isle of Corsica as a likely recipient of his undiluted teaching. Thus in his work on Poland he offered a model constitution which made major departures from his paradigm. Who could have been more "realistic" than Rousseau in advocating federalism, indirect democracy, and the delayed and gradual elimination of serfdom for Poland? As Frederick Watkins has noted, there is a "conservative" side to Rousseau's teaching, although as a political theorist he can be placed neither to the left nor the right of the doctrinal spectrum.

In espousing (after the manner of Polybius) the cyclical interpretation of history to explain the change of regimes in the early chapters of Book I of the *Discorsi*, Machiavelli was conceding the impossibility of the permanent establishment of his paradigmatic republic, in itself already diluted by comparison with the Platonic paradigm, within time. The following is a typical passage from his writings that illustrates how far removed he was from the utopianism of a messianic humanism that seeks to freeze time within the confines of a bogus eternity:

> And in all human affairs he who examines them well will see this: that one difficulty cannot be removed without another's coming up. . . . Hence in all our thinking we must consider where the fewest inconveniences are and take that for the best decision, because what is entirely clear, entirely without uncertainty, is never found.[16]

Of all the great modern political theorists, Hobbes skirts most closely on the brink of procrusteanism—i.e., the expectation that contingent, historical reality can be jammed into the confines of a

---

[16] *Discourses*, I, 6, in A. H. Gilbert, trans., *Machiavelli, The Chief Works*, 3 vols. (Durham, N.C., Duke University Press, 1965), I, 209.

rigid model. However, his paradigm has been diluted in advance, so to speak, and his sights lowered to consider the solid objective of temporal domestic peace as the goal. On the international scene, even a world of Leviathan states would be in a condition of war or cold war with each other, and in no sense is his paradigm a messianic or utopian construction. Furthermore, in at least one sombre passage, perhaps not sufficiently remarked upon by his interpreters, even Hobbes expresses considerable doubt as to whether his model commonwealth "derived from the principles of natural reason," will ever see the light of day:

> And now, considering how different this doctrine is, from the practice of the greatest part of the world . . . and how much depth of moral philosophy is required, in them that have the administration of the sovereign power; I am at the point of believing this my labour, as useless, as the commonwealth of Plato. For he also is of the opinion that it is impossible for the disorders of state, and change of government by civil war, ever to be taken away, till sovereigns be philosophers. But when I consider that the science of natural justice, is the only science necessary for sovereigns and their principal ministers . . . I recover some hope, that one time or other, this writing of mine may fall into the hands of a sovereign, who will consider it of himself . . . without the help of any interested, or envious interpreter; and by the exercise of entire sovereignty, in protecting the public teaching of it, convert this truth of speculation, into the utility of practice.[17]

As for Hegel, he makes abundantly clear in his *Philosophy of Right* that he is composing neither an exhortation in favor of the status quo nor a tract crying for reform. Like the owl of Minerva, philosophy flies only when dusk is falling; all philosophy is *Nachdenken*, or thinking in retrospect. Looking back on the development of the modern nation-state, Hegel attempts to discover its rational essence. No existing state can fully exemplify this rational essence, although some come closer to doing so than others.[18] Just as individual

[17] Michael Oakeshott, ed., *Leviathan* (Oxford, Blackwell, 1957), Part 2, p. 246.

[18] Hegel judged the Prussia of his times to be a highly advanced form of the modern nation state and therefore there are of course resemblances between sections of the *Philosophy of Right* (for example, that on monarchy,

men do not measure up in every respect to the representative or highest human type but have blemishes and imperfections, so individual states will only imperfectly incorporate the essence of the modern state which is the realization of freedom. The idea of the state never merges in Hegel's teaching with any particular individual state although there is no question that, compared to Plato, there has been a certain immanentization of the paradigm in that the Idea of Right works itself out and actualizes itself in world history. To say this is to do no more than to indicate that with Hegel, as with the other modern greats, we have moved from theocentric to anthropocentric humanism and from vertical to horizontal transcendence. In the latter tradition, immanent existence is itself apprehended as multidimensional and there is no attempt to flatten it out to a single experiential level.

Hegel's intentions as a political theorist are nowhere more adequately expressed than in the *Vorrede* to his masterpiece, the *Philosophie des Rechts:*

> This book, then, containing as it does the science of the state, is to be nothing other than the endeavor to apprehend and portray the state as something inherently rational. As a work of philosophy, it must be poles apart from an attempt to construct a state as it ought to be; it can only show how the state, the ethical universe, is to be understood.[19]

This passage is about as far as one can get from Professor Cobban's "party man," who writes for some immediate, practical purpose. It also serves to illustrate the fundamental agreement which all political theorists at least implicitly possess on the "is-ought" question, a

---

etc.) and Prussian institutions. However, this scarcely turns the *Philosophy of Right* into a defense of the Prussian State.

Hegel's positive evaluation of Prussia, where he (in Berlin) spent the last years of his life and career, is often misunderstood because "Prussia" has since become a symbol of reactionary forces, Junkers, and antidemocracy. What is forgotten is that Prussia is the father of modern bureaucracy and that with regard to constitutional liberties the Prussia of Hegel's time was remarkably progressive.

[19] Hegel, *op. cit.*, pp. 15-16. The translation used is that of T. M. Knox, Hegel's *Philosophy of Right* (London, Oxford, 1953), p. 11. Knox translates *"begreifen und darzustellen"* as "apprehend and portray"; "grasp and represent" would be a more literal rendering.

matter that will become so important for social thought influenced by positivism. For political theorists, *ens et bonum convertuntur*; they are all Thomists on this point, at least. There can be no other basis for a valid "ought" than that which (essentially—*not* existentially!) "is." That which "is"—that which has fully realized its essence —also "ought to be." For political theory, therefore, the ought is not a subjective, private value judgment, but the apprehension of the deepest, most enduring fact that men can experience. As Hegel expressed the matter in the Introduction to his *Philosophy of History*: "The insight . . . to which . . . philosophy is to lead us, is, that the real world is as it ought to be—that the truly good—the universal divine reason—is not a mere abstraction but a vital principle capable of realizing itself."

The most important problem confronting the contemporary revival of political theory is whether a new subtradition is required for the postmodern age. For many contemporary scholars, the advent of totalitarian regimes in our century has cast serious doubt on the sufficiency of anthropocentric humanism to withstand any longer the dangers of derailment into messianic humanism. One detects a new openness or receptivity to the reality of transcendent experience and a new interest in the theocentric humanist tradition of classical philosophy and Christianity. That tradition appears to have withstood successfully the full fury of the attack unleashed upon it by political messianism, neopositivism, reductionist psychology, and scientistic ideology, although it would be blind not to recognize that the attack continues with considerable force. Christianity and classical philosophy can no longer be dismissed as prescientific lore and superstition by methodological legerdemain.

However, no thoughtful person today asserts that postmodern problems can be adequately theorized by virtue of a simple and wholesale adoption of classical and Christian political theory, and the contemporary revival of political theory is not specifically a revival of Plato or St. Thomas Aquinas. Certainly, all the representatives of the new political theory would agree that at the least the problem is one of applying perennial principles to a new situation. One of the principal tasks of the new political theory is to assimilate valid teachings contained in the anthropocentric humanist tradition and in particular to show a new appreciation for the institutional achievements of modern liberalism. As critic and friend, postmodern political theory can also point out the deficiencies and limitations of this liberalism. Perhaps one might even hope that out of the dialogue of a postmodern political theory with both the theocentric and anthropocentric humanism which nourished modern liberalism, something that can be called "theocentric liberalism" is emerging and will continue to develop. This is a matter to which we shall return at greater length in the final chapter.

The Marks of Authentic Political Theory

We are now in a position to gather together the threads of our discussion concerning the nature of political theory as seen through its history. There are certain traits characteristic of all the paradigmatic political theorists from Plato to Hegel which taken together comprise a style of theoretical reflection about politics. These may be indicated as follows:

1. *Openness.* This implies awareness of the different levels of experience and of the possibility of man in some measure to gain a foothold outside his time in order to view it with detachment. "Openness" means the ability to transcend the confines of the contemporaneous political struggle, with its immediate issues and relevances, to discover—or rediscover—other issues and relevances. Openness results in the achievement of *critical distance* from the contemporaneous world of practical activity. It also results in a certain *tension* between the theorist and his environment. The theorist sees double in comparison with the political leader wholly immersed in the immediate problems of a specific institutional order. This second sight is no private gift of his, however. All men possess it, but the theorist develops it in a conscious way and attempts to explicate its meaning for politics. As critic, the political theorist is neither iconoclastic nor complacent. It is not that his allegiance to a concrete existing polity is simply replaced by one to theoretical truth. Unless it be corrupt beyond remedy, that allegiance remains and the tension between the two loyalties is not dissolved. This is true even for the Platonic Socrates who in the *Crito* refused to disobey the *nomoi* of his *polis* insofar as they governed his external, bodily existence. The theorist is, in varying degrees depending on the circumstances, a citizen-participant in a specific regime, but he is also, like Acton's historian, witness and judge of that regime. Because of this attitude some people accuse him of being a bad citizen, but he would regard himself in a different light—as a servant, and even as a lover, of his country.

2. *Theoretical Intention.* The political theorist reveals in his analyses the ability to view the reality he is investigating as, in the first instance, something to be understood rather than something to manipulate or operate on. The political theorist is not out to make reality conform to his will but to form his concepts so that they are adequate to the reality which he observes and in which he participates. No human mind can succeed completely in this respect—hence the quest for more adequate and highly differentiated symbols and concepts is a never-ending one—but without the objective being sought there is no hope for a genuine *epistēmē politikē*. As with all theoretical inquiry, political theory assumes an attitude of *dependence* on a reality which possesses a structure independent of the individual mind that is studying it. Theory presupposes a reality (and, following point (1) above, a multidimensional reality) to be observed and, insofar as possible, understood. The theorist strives always to resist the temptation to succumb to the *libido dominandi*, the *hybris* present in himself and in all men, which is the temptation to impose his own private wishes and desires on reality and to define reality in terms of them. The pure ideologist, on the other hand, accepts the *libido dominandi* on principle and seeks to re-create the human condition in his own image. Such an attempt is generally accompanied, or appears to be accompanied, by a sense of exultation and limitless extension of human powers, but in actuality the ideologist, like Plato's tyrannical man, is of all men the most enslaved by his illusions. In his passion to dominate, he is in fact most dominated.

3. *Focus on Universal, Perennial Problems.* The theorist seeks to provide at least a partial answer to such questions as, What is man? What kind of society is required for the full development of his humanity? What are the principles of right order for individuals and societies? These are universal questions, questions that confront man as man rather than particular men at a particular time and place. As Rousseau once wrote: "When it is a matter of reasoning about human nature, the true philosopher is neither Indian, nor Tartar, nor Genevan, nor Parisian; he is man."[20] Human societal existence is taken as a mystery to be explored, and man is the existent being endowed with the capacity to put these questions to existence,

[20] Jean-Jacques Rousseau, Letter to "M. Philopolis," in C. E. Vaughn, ed., *The Political Writings of Jean-Jacques Rousseau,* 2 vols. (New York, Wiley, 1962), vol. I, p. 225.

to discover meaning in that existence. The weight of the theorist's analysis falls on these universal, perennial questions rather than on the immediate, pressing, time-bound controversies of the day. Whereas the publicist is concerned with derivative, or second-order problems, taking the larger questions regarding the end of human life in society for granted or treating them only cursorily in relation to the pursuit of some immediate, practical objective, the theorist is above all pre-occupied with elucidating the principles of right order valid for men as men.

One example of publicistic writing is the work of Jeremy Bentham. From the perspective of political theory (and leaving to one side the question of the beneficence of his influence in humanizing the law, treatment of prisoners, etc.), Bentham is deficient in that he fails to treat the *summum bonum* as a problem for critical reflection, but dogmatically asserts pleasure to be the highest good, the remainder of his analysis concentrating on mechanisms for maximizing pleasure in a society. Bentham was an effective social reformer, but a very poor ethical theorist, for the supposition of pleasure as the highest good cannot be sustained for five minutes after a serious consideration of objections raised by Aristotle, and, indeed, at least implicitly, by John Stuart Mill.

Others who fall under the category of publicist rather than theorist are Dante, Marsilius of Padua, Jean Bodin, James Harrington, Edmund Burke, Joseph de Maistre, to cite only a few examples from major publicists—and to exclude literally hundreds ·of minor publicists whose names fill the footnotes of histories of political thought. Although Dante, Marsilius, and Bodin were all learned in political philosophy and attached an impressive apparatus to their works, the whole style of their thought is practical, oriented toward strengthening the position of the imperial or national monarchies they respectively defended. Dante explicitly states his practical intention in the preface of his *De Monarchia*. With regard to Marsilius, Jouvenel has correctly stated that the main purpose of the *Defensor Pacis* was to "sustain Louis of Bavaria, King of the Romans, in his struggle with Pope John XXII, and . . . to prove the supremacy of the empire. . . ."[21] Bodin is more of a borderline figure: his treatment

---

[21] Bertrand de Jouvenel, *Power: The Natural History of Its Growth* (London, Hutchinson, 1947), p. 39. Marsilius' "lack of disinterestedness" is clearly revealed in his treatment of the source of law. The argument is forced to

of sovereignty has the marks of a theoretical discussion, but the numerous inconsistencies of that doctrine, apparently designed to render the Salic Law and other features of the French polity of his time immune from change, give *Six Books on the Republic* a dated and publicistic character. On balance, it seems to have been more a tract (although a very learned one) on behalf of the *politique* faction in France than a treatise in political theory.

Of James Harrington's major work *The Commonwealth of Oceana*, Charles Blitzer has written that it was "an occasional work, written in the belief that it contained the only sure prescription for curing England's chronic constitutional ills and dedicated to Oliver Cromwell in the hope that he would undertake to effect the cure. . . ."[22] Matthew Wren, a contemporary, in discussing Harrington's treatment of the passions, highlighted the inadequacy of Harrington's philosophical anthropology when he wrote that "seeing the whole force of the argument rests upon the similitude of government with the soul of man, we may be instructed what the soul is, and what is the whole philosophy belonging to it. . . ."[23] In authentic political theory, the proportion of principles to institutional gadgetry is high; with Harrington the proportion is low.

Burke and de Maistre are examples of publicists who are engaged in a defensive action on behalf of an order of things which was passing away under the onslaught of the French Revolution. As leaders of the conservative reaction to the Revolution, their writings are drenched with polemical fury and their principles are not grounded in an adequate theory of man and society. Their discussion of the revolution is partisan and their conclusions exaggerated and colored. They are passionate combatants in the struggle. Their leading political ideas are simply the obverse of those of radical Enlightenment thought. As a result, it is difficult to regard their general notions about the relation of man to the community, the meaning of history, etc., as

---

run along the following lines: The source of law is the legislator, or the whole people (or weightier part thereof); yet the Roman people were representatives of the whole people of the empire and they delegated the legislative power to the Roman Princeps; the Holy Roman Emperor inherited this absolute power of his pagan predecessor. Therefore, Louis of Bavaria, the then Holy Roman Emperor, had by right despotic, unrestrained power.

[22] Charles Blitzer, *An Immortal Commonwealth: The Political Thought of James Harrington* (New Haven, Yale University Press, 1960), p. ix.

[23] *Ibid.*, p. 39.

serious contributions to the theoretical understanding of these subjects.[24]

With political theorists it is otherwise. Although Augustine and
Hooker began their chief works as *livres de circonstance*, they quickly
departed from the immediate practical purpose at hand to focus on
the perennial issues. Both the *City of God* and the *Laws of Ecclesiastical Polity* were treatises rather than tracts, and Hooker never even
got around to finishing the practical part of his masterpiece where
he was to defend the Church-State relationship established by the
Elizabethan settlement. Thomas Aquinas does little more than touch
on the burning question of the power of the papacy in temporal matters, and when he does so he is noticeably moderate. The weight
of his analysis is on such theoretical problems as the nature of law
(in the masterful treatise on law in Questions 90 ff., of the
Prima Secundae Partis of the *Summa Theolgica*), the common good,
etc. Machiavelli was deeply involved and interested in the affairs of
his time, but his overriding purpose was to express everything that
he knew and everything he had learned about politics. In his famous
letter to Vettori he describes how, in writing the *Prince*, he would
come into his study every evening, don regal clothes, and, having
banned all worldly anxieties from his mind, commune with the
ancients on the nature of political rule. He was much more than a
Renaissance man. Hobbes wrote that his *Leviathan* was "occasioned
by the disorders of the present time," but he made abundantly clear
his intention to set forth a teaching that was timeless in character.
His work was so unsuited for immediate propaganda purposes that
he brought down the wrath of both the royalist and antiroyalist factions in England, a not inconsiderable achievement. Thus, the great
political theorists continue to be read today virtually as if they were
contemporaries because they were centrally concerned with the problems which man as man encounters in leading his societal existence.

4. *Realism: the Dilution of the Paradigm*. Little needs to be
added on this point, given the previous discussion in this chapter of
the realism of the supposedly utopian and idealistic political theorists.
The political theorist is vividly aware of the inappropriateness of

[24] Francis P. Canavan in his book *The Political Reason of Edmund Burke*
(Durham, N.C., Duke University Press, 1960) ably argues a contrary view
with respect to Burke. My remarks apply mainly to Burke as author of the
Reflections on the Revolution in France, which is in my judgment by far
his most important work for the history of political thought.

seeking to impose his model of the good society directly upon a concrete historical situation. He is empirical rather than aprioristic, and his paradigm is just that—a paradigm for critical analysis, not a utopian blueprint to be implemented by an intrepid band of social engineers. The political theorist knows what utopian thinkers like Campanella and Owen never learned: that human nature cannot be changed by the black magic of institutional tinkering (e.g., by the elimination of private property) and that institutions must be adapted to the particular environment.

The dilution of the paradigm has since Plato been a preoccupation of political theorists. The stress upon the problem varies in relation to the "height" of the theorist's paradigmatic model: a Plato or a Rousseau will need to amend the initial model drastically, whereas a Machiavelli or a Hobbes, whose sights have, so to speak, been lowered in advance to take into account the antagonistic element in man's nature and the exigencies of the phenomenal power situation in general, will find that they have less work to do in this regard. In no instance is the political theorist blind to or naively overconfident about the difficulties involved in translating theory into practice. To a man, political theorists are realists about power. The description of power realities is only one of the tasks they envisage for a critical political science, however; they are also led to evaluate these realities in terms of a more comprehensive realism that discovers in man the potentiality for an ordered existence.

5. *Modesty: the Recognition of Limits to Knowledge.* Authentic political theory is never closed within itself, never pretends to be complete, all-inclusive, finished for all time. Despite frequent statements to the contrary, which one today encounters in the literature of political science, the political theorist does not construct an air-tight system; rather, he investigates in a critical manner the perennial problems of human existence in society. Knowledge of the inevitable limits to human knowledge is most profoundly grasped on principle by those thinkers formed by classical philosophy, Christianity, or both. Plato's *Republic*, Aristotle's *Politics*, Aquinas's *Summa*, and Hooker's *Ecclesiastical Polity* are, in the main, critically refined explorations of problems; these works are open to further elaboration and development and do not claim to furnish a certain knowledge covering all aspects of human existence. All these authors reason analogically from what is known to that which is the ground of all our being and know-

ing. The finite human mind is experienced as incapable of grasping ultimate, transcendent reality and holding it in its conceptual nets. As Richard Hooker, who in so many respects sums up the theocentric humanist tradition in political thought, expressed the radical humility of the theorists of transcendence:

> Dangerous it were for the feeble brain of man to wade far into the doings of the Most High; whom although to know be life . . . yet our soundest knowledge is to know that we know him not as indeed he is, neither can know him; and our safest eloquence concerning him is our silence, when we confess without confession that his glory is inexplicable, his greatness above our capacity and reach.[25]

Those theorists in the anthropocentric subtradition of political theory make no pretence of offering a total picture of reality in their teachings. Although Machiavelli, Hobbes, and Rousseau show a shift of direction in favor of consideration of world-immanent existence without explicitly relating such existence to the transcendental ground, they do not dogmatically deny the reality of transcendent Being. Machiavelli professes not to be expert in supernatural matters, while Hobbes puts forward a similar reservation, contending also that the innermost desires of individuals are beyond his ken. None of the modern masters of political theory claims to have subsumed all of reality in a system so as to leave no mystery, nothing further to be explored and explained. Hegel at first view seems an exception to this statement; his arrogance in claiming to be the culmination of the history of philosophy is by now legendary. Of all the great political theorists, he certainly falls closest to the danger of concocting a total system. However, Hegel is the epitome of modesty in his double refusal either to teach the state what it ought to be or to predict the course of history. Philosophy for Hegel is retrospective. Although he does not say so, the logic of his teaching would appear to be that world history, as it continues to unfold, will require the services of future Hegels to interpret its meaning after the fact. The *philosophia perennis* is itself a perennial, never-finished task.

When one compares the great political theorists with messianic humanists, such as Comte and Marx, one is made particularly aware of the fundamental modesty of theory. Both of these gentlemen claimed

[25] Hooker, "Sermon on the Certainty and Perpetuity of Faith in the Elect."

to possess the key to history and to have arrived at an infallible *gnosis* regarding the nature and destiny of man. With the messianic humanists, the "brain of man" (to revert again to Hooker) does indeed "wade into the doings of the Most High"; in fact, that brain becomes identical with It, and proceeds to abolish the entire superstructure of transcendent reality. To the messianic humanists, the third realm of history is about to commence in which time will become eternity, essence will replace existence, and alienation will be transformed into identity and complete world-immanent fulfillment. Man, no longer a mystery to himself, can shape his existence endlessly in the way he chooses to do so.

6. *Intellectual Honesty and Integrity.* The theorist is particularly concerned with rooting out self-deception, cant, and the ignoring of inconvenient or uncomfortable realities. He will not cover with sugary phrases facts which his audience would prefer not to hear nor will he make promises and predictions which are impossible of realization given the very nature of facts. This conscious effort to bring to light and expose prejudices, whether his own, or those of his time, or those inherited from the past, can make him unpopular and often misunderstood. Thus, over strong opposition, Augustine had to brand chiliastic interpretations of the book of Revelation as "ridiculous fancies." Hooker was unable to finish his *Laws of Ecclesiastical Polity* when he apparently decided that the Thomistic principles of Book I would not square with the Erastian conception of church government in Book VIII. He had the integrity not to offer a patched-up solution. None of the great theorists failed to face up to the dark side of human nature which must be taken into account by legislators, but Machiavelli in particular took it upon himself to present a candid portrayal of the force, fraud, deception, and unprincipled selfishness which are frequently involved in the exercise of power, thereby bringing down on himself an ignominy which has lasted even until today.

The great theorists are not without error, but through the study of their works we are vastly aided in struggling against our own errors and self-deceptions. For they accord us no cheap and easy solutions and refuse to succumb to the temptation to swindle themselves and mankind by concocting a picture of the human condition free of all its limitations, incongruities, deficiencies, uncertainties, and contingencies.

PART II ❧ THE ASSAULT UPON POLITICAL THEORY

THREE: THE IDEOLOGICAL REDUCTIONISM OF TRACY, COMTE, AND MARX

That political theory has for decades been in danger of being eclipsed is not a fact which can be explained by a simple loss of interest in an academic discipline by scholars and intellectuals. The "decline" of political theory after Hegel came in the wake of an unprecedented assault upon it by the most extreme and consistent of the nineteenth-century messianic humanists. This assault was so far-reaching and successful that it created problems from which thoughtful students of politics have been attempting to extricate themselves for decades. The challenge of ideology to political theory was complete and explicit. The nature of the challenge is contained in the fateful words of Marx, in the eleventh thesis on Feuerbach: "Philosophers have hitherto only *interpreted* the world in different ways; the point is to *change* it." Marx professed to see the very distinction between theory and practice as an illusion and to conceive of reality as simply "practical human-sensory activity."

In Marx's thought, the theoretical component of course does not disappear, but it is distorted and perverted so that it can no longer serve its critical function. From the merging of theory and practice, we have the destruction of both realms and their transformation into the bizarre world of ideological politics (which is in truth a non- or an antipolitics). Ideological thought in its most radical form is the converse of authentic political theory. Where theory is open to various dimensions of experience, ideology is the enemy of all openness, having reduced experience to the single dimension of *homo faber* and his needs. Ideology is in essence the fallacious attempt to wall in the opening to the cave.

Where theory is characterized by a built-in sense of limit and is antisystematic in nature, ideology overthrows on principle the very idea of limit. To the ideologist, reality has at last bared her secrets and the world is waiting for conquest by those who have the necessary knowledge that man himself is the ultimate creator of reality. Knowledge and power are joined in ideology in such a way that the only knowledge deserving of the name is that which is instrumental to attaining power and dominion over the environment and, ultimately, over man himself in his innermost being. Reality to ideological thought is something that needs to be "made up" rather than "made out." Man must recognize that he creates reality; given the application of sufficient intelligence, reality conforms to him, not he to it. There are no immutable and everlasting limits to human action, although in the benighted ages prior to the new ideology man has falsely imposed on himself superstitions and illusions (labelled "philosophy," "theology," etc.) which taught otherwise. Man is not creature, but creator; he is the "measure of all things" in a way which Protagoras would never have dreamed. In nineteenth-century messianic humanist and ideological thought, man becomes a newly styled Prometheus; unlike the Prometheus of the Greek myth, who was himself a god come to the aid of man, the new Prometheus is man himself become God. To the ideologist man has no nature, or constant core of his being; it is accordingly unnecessary to formulate an anthropology after the manner of political theory. To assign man a nature limits him; man is what he makes of himself through historical and societal action.

With the incorporation of the *libido dominandi* into the thinking of the ideologist, the very concept of the paradigm disappears. No essential reality remains to measure every attempt at existential embodiment of general principles of right order. Essence and existence, eternity and time, infinitude and finiteness, transcendent perfection and immanent fulfillment, are joined. The role of the political thinker now becomes the elaboration of a blueprint for the radical revolution: the one which will abolish all human dependency and usher in the perfect third realm of history. Instead of the paradigm of the *Republic* we have the program of the Communist Manifesto.

In the process of converting theoretical understanding into activist ideology, much is lost. Gone is the realism of political theory that recognized the inevitable gulf between paradigmatic and historical reality and the consequent necessity for the paradigm's dilution when applied to an existing historical situation. Gone is the tension between the theorist and any conceivable environment, the critical distance separating him from the partisan causes of his time. The lonely theorist becomes the man of the movement; he identifies himself completely with the movement that will implement the ideology of conquest. The denial of the Platonic position is complete; what Plato had discovered to be existential slavery to the world of flux and shadows is proclaimed by ideology as perfect freedom. The cave is not to be transcended—it is to be conquered, and all thought of the possibility of opening self or society to a reality beyond intramundane existence must be extirpated from the human mind. Man, Marx proclaims in the *Philosophical-Economic Manuscripts*, when he has transformed himself into a socialistic superman, will not ask metaphysical questions, or questions about the origin and ground of all existing things.

The radical elimination of every possibility of transcending the dimension of practical-productive activity and arriving at a critical theory of politics is the culmination of a lengthy and complex development which it is not our purpose to chronicle here. Such a chronicle would require an intellectual history of the entire modern period. In fact, as Eric Voegelin, Norman Cohn, and others have demonstrated,[1] an analysis of the roots of messianic humanism in the West would have to take us at least as far back in time as Joachim of Fiore and chiliastic mass movements of the high middle ages. These manifestations of *gnosis* were not messianic humanist movements in the technical sense because of the persistence of the theocentric component in their symbolization: the inner-worldly perfection would have to wait upon the thaumaturgic intervention of the divinity to achieve accomplishment. It is only later that the necessity of waiting on God is dispensed with, and man himself is declared the vehicle of his own salvation. Our purpose in this volume is rather to focus on the point in the history of political thought at which, because of the absolute and categorical reduction of all reality to the single

---

[1] Norman Cohn, *The Pursuit of the Millennium* (London, Oxford, 1957), and Eric Voegelin, *The New Science of Politics* (Chicago, University of Chicago Press, 1952).

dimension of sense experience, the very possibility of political theory and metaphysical reflection is denied. The critical distance maintained by the theorist between himself and his milieu is rejected on the basis of the assumption that he is the reflection of that milieu.

The "Ideology" of Destutt de Tracy

The term "ideology" was coined by Destutt de Tracy, whose book *Elémens d'idéologie* first appeared in 1801. Strictly speaking, there were no ideologists until the emergence under the Napoleonic regime of a school known as *idéologues* comprised of Tracy, Cabanis, Volney, Laucelin, Broussais, and others.[2] By ideology, Tracy meant the science of determining the origin of ideas. He espoused the view that all thought is a reflection of and is determined by sense experience, and that the world of physical sensation and tactile visibility is the only reality. As the "science of ideas," ideology denies that ideas have any source or object beyond the realm of physical sensation. Unlike Plato, who had described the *nous* as the faculty by which man gained vision of ultimate reality, Tracy saw the human mind as only another object in the world of nature. Ideological science was simply a part of zoology: "One has only an incomplete knowledge of an animal if one does not know its intellectual faculties. Ideology is a part of zoology, and it is above all with reference to the study of man that this science has importance. . . ."[3] The human intellect must be observed and described "as one observes and describes a property of a mineral or vegetable, or a remarkable circumstance in the life of an animal. . . ."[4]

According to Tracy, the traditional qualitative distinction between man and the lower animals must be overthrown, along with all metaphysical or religious conceptions of man—conceptions which regard man as something more than a phenomenon available to natural science research. Metaphysics, indeed, was equated with illusion and fantasy by Tracy. After explaining that ideology should be a natural

[2] See Fr. Picavet, *Les idéologues* (Paris, F. Alcan, 1891) for a detailed description of the movement.

[3] Destutt de Tracy, *Elémens d'idéologie*, 5 vols. (Paris, 1817), I, Preface.

[4] *Ibid.*

science whose objective is the discovery of laws governing the origin and development of ideas, he contrasts this undertaking with metaphysics, which has for centuries been engaged in the fruitless attempt "to determine the beginning and end of everything, to divine the origin and destination of the world. This is the goal of metaphysics. We count it among those arts of the imagination destined to please men but hardly to instruct them."[5]

The ultimate reality, the milieu in which the sentient organism called man is situated, was to Tracy nothing more than the total sum of

> chemical attractions and reactions which during a given time determine a particular order of facts and soon, under still unknown circumstances, are placed again under the rule of more general laws, those of inorganic matter: as long as this condition subsists we live, that is to say, we move and we feel.[6]

For Tracy, the truly scientific study of man would serve the function of exposing illusions and abstractions which had no basis in reality. Religion and philosophy would be overthrown, along with all forms of abstract thought such as deism and "natural rights" speculation. Only those ideas which could be clearly shown to relate to "real"— i.e., sensory—experience would be retained as constituting knowledge. Only through the new science of ideas could the political, moral, and pedagogical sciences be grounded in a proper manner.[7]

Tracy saw his movement as continuing a revolt begun by the sensationalist wing of French eighteenth-century thought; he frequently cites Condillac and Helvétius as worthy precursors. Helvétius had indeed prefigured Tracy's reductionism with his conclusion that, "Our ideas are the necessary consequences of the societies in which we live."[8] The target of the revolt was the thesis that there is any source of ideas other than sensation. Tracy emphatically rejected what he understood to be Descartes's teaching that there were three kinds of ideas: innate, self-created, and impressions derived from

[5] Ibid.

[6] Quoted in the introduction by Gilbert Chinard to Emile Caillet, La tradition littéraire des idéologues (Philadelphia, American Philosophical Society, 1943).

[7] Tracy, op. cit., pp. 19, 20, 301.

[8] Quoted in Hans Barth, Wahrheit und Ideologie (Zurich, 1945), p. 62.

observing the outer material world. The notion of innate ideas in particular was Tracy's *bête noir*. For Tracy, all thinking can ultimately be
reduced to feeling: *"Penser, c'est toujours sentir."* He replaced the
famous *cogito ergo sum* of Descartes with the dictum *sentio ergo sum*
(I feel, therefore I am).

To Tracy, the science of ideas, ideology, would attain the same
grade of certainty and precision which he thought the physical and
mathematical sciences possessed. By tracing all ideas to sensory experience, a new science of man would be created to guide the entire
political and economic life of human beings. The lawgiver would
then have the necessary knowledge for erecting a just and reasonable
social order.

The *idéologues*, or *idéologistes* as Tracy preferred to call them,
hoped to be the acknowledged guides of social action in postrevolu-
tionary Europe. Quite consistently with their general orientation, they
regarded their doctrine as practical in origin and goal. As Hans Barth
expressed it, their "radical dissection" of ideas (tracing them back
to their origins in sense experience) "was no end in itself, but rather
only the means to construct an all-embracing system for the education
and shaping of human beings."[9]

By rejecting metaphysics, Tracy cut himself off from the sources
of critical reflection about the ends of human life. He failed utterly
to achieve the objective social science he had promised. Rather, what
happened was that the general goals of Enlightenment political
thought were admitted uncritically into the corpus of knowledge. The
symbols of his immediate political environment were substituted for
the concepts of *epistēmē politikē*. Hans Barth has admirably summarized this development:

> Despite its basic enmity to metaphysics and despite its claim
> to ground itself exclusively on experience and methods of the
> natural science of man, Destutt de Tracy's science des idées
> incorporated the general intellectual presuppositions of the En-
> lightenment.[10]

The political program of the *idéologues* reads like a catalogue of
eighteenth-century French progressivist thought, including as it did
faith in mass education as the ultimate social panacea, the destruction
of all privileged bodies, the exclusion of priests from public positions

[9] *Ibid.*, p. 23.

[10] *Ibid.*, pp. 30-31.

(and from receiving state salaries or teaching moral philosophy in the schools), uniformity of laws, customs, administrative procedure, and weights and measures, the unqualified right of divorce, absolute freedom of the press, and the removal of all trade restrictions.[11]

Despite their claim to be radically empirical, the *idéologues* were actually highly abstract and deductive thinkers. It was their rigid, aprioristic style of thought coupled with their dogmatism on political and religious questions that led Napoleon to dismiss them as idle dreamers and cranks. Ideology became for Napoleon a pejorative term, equivalent to visionary speculation without any grounding in reality. While Napoleon's characterization of ideology is the opposite of that which Tracy had so strenuously proclaimed, it in fact comes quite close to describing the result which Tracy and the *idéologues* actually achieved.[12]

Although the meaning of "ideology" has become extremely vague today, and more often than not stands for any set of ideas claiming to support or justify a given political or economic system (here it is virtually synonymous with what is referred to in this volume as "political doctrine"), it may be doubted whether it is a sound procedure to employ the term in this loose way, especially in political science. Instead, being faithful to its origins with Tracy, ideology is used in this volume to refer to a set of ideas about the ordering of society claiming the prestige of (phenomenal) science, based on an immanentist, reductionist epistemology, and aiming at the transformation of the world through making it conform to abstractions divorced from the realities of human existence in society. Ideology develops in the context of the nineteenth-century revolt launched explicitly against theory.

The Scientistic Messianism of Auguste Comte

Another key figure in the attack upon political theory by ideological reductionism was Auguste Comte. Like Tracy, Comte was inventive in coining new words to describe new movements; whereas Tracy graced the political vocabulary with "ideology," Comte added

[11] Picavet, *op. cit.*, p. 297.

[12] In a speech delivered December 29, 1812, Napoleon denounced "l'idéologie . . . cette ténébreuse métaphysique" for its ignorance of the "human heart" and the "lessons of history." Ideology, he said, sought to legislate for abstractions rather than for human beings.

the term "positivism." Although Tracy had looked eagerly to the advent of a new age dominated by those who had become expert in the new science of ideology, it remained to Comte and Marx to draw out the full messianic implications of ideological thinking. Tracy remained essentially bound to Enlightenment progressivism, with its faith in the efficacy of education gradually and inexorably to lead men to the new order. The new order itself, although inaugurating a radical break with all previous history would not transfigure worldly existence beyond all recognition. The new age would be enlightened, egalitarian, secular, prosperous, and contented. However, the *idéologues* were too individualistic to recognize the boundless possibilities for remaking man himself by modifying his environment through the total control of society. Tracy did not fully exploit the possibilities of his "discovery" that man is the product of his material environment. Marx was to recognize that if the environment makes man, man can make the environment, and ideological reductionism opens up the secret to complete mastery over himself and his world. Man could create himself anew and shape a qualitatively superior existence. Thus, although ideological reductionism was in the first instance deterministic (man as the product of his material environment), it easily lent itself to transformation into antideterminism (because man himself had discovered that he was the product of his environment, now, thus enlightened and equipped with the power of the natural sciences, he could determine that environment and thus determine himself). The leap into full-fledged messianism, into a world in which man—or the right men, the gnostic savants—can have unlimited control of the *conditio humana*, was taken by Comte and Marx.

Comte, who by the end of his life was convinced that he was the high priest of Humanity, showed to what lengths one can go after systematically rejecting the notion that there are inherent limits to human knowledge and power. Like Tracy, Comte was preoccupied with constructing a new master science of man (he coined the word "sociology" to describe it) to be grounded on the discovery that sense experience alone was real. All theological, metaphysical, and ethical reflection was relegated to the rubbish heap of history. History itself was interpreted according to the famous law of the three stages. The "theological stage," extending from the dawn of time to the Protestant Reformation and subdivided into the ages of fetishism, polytheism, and monotheism, was characterized by the anthropomorphic representation of allegedly divine forces. This first period of history was the age of the infancy of the human mind when blatant superstition paraded as knowledge. The second or "metaphysical stage" tended toward the replacement of animistic and anthropomorphic symbolization with abstract concepts, such as natural rights and the depersonalized God of deism. It was an age of criticism and revolt, ending in the destructiveness and terror of the French Revolution. Only with the "positive" or "scientific stage," inaugurated by Comte himself, would knowledge about man and nature replace the ignorance, superstition, and illusion that had prevailed throughout the prehistory of the human race. The third age would synthesize "order and progress."

In his *Discours sur l'ésprit positif* of 1844, Comte expounds the meaning of the term "positivist." He gives various significations of the word, contending that it designates the "real" as opposed to the "chimerical," the "useful" in contradistinction to the "parasitic," the "certain" instead of the "vague and indecisive." Other qualities of the positivist as opposed to the metaphysical mentality are precision, constructive power, and relativism.[13] To Comte's way of thinking, sociology would discover—indeed, with him as its founder, had discovered—laws governing human behavior as precise and definite as those pertaining to natural phenomena. Positivism was the application of empirical and scientific methods to every field of inquiry. It marked the rejection of every form of knowledge based on the supposition that there was any reality beyond inner-worldly material existence. As with Tracy and Marx, so with Comte, we witnessed the seeming paradox of determinism and liberation. By discovering that the real world of immanent existence was governed in its evolution by inexorable laws, man would be free to take advantage of and accelerate their operation, which in any case was beneficent. As the grand, fundamental law of the three stages made clear, the evolution of nature was wholly progressive, its decree being that human beings "are always becoming more intelligent, more active, and more loving."

To Comte, all ethical, metaphysical, and theological speculation was worthless, and its persistence retarded the beneficent liberating thrust of nature. Positivism, he wrote, recognizes as a fundamental methodological principle that "every proposition which is not strictly reducible to the enunciation of a fact . . . is unable to offer any real

[13] Auguste Comte, *Discours sur l'ésprit positif* (Hamburg, 1956), pp. 84 ff.

and intelligible sense."[14] Thereby he anticipated the verification principle adopted by the Vienna Circle in the next century. However, he went far beyond any methodological considerations based on the distinction between sense and nonsense propositions to insist that all teaching and publication at variance with positivism be banished from the face of the earth. To insure that no individual would be so unfortunate as to fall back into the intellectual and spiritual darkness of the prepositivist age, he commanded that all works at odds with positivism be destroyed and the language cleansed of such metaphysical terms as "right" and "first cause." In the new society as reconstructed under the Comtean dispensation, classical, Christian, and modern political theory would have been legislated out of existence. The result, as John Stuart Mill observed, would have been the most perfect example of spiritual and temporal despotism yet known to man.

Comte convinced himself that his own mind had become coextensive with reality, and that he had only to feel or think something, to interrogate himself, in order to know reality completely. He substituted for the concepts of classical and Christian philosophy the symbols "Humanity" and "Great Being" to represent the totality of things and sometimes thought of himself as a prophet of and at other times as identical with this reality. Of all the gnostic system-builders of the nineteenth century, he was perhaps the most extravagant in his claims. The titles of his works reveal the enormity of the distance separating Comte from the political theorist. No one can doubt that he believed all reality to have been perfectly encompassed in his system after perusing the following list of titles:

> Système de politique positive
> Système de logique positive
> Système de morale positive
> Traité de l'education universelle
> Système d'industrie positive
> Traité de l'action totale de l'humanité sur sa planete.

Like Tracy, Comte saw all thought as having the practical objective of mastering and transforming the human environment. Man's inexorable development toward omnipotence and omniscience had reached its goal with his own person. Perhaps his most famous

[14] *Ibid.*, p. 26.

slogan, and the one most inimical to the theoretical spirit, was *savoir pour prévoir* (to know in order to predict). Science and theory were intended to serve practice, as he explains in a section of the previously cited *Discours* of 1844 on the "Harmony between Science and Art, and between Positivist Theory and Practice."[15] The purpose of all science was to serve the practical-productive needs of humanity, a humanity which at last was on the verge of achieving total conquest of the environment.

Positivist theory was not to remain an affair of the leader and his disciples: it must be presented in catechismic form for dissemination among the masses. To revert once more to his *Discours sur l'ésprit positif*, one finds in the section on "Organization of the Revolution" the plans for an alliance between philosophy and the proletariat similar in many respects to that conceived by Marx. The entirety of Part III of the same work is devoted to a discussion of techniques for popularizing positivist teaching. A later work by Comte with the same objective was entitled the *Positivist Catechism for Women and Workers.*

As befits the discoverer of a complete science of man and the universe, who styled himself high priest of Humanity, the Comtean vision of history's third age was as wild and stupendous as anything in the entire literature of political messianism. The kingdom of the secular saints would be characterized by the emancipation of man from all necessary work, the withering away of the destructive impulse, universal chastity (birth would emanate from woman alone), the end of fear and anxiety. A new religion, fabricated by himself and propagated by priestesses, would give man a total spiritual comfort far surpassing even that promised by the peace-of-mind cult in present-day America. In the positivist religion, which, of course, was thoroughly consonant with positivist science, a new trinity composed of the Great Being (Humanity), the Grand Fetish (the Earth) and the Grand Medium (Space) replaced the triune God of Christianity. A new positivist calendar of thirteen months, with each month and day named after a great scientist or artist, was also decreed. Group meetings were to be held in addition to private meditations; on these occasions antisocial and unproductive emotions such as hate, despair, and insecurity would be worked off in a veritable orgy of emotional release. The tricky problem of how to square the newly won divinity

[15] *Ibid.*, pp. 56-57.

of man with the fact of his continuing mortality was solved by the banishment of death as an idea: people did not die in the Comtean paradise, but simply achieved the exalted status of "incorporation into the Great Being," at which time their names were inscribed upon a gigantic plaque containing the names of all others who had previously been accorded this honor. (Social misfits were not accorded this distinction and simply disappeared into the void of anonymity.)

To a certain extent the wildness of Comte's vision can be attributed to idiosyncrasies of personality and even to lapses into insanity (as clinically defined), but there is a connection between his scientism and his messianic schemes. The fantastic dreams of a future perfect society on earth, together with the bone-chilling accounts of the terror apparatus that could be called into play to create and maintain it, are in a profound sense merely expressions by an imaginative mind of the *hybris* of scientistic ideology. For if reality is nothing but a field of material forces waiting to be exploited and manipulated by any organism intelligent enough to exploit it, there is nothing intrinsically objectionable in a proposal designed to exploit it with maximum efficiency. Of course, in the process we witness what C. S. Lewis has called the "abolition of man." As reality is reduced, so is man. Gone is the possibility of authentic multidimensional experience; religion, theory, art, literature, all are harnessed to the needs of the immanent productive process. Man becomes a laboring animal, the equivalent of the industrious beaver (it was no accident that St. Simon, who was Comte's mentor before the latter broke with him, described the beaver as his favorite animal). Society is conceived as one vast factory and, like a factory, the end for which it functioned was beyond debate. That end was the production of the maximum conceivable physical and mental comfort for man. Those who might be inclined to reject the blandishments of this terrestrial paradise would be dealt with appropriately although in time, with the purification of the vocabulary and the reeducation of the masses, it would be virtually impossible even to think negative thoughts about the positive society, or such, at any rate, was the expectation of its author.

The Culmination of Ideological Reductionism: Karl Marx

No writer has been so thorough in his rejection of political theory, authentically conceived, as Karl Marx. All previous partial revolts against theory and theoretical existence are completed and fulfilled in Marx. Marx had one of the most brilliant minds in the history of political thought. Properly oriented, this mind could have produced a great work of political theory. Instead, he produced the great work of antitheory, and provided mankind with the most radical and consistent formulation of messianic and ideological thinking.

The relationship of Marx to the *idéologues* of the post-Revolutionary era is direct. During his Paris exile between 1844 and 1845— a crucial year for his intellectual development—he studied closely Tracy's *Elémens d'idéologie*.[16] The ensuing analysis will concentrate primarily on Marx's early writings (from 1843 to 1850), which have been too long neglected in favor of his later works or, more recently, by Erich Fromm and others, misinterpreted as comprising a supposedly democratic and humanistic phase of his thought. J. L. Talmon is correct to lay emphasis on the "Messianic postulate" of the young Marx and to regard the later economic apparatus of *Das Kapital* as intended to justify the "Messianic expectation."[17]

Marx held that reality has no structure outside that imposed by human practical-productive activity. Man himself has no essence or nature but changes through interaction with his natural and social environment. All thought is a reflection of the immanent environment in which man finds himself. This environment is not static but is malleable, changing as *homo faber* acts on the world to produce new tools, modes of production, institutions, and justificatory ideas. The full truth about the human condition is two-sided: circumstances determine man, but man determines the circumstances, the total milieu for man being nothing but the result of human practical-productive activity. Throughout previous history, man has been alienated from nature, his fellow beings, and himself: he has been the slave of extraneous economic forces and of illusory religious, philosophical, and political ideas which assume a world of objective right and truth transcending human activity itself. The conditions for the fundamental transformation of the human situation from slavery to mastery have been prepared, through the elaboration of the proletariat, out of the context of capitalist society. Communist (Marxist) science, which has solved the riddle of history, will lead the way to the final revolution.

---

[16] Barth, *op. cit.*, p. 87.

[17] J. L. Talmon, *Political Messianism* (London, Secker & Werbarg), p. 205.

This revolution will differ qualitatively from all other revolutions in history in that it will be universal in scope, will eliminate "wrong as such" rather than this or that particular wrong, will free man for endless self-determination rather than subjecting him to yet another alien power, and will make possible—indeed inevitable—the full and complete control and conscious domination of all the forces of nature and society (of reality as such) by and for man. It will not substitute one ruling class for another but will elevate mankind (the proletariat) to a position where it can rule itself. The final revolution will be the result of the successful application of Marx's discovery that man is not creature but creator and, as a "species-being" is completely free to remake the world according to his creative will. The final revolution, in the words of Marx's collaborator, Engels, will be the "leap from necessity into freedom." Man, from being a dwarf will become a giant, and the new man will have no need of the institutions that served as fetters in his prehistory. Along with the Church, private property, and the family, the state as an engine of force and repression above society will wither away. The brotherhood of autonomous persons will arrive with the completion of the revolutionary process under the guidance of the vanguard of the proletariat—the unified and tightly organized Communist party.

Marx systematically rejected the three great sources of the theocentric humanist tradition in the West. Greek philosophy was discarded in his doctoral dissertation, Judaism in his essay on Bruno Bauer's *The Jewish Question*, and Christianity, and indeed any religious understanding of the world, in the *Critique of Hegel's Philosophy of Right*. "The critique of religion," he wrote in the preface to the latter work, "is the presupposition of all critique." Man, who sought a "superman" (God) in a fantastic heaven, really saw only himself mirrored there. "The foundation of irreligious critique is this: Man makes religion, religion does not make man." Furthermore, by "man" is meant no abstract individual but "the world of man, the state, society. This state, this society produces religion, which is a *perverted world-consciousness*, because it itself is a perverted world. Religion is the general theory of this world, its encyclopedic compendium, its logic in popular form, its spiritualistic *point-d'honneur*, its enthusiasm, its moral sanction. . . ."

After portraying religion as a societal product or, more precisely, as the product of an alienated and perverted social existence, Marx goes on to characterize religion, in words that have become famous, as "the expression of real misery and the protest against real misery. Religion is the groan of the oppressed creature, the heart of a heartless world, the spirit of an unspiritual condition. It is the opiate of the people." It therefore becomes the task of history

> after the other-worldly truth has disappeared, to establish the truth of this world. It is the immediate task of philosophy, which stands at the service of history, after the holy form of human self-alienation has been exposed, to expose self-alienation in its unholy form. The critique of heaven transforms itself into a critique of earth, the critique of religion into the critique of law and right, the critique of theology into the critique of politics.[18]

In the coming period of the great revolution, the function of philosophy, and specifically German philosophy, would be to serve as the potent weapon of social change: "as philosophy finds in the proletariat its material, so the proletariat finds in philosophy its spiritual weapon." Theory and practice, philosophy and the proletarian mass movement, would be united.

> The emancipation of the German is the emancipation of man. The head of the emancipation is philosophy, its heart the proletariat. Philosophy cannot actualize itself without the development of the proletariat, while the proletariat cannot develop itself without the actualization of philosophy.[19]

The *Critique of Hegel's Philosophy of Right* was composed in 1843; during the following year he drafted a manuscript entitled *Nationalökonomie und Philosophie*. This uncompleted work, which was not published until 1932, is of fundamental importance for the understanding of Marx's entire teaching. Nowhere in the entire Marxian corpus is the proposition that material existence is the totality of existence and that man's inner life is entirely derivative from his material environment more emphatically proclaimed. "Religious alienation as such exists only in the realm of consciousness, or in the interior life of man," he wrote, "but economic alienation

---

[18] "Zur Kritik der Hegelschen Rechtsphilosophie" in S. Landshut, ed., *Karl Marx: Die Frühschriften* (Stuttgart, Kroner, 1953), pp. 207-224 at pp. 207-209.

[19] *Ibid.*, pp. 223-224.

exists in *real life*—therefore, its abolition includes both sides."[20] Ideological reductionism could receive no clearer expression.

As with Tracy and Comte, Marx was certain that a "science of man" using the methods and constituting a part of natural science was coming into being before our eyes:

> *Sense experience (see Feuerbach) must be the basis of all science. Only when it proceeds from the two forms of sensory consciousness and sensory needs—and therefore only when it proceeds from nature—is it truly science. The entire historical process is a development toward man's becoming an object of sensory observation and the recognition of the needs of "man as man." History itself is nothing but a real part of natural history, as the unfolding of nature toward man. Natural science will later include the science of man, as the science of man will include natural science: it will be one science.*[21]

This very conception was the basis of Marx's insistence on the "scientific" character of Communism. Communism, the "appropriation of the human essence through and for man," is nothing but a "fully developed naturalism." This naturalism is in turn nothing but the "fully developed humanism." Communism is the "true resolution of the conflict between existence and essence, objectification and self-activity, freedom and necessity, individual and species. Communism is the solved puzzle of history and knows itself as this solution."[22]

Marx's gift for going to the root of things is nowhere more strikingly revealed than in his discussion of the necessity of expunging metaphysical questions—questions concerning the origin and ground of being—from the consciousness of man. These passages contain perhaps the most unbridled expression of the intellectual *libido dominandi* in the entire history of thought. With irresistible logic—given his premises—Marx reasons that if in fact "man is the essence for man," then in no sense is it conceivable for man to be dependent on an order of being which he did not create. The idea of creatureliness is condemned as a perverted idea; man cannot be truly man until he grasps the truth that he makes his own truth, that he creates

[20] "Nationalökonomie und Philosophie" in *Ibid.*, pp. 225-316 at 236.

[21] *Ibid.*, p. 245.

[22] *Ibid.*, p. 235.

himself. The metaphysical question about the origin of man, about the source of all existing things, is the product of abstraction. Only man in his alienated condition, the condition in which he finds himself prior to the final, apocalyptic Communist revolution that will negate this alienation, can think about or ask such a question. In the new world of the classless society and with the socialization of the means of production, a new man will be produced who is immune from the temptation to ask or conceive of metaphysical questions:

> for socialistic man the whole of so-called world history is nothing but the creation of man through human labor, of the development of nature for man, and in this process he has the visible, incontestable proof of his creation: through himself, through his own process of development.[23]

Once the interdependence of man and nature and the truth of man's self-creation have been recognized, have been experienced in real, i.e., practical life, then philosophy, theology, and political theory (inquiries grounded on the experience of man as having an origin beyond himself) "become impossible in practice." Communism, declares Marx, does not need to deny God in order to affirm man: rather, it affords the mechanism for negating the society of exploiters on which the idea of God is based. Communism begins with the "theoretical and practical sensory consciousness of man and nature." Reality to Marx is a seamless web, and all distinctions between objectivity and subjectivity, theory and practice, the individual and the species, nature and man, are dissolved. Reality is compressed into one-dimensional form, and all experience which claims to point beyond the world of immanent *praxis* is branded as illusory and as the product of practical conditions that must be changed by man himself.

Therefore, it is scarcely any surprise to find theoretical reflection, conceived of as having its own justification beyond its capacity to affect practical life, dismissed as a subterfuge for an ulterior practical concern. Disinterested *theōria* is a complete impossibility in the

[23] *Ibid.*, pp. 247-248. The whole section 5 of the *Philosophical-Economic Manuscripts* (pp. 246-248) is of crucial importance. Here is the kernel of Marx's "proof" of the impossibility of open existence and of metaphysical and ethical experience transcending the confines of immanent, human practical-productive activity.

Marxian world-view. *All* thought has its origin and end in the cave of practice. The antitheses which theory discovers can find their resolution "only in a practical manner," only through the "practical energy of man." The contradictions of theory cannot be resolved intellectually. There are no problems of pure knowledge. Every so-called theoretical problem must be seen as in truth a real problem of life which pre-Marxian philosophy could not solve precisely because it vainly sought to treat all propositions from an exclusively theoretical perspective.[24]

Marx's views on the "unity of theory and practice" (a phrase which was to be frequently invoked by Lenin and to serve as the keystone of all Communist ideology) are presented most fully in his important essay *The German Ideology*, composed between 1845 and 1846. The Marxian position is summarized in eleven dogmatic pronouncements or theses preceding the essay itself. The theses are criticisms of Ludwig Feuerbach's materialism, for which Marx had great respect but which he thought did not sufficiently demonstrate the immeasurable enhancement of human power which the materialist hypothesis inevitably portends. According to Marx, Feuerbach's materialism was excessively contemplative and theoretical:

> *The chief deficiency of all materialism up to the present time . . . is, that material reality is comprehended only in an objective or speculative fashion, instead of subjectively, as a material-human activity, or praxis.*[25]

Whether human thought can arrive at objective truth is a practical rather than a theoretical question. "It is in *praxis* that man must prove the truth, that is the reality and power, the this-sidedness, of his thinking." The teaching of Feuerbach about the fundamental importance of altering man's material circumstances and educating him in the truth of the materialist world-view "forgets that the material circumstances must be altered by man himself and that the teacher himself must be educated." This alteration in man's condition can be brought about only through "revolutionary *praxis.*" Objectivity and subjectivity are in revolutionary *praxis* dialectically united:

[24] *Ibid.*, p. 243.

[25] "Die Deutsche Ideologie" in *ibid.*, pp. 339-485 at 339. This is the opening sentence of the entire work. The "Theses on Feuerbach" are found on pp. 339-341.

man both acts (subjectively) and is acted upon (objectively). Reality is not to be understood but to be transformed.

Theory and practice constitute a unity. It is not sufficient to destroy the idea of God to prove, as Feuerbach did, that God is an anthropomorphic projection of human needs and aspirations, that other-worldly religion results from human suffering and alienation in this world, and that "the earthly family is the key to understanding the secret of the holy family." Rather "the earthly family itself must be practically and theoretically negated." By changing practical reality, theories and ideas of human beings are also changed, because reality is nothing more than "practical human-sensory activity" (*praktische menschlich-sinnlich Taetigkeit*).

Marx's reductionism leads him to contend that the essence of man is derivative from his societal relationships, and these relationships are in turn the result of man's material, practical activity. All human life is societal life, the isolated individual of liberal thought being a mere fiction, and "all societal life is essentially practical life. All mysteries . . . find their rational solution in human *praxis* and in the proper apprehending (*Begreifen*) of this *praxis*." Religious feeling is itself only a "societal product." He ends with the previously cited battlecry of the antitheoretical spirit: "The philosophers have only *interpreted* the world in different ways; the point is to change it."

The body of the essay entitled *The German Ideology* relentlessly develops the position that all thought concerning man and society —whether religious, ethical, aesthetic, metaphysical, or political—is ideological in character. Although he was familiar with Tracy's definition of ideology as the "science of ideas," Marx chose to use the term to indicate the false content of all thought prior to Communist science. Ideology to him was a "false consciousness" and it was the task of Communism to unmask the economic basis of supposedly disinterested and objective speculation. Consciousness, declares Marx, is itself a societal product and has no independence from material interests. What is called "spirit" or "mind" (*Geist*) is actually "burdened" with matter, and speech itself is basically "layers of air" and "sounds" in motion.[26]

It is in this essay that we find the famous formulas of Marxist reductionism, such as "what individuals are depends upon their mate-

[26] *Ibid.*, p. 357.

rial productive circumstances" and "it is not consciousness that determines life, but life that determines consciousness."[27]

"Morality, religion, metaphysics," and all such "ghosts of the human brain" are to Marx "ideological reflexes and echoes of the life process." When men interact with nature so as to change the material basis of their lives, they create thereby a new reality, resulting also in a change of "their thinking and the products of their thinking."[28] The very fact that men ever invented the false distinctions between theory and practice, spirit and matter, this-worldly and other-worldly existence has its origin in a material, societal development, viz., the division of labor. From the moment that work was divided into manual and mental categories, "the consciousness was capable of emancipating itself from the world and proceeding to develop 'pure theory,' theology, philosophy, morality, etc."[29] Communism, which will abolish class society with its division of labor, will also abolish pure theory, metaphysics, religion, etc. The illusory assumption that philosophy, religion, etc. are autonomous activities having been exposed, they will vanish as the material circumstances (division of labor, class structure) that formed the alienated consciousness on which they in turn were dependent become negated through the Communist Revolution. Through the Revolution the "all-sided dependence" of human beings on powers beyond man will be replaced by "control and conscious domination of these powers." Man is a societal being and as such men "make one another, both in the physical and intellectual [*geistig*] sense."[30]

In the Marxian formulation, theory loses its critical function and is described as the handmaiden of practical material interests. Thus, in the area of political thought, Marx holds the idea of the separation of powers to be a reflection of the struggle for power in Europe at a particular point in time rather than being the expression of some perennial truth. The struggle among the monarchy, nobility, and the bourgeoisie was the material reality which produced the ideology of the separation of powers. Thus, "the thoughts of the ruling class are in every epoch the ruling thoughts" and "the class

[27] *Ibid.*, pp. 347, 349.
[28] *Ibid.*, p. 349.
[29] *Ibid.*, p. 358.
[30] *Ibid.*, p. 366.

which constitutes the leading material power of the society is at the same time its leading intellectual power." The "ruling thoughts" of an epoch are therefore "nothing else but the ideal expression of the ruling material relationships."[31] This proposition is universal and admits of no exception. The Platos and Hegels, along with all the propagandists and time-servers in the history of mankind, are indiscriminately lumped together as the dupes or servants of the powers that be in every age.

Marx's most vivid illustration of what he understands to be the unity of theory and practice, the alliance between philosophy and the proletariat, is the *Communist Manifesto* itself. Here, in contrast to the pure theoretical treatise, such as Hobbes's *Leviathan* or Plato's *Republic*, we have a catechism for the widest possible dissemination among the masses. The *Manifesto* is not simply a polemical tract aiming at the adoption or prevention of concrete institutional change; it is also a high-flown statement of theoretical principles underlying the call to total action on behalf of the final victory for humanity. The *Communist Manifesto* was clearly intended by Marx and Engels as an illustration of the unity of theory and practice. Section two of the document, which enunciates well prior to Lenin the notion of the Communist party as the vanguard of the proletariat, describes the party as the most decisive, advanced, and progressive element in the working class movement in both the practical and the theoretical sense. Its title to lead is a consequence of its scientific understanding of the historical process and the inevitability of the destruction of capitalism and with it all forms of exploitation of man by man.[32] Communist "theory" is the necessary weapon for the demolition of class society; it is not a mere description of the realities of human life in society but a blueprint for establishing a new world, based on the knowledge of man's self-creation. Marx here emerges as the supreme partisan, as an intellectual who will spare nothing in the service of the mass movement. He consciously repudiates the aspiration of the theorist to a disinterested approach.

From the Marxian tomb of *praxis* there is no escape. Man, in the totality of his being, is absorbed into the new society which is nothing else than the organized, conscious, collective domination by the

[31] *Ibid.*, pp. 373-374.

[32] "Manifest der Kommunistischen Partei," in *ibid.*, pp. 524-560 at 539.

human species of the real material world. Even if Marx's goal of final
Communism, characterized by the withering away of the state, spontaneity, self-determination, and the end of alienation could be
achieved in history (which it on principle cannot be, because man
remains man with all his nobility and his vices and every society
requires a ruling minority for its functioning and, in sum, temporal
existence does not change its character upon the orders of prophets
of ideological second realities), what would be the result? Quite
simply, the result would be a world inhabited by men whose spiritual
substance has been exhausted in the process of conquering and dominating the environment. The "unity of theory and practice" would
achieve the destruction of the *bios thēoretikos*. The total victory of
revolutionary *praxis* would mean the creation of a world in which life
in the openness of philosophy (the "asking of metaphysical questions") would be impossible. Marx's totalitarian ideology which
promises men the "leap from necessity to freedom" actually indicates
the route from the freedom of spirit discovered in Greek philosophy,
Judaism, and Christianity, to enslavement, to the practical-productive
world-view. The only obstacle in the way of the emergence under
Marxism of the one-dimensional man, wholly absorbed in problems
of production and "Communist construction," would be man himself, who even in the face of enormous societal pressure retains the
spark of inner resistance capable of being kindled into a flame.

Theory versus Ideology

When one considers the magnitude of the messianic attack,
together with the grim institutional reality which followed in its wake
during our century, the importance of the survival of political theory
becomes obvious. For if political theory becomes impossible, then
the open society will have become an impossibility. The attacks of
the three ideological reductionists whom we have cited in this
chapter reveal that the fortunes of political theory are bound up
with those of philosophy and theology in general. Indeed, political
theory and political science may properly be seen as drawing on these
disciplines and as closely related to them. Political theory is the study
of the principles of right order in the psyche and in society. It is
not an isolated academic discipline, a subfield within the discipline
conventionally called today political science. Any serious thinker,
whether he be labelled theologian, philosopher, social scientist, or

what not, who contributes to the articulation of critical principles of right order is a political theorist. But to arrive at critical principles means going beyond partisanship, beyond immersion in the stream of practical-productive activity, beyond polemics, tactics, or projects of revolution. The final death of political theory, which is one of the goals of ideological reductionism, would mean far more than the demise of a specialized academic discipline which under another name might later reappear. The death of political theory as the science of the critical principles of order would mean the unchallenged victory of a totalitarian world-view.

Marx was the most radical reductionist in the history of political thought. Today the vital question is whether the validity and independence of ethical and theological experience can be recovered. Can the tide of reductionism be turned so that the full amplitude of the experience of the existing human person in his relationship to transcendent reality be understood again and once more permeate the intellectual atmosphere? It would appear that there is cause for optimism, and that we are at present in the West in the midst of a process of de-ideologizing the political vocabulary. However, in intellectual circles the reductionist attitude, usually but not always without the messianic component of Marxism and Comteanism added, continues to be powerful. The methodology of post-Comtean positivism remains a major obstacle to the revival of a science of right order open to transcendence, and it is on this phenomenon that attention is focused in the following chapter.

FOUR: POSITIVISM, THE NEW POLITICAL SCIENCE, AND THE DECLINE OF POLITICAL THEORY

The impact of Comte's positivist idea on the social sciences during the century since his death has been enormous. Although positivism failed to make a clean sweep of the field, it is nonetheless true to say that from the latter half of the nineteenth century until the midpoint of the twentieth a process that can be described as the "positivization of the social sciences" was taking place. Meanwhile, outside the academy, aggressive ideological mass movements of left and right proliferated. During this period, critical political theory did not disappear (as we shall attempt to demonstrate in Chapter 5), but it did decline significantly as the intellectual energies of many who in former times would have been political theorists were siphoned off by the new "value-free" social sciences.

It is not our concern here to write an account of this positivization process. Arnold Brecht has fulfilled this task admirably in his mammoth work *Political Theory*, and Bernard Crick has provided an acute analysis of the process as it took place in American political science since the 1930s.[1] In this chapter the focus will rather be on the basic features of neopositivist[2] methodology and the incompatibility of political theory with those principles. For to the extent that positivist methodological assumptions prevail in the social sciences, political theory is made impossible. A full recovery of critical political theory within the positivist universe of discourse cannot be achieved. This point needs to be made with some emphasis, because it is becoming rather fashionable in some quarters to speak of "reuniting" the traditionalist and behavioralist components of the discipline and to seek to build bridges between the rival positions.[3] While there can be nothing wrong, of course, in the attempt to build bridges, I regard the

[1] Arnold Brecht, *Political Theory: The Foundations of Twentieth-Century Political Thought* (Princeton, Princeton University Press, 1959); Bernard Crick, *The American Science of Politics* (Berkeley, University of California Press, 1959). The accent of Crick's analysis is on the adjective in his title. It is the great merit of Crick's work to have demonstrated the degree to which the "new" political science in the United States has been based on a rather thoughtless universalization of certain specifically American predilections and concerns.

[2] By neopositivism, I mean the Vienna circle and those who have been influenced by its orientation. Neopositivism is, or attempts to be, more sophisticated than was either the messianic Comtean positivism or the militant antireligious positivism of the *fin du siècle* in Europe about overtly parading value-judgments as science. Neopositivism strives to achieve methodological purification. However, as we shall see in Chapter 9, old-style Comtean attitudes are still very much alive even in some people who proclaim themselves as adherents of neopositivist methodology.

[3] William T. Bluhm, *Theories of the Political System* (Englewood Cliffs, N.J., Prentice-Hall, 1965), is the most fervent recent call for bridge-building and synthesis in political science.

effort as premature. Indeed, if a bridge does eventually unite the philosophical and behavioralist wings of the profession, it is most likely to emerge, without our consciously constructing it, out of the very process of serious intellectual debate between strongly held positions. There is something artificial about building an intellectual bridge for its own sake. The end of scholarship is truth, not amity.

Positivism is an indispensable label, but it must be recognized that among those who share its methodological postulates there are significant differences. Its finest representatives, men like Max Weber and Arnold Brecht, are sensitive to the limitations and difficulties attendant on the separation of fact and value and actually succeed in rescuing a small strip of reality in which critical, rational principles have some bearing. A second category of positivists, about which more will be said in Chapter Nine, remains afflicted with the Comtean *hybris* and supports under the guise of objectivity a closed, manipulative society all too reminiscent of the ideological reductionism discussed in the last chapter. Against all the rules, values are smuggled in under the guise of facts or conceptual schemes. Within this group are to be found the extreme behavioralists and apostles of social engineering. A third school of positivist social scientists may be labelled the hyperfactualists; although rather numerous, they are not very important and are recognized to be lacking in intellectual sophistication by the more able representatives of the positivist camp. Their work tends toward triviality and the accumulation of factual minutiae. Research on the facts without any clear understanding of how to order or relate them is characteristic of this group. A fourth group may be termed the axiological positivists, who, while agreeing that value-judgments are not and may not become scientific, nonetheless insist upon the propriety and indeed inevitability of value speculation on the part of the social scientist. Because it is not possible to achieve a completely value-free social science, it is maintained that the investigator should frankly state and develop his value assumptions, carefully labelling them as such.

To summarize, there appear to be four principal varieties of positivist social science: relatively open and undogmatic, hybristic, hyperfactualist and descriptive in the trivial sense, and axiological or oriented to value as well as to fact. While the differences between the four types are important, it remains true that a full-fledged critical theory of politics and society is impossible even for the most open

representatives of the positivist persuasion, because such an attempt
is stifled at its inception by the cardinal methodological postulate
of positivism: the separation of fact and value.

Arnold Brecht, in the study to which reference has already been
made, has chronicled the process of "methodological purification"
which took place in twentieth century social science. The purification
consisted in the careful distinction between factual propositions and
value-judgments together with the insistence that the latter be treated
as beyond the purview of scientific, verifiable, or intersubjectively
valid knowledge. As Richard Schmidt, writing at the turn of the
century in Germany, described the goal of positivist political science:

> The new political science frees itself from the speculative view-
> point, leaves the metaphysical question about the idea of the
> State to one side, and confines itself to the world of experience.[4]

By experience, *Erfahrung*, Schmidt meant the world available to
sensory observation. The inward seeing of the theorist, the multidimensional experience of the existing human person is excluded
from science because it is not empirical. This meant that for positivism propositions about the right order of the psyche and society,
the central questions for political theory, were matters of subjective
opinion. Thus, the entire enterprise of elaborating a critical *epistēmē
politikē*—the objective of traditional political theory—was shaken to
its foundations. What is called political theory then becomes within
the positivist universe of discourse either the formulation of hypotheses and conceptual schemes for aid in empirical research or the
propagation of unscientific value-judgments. The new science of
politics will admit theory into its confines only as methodology, as
the handmaiden of empirical research. Old-style political theory with
its excess baggage of metaphysics, ethics, etc., is transformed into
political doctrine, utopian speculation, or the ideological reflex to a
given practical set of circumstances. Thus, there could be scientific
theories of voting behavior, decision-making, social change and the
like, but no theories of the principles of right order because the latter
would be unverifiable and untestable with regard to sense observation.
Theory as science, the validity of whose principles can be tested in
terms of the inner experience of the mature man (Aristotle's *spou-*

[4] Richard Schmidt, *Allgemeine Staatslehre*, 2 vols. (Leipzig, 1901), vol. I,
p. 117.

daios), is destroyed in favor of a conception of all science as consisting of propositions capable of verification with reference to sensory experience.

The meaning of the fact-value dichotomy for political science is made perfectly clear in numerous works of the positivist persuasion, but two quotations, one from David Easton and the other from Herbert Simon, will suffice to illustrate the point that value-judgments are placed beyond the scope of science. Easton, whose book, *The Political System*, has attracted considerable attention in contemporary social science circles, states that the "working assumption . . . generally adopted in the social sciences" maintains that "values can ultimately be reduced to emotional responses conditioned by the individual's total life experiences." This commonly accepted assumption (which he also endorses) regards facts and values as "logically heterogeneous."

> [The] factual aspect of a proposition refers to a part of reality, hence it can be tested by reference to the facts. In this way we can check its truth. The moral aspect of a proposition, however, expresses only the emotional response of an individual to a state of real or presumed facts. . . . Although we can say that the aspect of a proposition referring to a fact can be true or false, it is meaningless to characterize the value aspect of a proposition in this way.[5]

Simon has summarized his basic methodological position as follows: "The process of validating a factual proposition is quite distinct from the process of validating a value judgment. The former is validated by its agreement with the facts, the latter by human fiat."[6]

Both authors are in essential agreement with Gustav Radbruch in his relativist phase when he declared that values "are not capable of cognition but only of confession."

Simon, Easton, Lasswell, Felix Oppenheim, and the host of other political scientists who today join the chorus affirming the fact-value separation as the inviolable methodological canon of scientific scholarship have derived their position from a school of thought known as logical positivism. Closely associated with this movement, although

[5] David Easton, *The Political System* (New York, Knopf, 1953), p. 221.

[6] Herbert Simon, *Administrative Behavior: Study of Decision-Making Process in Administrative Organization*, 2nd ed. (New York, Macmillan, 1957), p. 56.

not precisely identical with it, is linguistic analysis, another intellectual development of considerable importance in illuminating the present condition of political theory. It will be necessary in this chapter to consider these schools of thought in order to indicate, in a more satisfactory manner than would otherwise be possible, the sources of the methodological postulates of contemporary positivist political science and to discover why this political science must remain an obstacle in the way of the revival of political theory. For the differences between the proponents of the revival of political theory and positivism are fundamental in nature. They are not idiosyncratic or personal, but epistemological and philosophical. They have to do with interpretations of experience and the ways of knowing, and they cannot be glossed over with some fuzzy compromise or a contrived synthesis of incompatible elements. Few people enjoy internecine strife for its own sake, but in the case of the positivist-classicist controversy in political science, the conflict has a deep and valid basis and turns on absolutely fundamental questions. If there is to be a détente and eventual rapprochement within political science it must be preceded by a frank recognition of the nature and extent of the quarrel.

Logical Positivism

Logical positivism as a term was coined in the 1920s "to characterize the standpoint of a group of philosophers, scientists and mathematicians who gave themselves the name of the Vienna Circle."[7] The mainstay of the Vienna Circle until his murder by a disgruntled student was Moritz Schlick, Professor at the University of Vienna and later at Prague. Other members of prominence were Rudolf Carnap, Otto von Neurath, Victor Kraft, and Herbert Feigl. Still others who from time to time were loosely affiliated with the group but who were not members in any strict sense were Ludwig Wittgenstein, Hans Kelsen, and Karl Popper. Wittgenstein is of particular importance in that he served as a kind of intellectual link between the circle and the school of linguistic philosophy that has flourished in Oxford and other English universities.

Logical positivism is a blanket term covering a multitude of

[7] A. J. Ayer, Introduction to *Logical Positivism* (New York, Free Press, 1959), p. 3.

thinkers; there is considerable diversity in both the scientific and political views of those who willingly accept the label and to whom it may be accurately applied. However, logical positivists all share a certain basic orientation about the criteria to be employed for determining what kinds of statements can constitute knowledge, and they are unanimous in rejecting the claims of traditional metaphysics to cognitive status. With varying degrees of dogmatism, they would share Carnap's experiential reductionism as expressed in statements like the following:

> I will call metaphysical all those propositions which claim to represent knowledge about something which is over or beyond all experience, e.g., about the real Essence of Things in themselves, the Absolute, and such like.[8]

> Metaphysicians cannot avoid making their propositions non-verifiable, because if they made them verifiable, the decision about the truth or falsehood of their doctrines would depend upon experience and therefore belong to the region of empirical science.[9]

The above statements are perfect examples of the dogmatism and experiential reductionism of the extreme logical positivist position. Carnap's rigid and narrow principle of verification is itself unverifiable and is ultimately no more than a stipulated definition. To get around this objection, Carnap grounded the verification principle on its acceptability to a given "culture circle," but this argument is also arbitrary and shows the way in which logical positivism reinforces the idea of a closed society and is inimical to political theory, which strives to maintain a critical distance from one's culture circle.

In his perceptive volume *Words and Things*, Ernest Gellner describes the basic tenet of logical positivism (shared by linguistic philosophy) as follows:

> . . . all knowledge, or, in the linguistic formulation, all meaning-ful discourse, consists of two kinds: first, reports of experiential fact, whose claim to truth resides exclusively in that the facts bear them out; and, secondly, logic, interpreted as consequences of calculations within systems whose rules are conventionally estab-lished.[10]

---

[8] R. Carnap, *Philosophy and Logical Syntax* (London, 1935), p. 15.

[9] *Ibid.*, p. 17.

[10] Ernest Gellner, *Words and Things* (London, 1959), pp. 78-79.

To the logical positivist, then, scientific propositions are of two kinds: analytic or synthetic. An analytic statement is logical or mathematical in nature: it "adds nothing to the meaning of a given term or proposition, but merely makes explicit [as in a syllogism] what is implied in that meaning."[11] However, when "a proposition adds something to the meaning of a given term or proposition it is not analytic but synthetic." Synthetic propositions cannot be arrived at simply by deductive reasoning from an a priori statement.

Logical positivism set out to discover the criteria of "verifiability" for synthetic—or substantive and factual—statements. According to the earliest, most rigorous formulations of members of the Vienna Circle, a synthetic proposition had "meaning" or "sense" only if it were on principle capable of empirical verification, empirical in this context meaning availability to the sensory or "direct" experience of two or more independent observers. If a statement is not verifiable in the above manner then it can be proved to be neither true nor false, and so is "meaningless," or, in A. J. Ayer's formulation in his celebrated tract *Language, Truth, and Logic*, is "nonsense," i.e., unverifiable by sense experience.

From the perspective of logical positivism, therefore, the core of traditional political theory, constituting as it did reflection on the good life for man and society, was rejected as unverifiable and, therefore, meaningless. Indeed, as various critics of this perspective have noted, if the standards of valid meaning adopted by the most rigorous logical positivists were accepted it would be difficult to ascertain what would be left within the domain of science. As Michael Polanyi has observed, "strictly speaking, nothing that we know can be said precisely." We must not, he continued, "invoke quixotic standards of valid meaning which, if rigorously practiced, would reduce us all to voluntary imbecility."[12]

Indeed, strictly speaking, the principle of verifiability is itself unverifiable and amounts to a momentous dogmatic assumption —readily disproved by the totality of our experience—about the physicalistic nature of human experience. Smuggled into the canons of science is the antimetaphysical metaphysics of the Tracy-Comte-

[11] See the discussion in Brecht, *op. cit.*, pp. 55 ff.

[12] Michael Polanyi, *Personal Knowledge: Towards a Post-Critical Philosophy* (Chicago, University of Chicago Press, 1958), p. 88.

Marx type of sensationalist reductionism. It is such considerations as these that have led Leo Strauss to characterize positivism as being "more dogmatic than any other position of which we have records."[13]

Unless it be thought that the principle of verification is being misinterpreted here, let us listen to its formulation at the hands of A. J. Ayer. That principle of verification, we are told,

> lays it down that the meaning of a statement is determined by the way in which it can be verified, where its being verified consists in its being tested by empirical observation. Consequently, statements like those of metaphysics to the truth or falsehood of which no empirical observation could possibly be relevant, are ruled out as factually meaningless.[14]

This, of course, is a decidedly curious way of proceeding, because it defines meaning in advance by the method employed to reach it, instead of viewing method—or better methods—as the procedure(s) by which we arrive at meaning. In such a curious view of the world, method replaces substance as the central concern of the investigator. This attitude of mind has been described with accuracy as "methodolatry."

The influence of the neopositivist verification principle on contemporary political science of the behavioralist variety has been of immense proportions. Examples from the literature could be multiplied to show the frequency with which the verification principle is invoked as the criterion by which propositions are accorded scientific status. The role of this principle and the fact-value dichotomy in the teaching of Lasswell, Simon, and other contemporary behavioralist political scientists will be discussed in Chapter Nine. For the present, it is sufficient for purposes of illustration to cite the following statement by an adherent of the behavioral school of political science in a volume referred to in Chapter One:

> There is . . . another manner [in contrast to "normative theory"] in which the study of man may be approached. We shall call this empirical theory. Its primary focus is on an explanation of how man, in fact, does behave rather than how he should or

[13] Leo Strauss, "The Liberalism of Classical Political Philosophy," *Review of Metaphysics* XII (March, 1959), 390-431 at 430.

[14] Essay in Gilbert Ryle, ed., *The Revolution in Philosophy* (London, 1956), p. 74.

ought to behave. Empirical theorists attempt to determine, with as few unproven assumptions as possible, factors which help to explain man's activities on this earth. They do this with the following criterion as a guide: that any explanation which is given may be verified on principle through the use of man's sense apparatus (the five senses of seeing, smelling, hearing, touching, and tasting), without relying on a sixth sense.[15]

Linguistic Philosophy

Another intellectual movement of importance which has contributed to the decline of traditional political theory has been linguistic philosophy. There is considerable diversity among linguistic philosophers (which leads them to rejoin that they do not comprise a school and that any generalization about their position is inaccurate), but despite these variations certain characteristics are common to them. Most linguistic philosophers have agreed with the logical positivists that metaphysical statements are outside their province, as are value-judgments, which have emotive but not cognitive significance.[16] Philosophy is conceived to be a "second-order study," a "conceptual and not a substantive inquiry."[17] Its findings cannot be about first-order principles. Philosophy takes the world as it is—i.e., as known to natural science and common sense, and attempts to clear up linguistic confusions and muddles, whether in the language of science or everyday activity, including political activity.

Despite the fact that linguistic philosophy exhibits a marked similarity in orientation to the logical positivism of the Vienna Circle, it tends to exhibit a slight degree of openness to metaphysical experience. This is probably due in part to the influence which Ludwig Wittgenstein exerted on the movement at least in the early phase of his thought. Wittgenstein, who taught at Oxford for some years,

[15] Lewis W. Froman, Jr., *People and Politics* (New York, Prentice-Hall, 1962), pp. 16-17. A. J. Ayer's *Language, Truth and Logic* is cited in his footnote along with Hans Reichenbach and Arnold Brecht.

[16] To quote Ayer once more: ". . . it is not especially the business of the philosopher to make value judgments, to tell people how they ought to live. He is free to make value judgments, like anybody else, but he is not professionally entitled to a special hearing." *Ibid.*, p. 78.

[17] Gellner, *op. cit.*, pp. 100-101.

suggested at the end of his famous *Tractatus* that there may be truths beyond those capable of being expressed in "ordinary language" —i.e. language of sense experience. As he cryptically stated it, "One must be silent about that of which he cannot speak." (*Wovon man nicht sprechen kann darüber muss man schweigen.*) This counsel, it is true, is preceded by a passage in which Wittgenstein instructs the philosopher to "say nothing except what can be said"; metaphysics does not come within his province. The proper method of philosophy is to clear away the rubbish of linguistic misconceptions; should the task ever be completed, philosophy would cease to have a *raison d'être.* "He who understands" would "throw away the ladder after he has climbed up on it."[18] Despite the nearly complete emasculation of philosophy implied in such an orientation, more dogmatic logical positivists were aroused by his final intimation of a "something" to be silent about—of a reality beyond sense experience—which could only be hinted at in ineffable language. Von Neurath exploded that "one must indeed be silent, but not *about* anything." And an English logical positivist commented acidly, "What we can't say we can't say, and we can't whistle it either."[19] These gentlemen would have agreed with Moritz Schlick, who in his *A New Philosophy of Experience* (1932) wrote: "To regret the impossibility of metaphysics becomes impossible; it would be the same as regretting the impossibility of a round square."

Although most of the original logical positivists of the Vienna Circle group appear to have been left-wing in their political views, the tendency of their methodology and view of science was toward political conservatism for the simple reason that they removed from political philosophy, as from philosophy in general, the possibility of elucidating any critical principles of substantive importance. Although they all agreed that a philosopher or scientist is free to volunteer and to advertise his personal preferences on political or moral questions, his opinions were no more authoritative than those of anyone else, being unprovable and grounded on his visceral reactions and emotional preferences. Since the main activity of a philosopher or scientist is to be precisely that, and since political and ethical speculation was ultimately arbitrary and opinionated, the logic of logical positivism

[18] L. Wittgenstein, *Tractatus Logico-Philosophicus*, p. 189.

[19] Quoted in Ayer's essay in Ryle, *op. cit.*, p. 75.

is to stick to one's last and to leave evaluation and exhortation to others.

The latent conservatism in logical positivism becomes more explicit in linguistic philosophy—and is apparently personally congenial to most British linguistic philosophers, who seem, in contrast to the Vienna Circle members, actually to be highly conservative in their political convictions. This has caused considerable uneasiness to an individual like A. J. Ayer, who has taken to writing political columns for the Sunday newspapers. He is a conspicuous exception to the rule that, in Britain, linguistic philosophers tend to be politically conservative, and he may be counted in the left wing of the British Labour Party.

Ernest Gellner, who is also disturbed (to employ an understatement) about what he detects to be the implicit conservatism in British linguistic philosophy but who finds this situation inherent in the very nature of the enterprise, has indicted the movement in the following terms: "An alienation from the modern world and real issues, a curious artificiality, pedantry, an ivory-towerism, procrastination, all these are characteristics and values shared by . . . linguistic philosophers."[20] Reflecting upon G. E. Moore's statement that he was not puzzled by the world but only by other philosophers' sayings, and John Wisdom's dictum that "Philosophy begins and ends with platitude," Gellner observed that the "old kind of philosophy took language for granted and puzzled about the world. Linguistic philosophy takes the world for granted and puzzles about language."[21]

The conservative propensities of linguistic analysis for political thought are nowhere more clearly revealed than in what is probably the outstanding work of a linguistic philosopher on politics: T. D. Weldon's *Vocabulary of Politics*. Weldon's position is that philosophical writings in any case have no effect on practical life and that regardless of developments in philosophy, general human interests, as Kant once put it, "remain in the same position as before."[22]

In an essay that is less well-known than his book but which expresses the same viewpoint, Weldon wrote of the function of political philosophy:

> It is not the job of philosophy to provide new information about politics . . . or any other matter of fact. Philosophical problems

[20] Gellner, *op. cit.*, p. 92.

[21] *Ibid.*, p. 96.

[22] T. D. Weldon, *The Vocabulary of Politics* (London, 1953), p. 145.

are entirely second order problems. They are problems, that is, which are generated by the language in which facts are described and explained by those whose function it is to construct and defend scientific, historical, or other types of theory.[23]

Political philosophy, Weldon insists, should not be expected either to establish or demolish political principles; its conclusions have no bearing on the decisions of practical politicians. In particular, political philosophers should not be expected to suggest reforms of the electoral system, or new legislation in any area.

> The purpose of philosophy, then, is to expose and elucidate linguistic muddles; it has done its job when it has revealed the confusions which have occurred and are likely to recur in inquiries into matters of fact because the structure and use of language are what they are. "Modern political philosophers do not preach," we say, "That was the heresy of the nineteenth century. We are plain, honest men who tidy up muddles and have no axe to grind."[24]

This statement reveals as well as any other the tendency of linguistic philosophy to buy a condemnation of ideological fanaticism at the price of a monumental complacency. This position which Weldon defends is tenable, if at all, only in a well-ordered society with a strong sense of tradition, as is the case with Great Britain. But what if the language one is analyzing is that of Italy in 1922 or Germany in 1933? What about just doing one's job and linguistically fiddling while Rome burns in that historical context? In this area, linguistic philosophy is clearly a result of overreacting to the massive poisoning of the intellectual atmosphere by the arrogant system-builders and messianic thinkers of nineteenth-century Europe. Although understandable as a phenomenon and in a way admirable for its condemnation of utopian messianic pretensions, it utterly destroys the distinctive critical function of political theory as it has been understood.

Linguistic philosophy shares with logical positivism a monumental conceit, for it seriously maintains that by far the greater part of philosophical thought prior to the Wittgensteinian-Vienna Circle

[23] "Political Principles" in P. Laslett, ed., *Philosophy, Politics, Society*, first series (New York, Barnes & Noble, 1957), p. 22.

[24] *Ibid.*, pp. 23, 24.

revelation is a misconceived inquiry, an inquiry concerned with the wrong questions. Aristotle's view that philosophy originated in "wonder,"[25] must be replaced with the idea that traditional philosophy arose out of verbal confusion. The task of the new philosophy is therapeutic: to point out to the befuddled traditionalist that "when verbal confusions are tidied up" most of his questions "are not unanswerable."[26]

Thus, the apparent modesty of linguistic philosophy actually masks a stupendous arrogance: the claim to have eliminated the major problems of previous philosophy by a bit of verbal clarification.

Faced with a doctrine of this type, one is impressed by the wisdom of the following statement by R. G. Collingwood:

> *Assumption for assumption, which are we to prefer? That in sixty generations of continuous thought philosophers have been exerting themselves wholly in vain and have wanted for the first word of good sense until we came on the scene. Or that this labor has been on the whole profitable, and its history the history of an effort neither contemptible nor unrewarded?*[27]

A. J. Ayer has done the service of pointing up the major issue involved in the contemporary attempt to restore philosophy and political theory to their historic dimensions. It is all very well, he has written, for the metaphysician to say that there may be "other worlds besides the world of science and common sense, and that he makes it his business to explore them. But then the onus is on him to show by what criterion his statements are to be tested: until he does this we do not know how to take them."[28] It could perhaps be argued more plausibly that the "onus" is on the reductionists to show why they can arbitrarily confine experience to sense experience. But Ayer is right that an explication of the criteria by which metaphysical statements are to be tested is an essential task for those engaged in the revival of political theory in the traditional sense. As we shall see, this problem has been of central concern to Eric Voegelin, a

[25] *Metaphysics*, Book A, chap. 2: Philosophy arose "as it arises still, from wonder." Man is "astonished" and "perplexed" about things; he is conscious of his own ignorance.

[26] *Vocabulary of Politics*, p. 192.

[27] R. G. Collingwood, *Essay on Philosophical Method* (Cambridge, Oxford University Press, 1933), p. 225.

[28] Ryle, *op. cit.*, pp. 75-76.

key figure in the contemporary effort to restore political theory as the science of right order in the psyche and in society.

Axiological Positivism

Not all social scientists were happy about the purification of their disciplines due to the demands of logical positivism. Even among many of those who accepted the positivist fact-value dichotomy and who therefore denied value-judgments cognitive status, there was a movement to win back for the political and social scientist his concern for the significant and relevant questions with which he had previously dealt. An early attempt was made in Europe, where a sizeable school of neo-Kantian writers began to insist on the inevitability of value-judgments in scientific investigation and on the *Wertbezogenheit* ("value-relatedness") of factual statements. In the United States, only since World War II has there been a major effort along somewhat similar lines to solve the dilemma posed by the emasculation of political theory that accompanied the positivist ascendancy. David Easton has been prominent among those who have argued for the retention of "value theory" as one of the major concerns of the political theorist. At least this was true for his book *The Political System*. In his more recent works he has had less to say about value theory and more about models and types, what he calls empirical theory.

The principal contention of Easton's earlier position (which might be called the axiological-positivist position) is that the fact-value dichotomy need not and should not mean that the political scientist qua "political theorist" will eschew value-judgments in a bootless chase for the *wertfrei Wissenschaft* ("value-free Science"). On the contrary, political theorists should gladly seize the opportunity to throw off the encumbrance of having to claim cognitive status for their ethical reflections, a necessity under the old prepositivist dispensation. The theorist will now be free to become an "imaginative moral architect." In addition to producing "causal theory" he can indulge in "moral theory." Political theory in the latter sense will be "a projection of an individual's total scheme of preferences." The Eastonian axiological position has been expressed by Dwight Waldo who, also subscribing to the notion that value is a "positive or negative preference," has insisted that "Political theorists should undertake 'imaginative moral architecture,' and indulge their creative imaginations in utopia-building. . . . Whose function is it, if not the political theorist's, to project ways of organizing the political aspects of our lives?"[29]

Contemporaneously with Easton (although Easton goes into the matter much more deeply), Alfred Cobban propounded the same remedy for the rejuvenation of political theory in his previously cited essay. Cobban sharply separated political science from theory. ("The object of science is to show how things happen, and why, in the nexus of cause and effect, they do happen. . . .") "What I mean," he wrote in an article in 1953, "is simply that it is not the function of science to pass ethical judgment. . . . The political theorist, on the other hand, is essentially concerned with the discussion of what ought to be. His judgments are at bottom value judgments."[30]

The only difficulty with the proposed solution is that it perpetuates the very intellectual crisis which it is designed to alleviate. Whatever comes of this axiological revisionism (and positivists like Arnold Brecht are by no means disposed to accept it),[31] it cannot possibly have the effect of restoring political theory, because true political theory is not to be confused with value projection and utopia construction. As an experiential science, political theory undertakes to discover the place of political activity in the structure of reality as a whole. Like his positivist counterpart, the theorist must test his propositions by recourse to experience, only the range of the experience which he regards as suitable for control is broader than the single plane of physical sensation and tactile visibility. One can search the vocabulary of political theorists from Plato to Hegel but he will not find a single reference to the specific term value-judgment or to the concept for which it stands under some other name. As one of the leading members of the movement to restore political theory as an experiential science has expressed it, the terms value-judgment and value-free science

> were not part of the philosophical vocabulary before the second half of the nineteenth century. The notion of a value-judgment

[29] Dwight Waldo, " 'Values' in the Political Science Curriculum," in Roland Young (ed.), *Approaches to the Study of Politics* (Evanston, Illinois, 1958), pp. 96-111 at 111.

[30] Alfred Cobban, "The Decline of Political Theory," *Political Science Quarterly*, LXVIII (September, 1953), 335.

[31] See Brecht's comment on Easton's book in *Political Theory, op. cit.*, p. 502.

(*Werturteil*) *is meaningless in itself; it gains its meaning from a situation in which it is opposed to judgments concerning facts* (*Tatsachenurteile*). *And this situation was created through the positivistic conceit that only propositions concerning facts of the phenomenal world were "objective," while judgments concerning the right order of the soul and society were "subjective."* . . . *This classification made sense only if the positivistic dogma was accepted on principle.* . . .[32]

The theorist is not at liberty to advocate any preferences which, for whatever obscure reason, may strike his fancy (or, in more sophisticated language, have an emotive appeal for him), for he takes his bearings from his understanding of the reality in which he participates. All the great political theorists of the past would have subscribed in principle to the Thomistic dictum that *bonum et ens convertuntur*, and they would have agreed that the answer to the axiological question of what ought to be is contained within the answer to the ontological question of what essentially is.[33] When the theorists offered their propositions about the good or natural life for man in society, they were, it is true, speaking about what he ought to do, but this "ought" was not regarded as a subjective preference or value-judgment but as an experiential fact; the ought is the "experienced tension between the order of being and the conduct of man."[34] (The differences among the various political theorists concerned their divergent reading of what experience teaches about the ontological structure itself.)

The axiological positivist position can never succeed in rescuing political theory from the oblivion to which "value-neutral" positivism has consigned it. If it accomplishes anything, it can only be to turn political theorists into opinionated ideologists. The axiological approach, while aspiring to redeem political theory, can only consummate its destruction. If a scholar really accepts the dogma that

[32] Eric Voegelin, *The New Science of Politics* (Chicago, University of Chicago Press, 1952), p. 11.

[33] Which is not the same as asking "what exists." Cf. J. H. Hallowell, *The Moral Foundation of Democracy* (Chicago, University of Chicago Press, 1954), pp. 24-25: ". . . being and goodness belong together. Through knowledge of what we are, we obtain knowledge of what we ought to do. To know what man is, is to know what he should be and do."

[34] Eric Voegelin, "*The Nature of Law*," unpublished treatise, p. 66.

all speculation about right order in society and psyche is hopelessly subjective, ultimately nothing more than a reflection of his unique total life experiences, what justification does he, as a scholar and an aspiring scientist, have for engaging in such speculation? If he believes his conclusions on such matters to have no more foundation than his ultimately arbitrary personal preferences, he will as a scientist leave most of what used to be the field of political theory to demagogic exhibitionists and concentrate on a topic for investigation that will be sanctioned by the profession as a scientific endeavor. Indeed, it was precisely for the reason that he was distressed over social science becoming a battleground for competing subjective value-systems that Max Weber issued his plea for "value-free" social science in the emotion-drenched university atmosphere in Munich after 1918. Surely the answer to political theory's difficulties—brought on by the victory of the positivist orientation—does not lie in heeding the siren call of those who say that political theory must become the deliberate advocacy of personal political preferences. The answer can only lie, rather, in the questioning of the positivist dogma itself. For it is the dogma, after all, with its experiential reductionism that is at the root of the aforementioned difficulties.

Max Weber and the Positivist Cul-de-sac

The inherent limitations in the positivist position are revealed most clearly in its greatest representative, Max Weber. He did as much as anyone possibly could within the positivist universe of discourse to avoid the pitfalls of either a sterile or reductionist factualism (logical positivism) or an uncontrolled indulgence in opinionated and uncritical value speculation (axiological positivism). And yet he must be judged as having failed. When even a Weber cannot overcome the restrictions of the positivist perspective to establish a significant and critical social science, the position itself must surely be fundamentally defective. Neo-Positivism or post-Comtean positivism at its best is a flight from ideology toward science; but it never reaches a critical *epistēmē politikē* and so as a movement must be declared a retrogression in the history of political and social thought.

It was Max Weber who discussed most profoundly the problems, dilemmas, and agonies which the fact-value dichotomy imposes on the social scientist. Weber was a prodigiously gifted man, who almost certainly would have been a political theorist of the first rank had he been able to overcome the positivist methodological position. He deserves to be read as a sensitive human being with enormous political acumen and at the same time as the most able exponent of value-free social science (*wertfrei Wissenschaft*).

By *Wertfreiheit* Weber meant anything but the naive view that values had nothing to do with science. He agreed with the axiological positivists on the "value-relatedness" (*Wertbezogenheit*) of all science. Our very selection of a problem for scientific research is the result of a positive choice, or "interest." The mind does not observe facts at random; we select that area of reality which commands our interest. As a result of the "knowledge-interest" that motivates us to do research on a particular problem in the first place, we then order the facts in terms of a conceptual framework. If this ordering is done successfully, an "ideal type" will be fabricated by the researcher which will bring out connections, or interrelated patterns, in the social process.[35] These ideal types are empirical rather than normative, however:[36] their purpose is to illuminate social reality by helping us to understand how a particular phenomenon developed, came to be what it is and not something else. It is precisely here that what one scholar has called the "small strip" of value-free science existed for Weber.[37] Ultimately irrational interests have led us to investigate a particular phenomenon (such as the rise of capitalism) in the first place, and our judgment on the value of the movement

[35] Weber stressed the instrumentalist and consciously constructive character of ideal types. They were not copies of reality but uniformities and regularities *imposed* on reality by the human mind in order to bring out real causal connections which would go unnoticed without such conceptual simplifications. As he expressed it, the proper domain of science is to discover the "subjective interrelatedness of problems." The "new science" will with "new methods" uncover "new problems" and "truths"; the achievement of the new science will consist in "opening up new meaningful historical perspectives." Only the application of the type or model to empirical reality itself will confirm whether it is a mere "Gedankenspiel" or "*eine wissenschaftliche fruchtbare Begriffsbildung.*" From "Die Objektivitaet sozialwissenschaftlicher Erkenntnis" in J. Winckelmann, ed., *Max Weber* (Stuttgart, Kroner, 1960), pp. 206-207.

[36] "*Es gibt Idealtypen von Bordellen so gut wie von Religionen,*" he observed in his famous essay on "Objectivity" cited above.

[37] See the penetrating essay on Weber in Franz-Martin Schmoelz, *Zerstoerung und Rekonstruktion der politischen Ethik* (Munich, 1963).

in question—whether we approve it or not—is also ultimately arbitrary. Between the two layers of irrationality, however, stands the small strip of the "objectivity of social knowledge."

Weber never tired of repeating that, although science was related to values it could not validate them. He was opposed in particular to the mixing of scientific research and propagandistic appeals to this or that "ism" (whether socialism, pacifism, or nationalism). A science of social reality could treat the values of men as an object of research, could possibly demonstrate the practical consequences of adopting a particular value position, and could clarify inconsistencies in a given value system (i.e., it could show when subsidiary value-judgments did not follow logically from ultimate norms).[38] What science could not do and never would be able to do was to validate one set of values against another or against all others. "An empirical science can teach no one what he *ought* to do, but only what he *can* do, and, under certain circumstances, what he *wants* to do," he wrote. The validation of values "is an affair of faith, and besides this *perhaps* a task of speculative thinking about life, the world, and its meaning, but certainly never an object of a science that is based on experience [*Erfahrungswissenschaft*]."[39]

Weber's objective in all this discussion was to reduce the role which uncontrolled passion, ignorant enthusiasm, and vulgar prejudice played in the contributions of some so-called scholars and social scientists. He himself succeeded admirably in this respect. Whether in his provocative and immensely fruitful *Protestant Ethic and the Spirit of Capitalism*, or in his essays on socioeconomic institutions informed by his analyses of the traditional, charismatic, and rational-legal types of authority, or in his masterful lecture on "Politics as a Vocation," Weber unfailingly displayed a truly remarkable sobriety, humaneness, and discriminatory ability.

One of his most valuable distinctions was between the ethics of intention (*Gesinnungsethik*) and the ethics of responsibility (*Verantwortungsethik*). Indeed, his concept of the ethics of responsibility, or consequences, contained within itself the seeds of a critical principle which, had it been permitted to develop, would have given

[38] See "Der Sinn der 'Wertfreiheit' der Sozialwissenschaft" in Winckelmann, *op. cit.*, pp. 263-310.

[39] In Winckelmann, *ibid.*, pp. 190, 191. See also Karl Jaspers, *Max Weber* (Munich, Piper, 1958), pp. 54-55 for a discussion of his views on science.

Weber a scientific basis for objectively invalidating the various messianic creed movements growing up around him. To the last, however, Weber refused to entertain the possibility that the scientist qua scientist could provide men with any knowledge concerning the relative validity of the ends and goals proffered for human action. As the famous final sentence in his lecture "Science as a Vocation" stated: "Meeting the demands of the day is . . . simple if each man discovers and follows the demon that holds the threads of *his* life."[40] Small wonder, then, given his understanding of ultimate values as "demonic," that Weber wanted, insofar as possible, to exclude them from science.

Max Weber offered a teaching that was as rich as it possibly could be given the burden of the positivist taboo on normative reflection. His abstinence in the face of widespread "left" and "right" value-mongering is in many respects similar to that of the authentic theorist. But in his zeal for methodological purification, Weber excluded *both* theory *and* ideology. To Weber it could "never be the task of *Erfahrungswissenschaft* to offer binding norms and ideals" or "to provide recipes for practice."[41] In the lumping together of "norms," "ideals," and "recipes of practice," we see a tragic lapse in Weber's discriminatory powers. The equating of general principles of action—of norms arrived at by critical reflection on the totality of human experience by a philosophically formed character type—with uncritical ideals and detailed institutional blueprints by a man of Weber's intellectual stature should prepare us for the fundamental misunderstanding of the nature of political theory we encounter among the lesser luminaries of the positivist world. The revival of political theory will depend on the rediscovery of theory's decisive differentiation from utopia and practical political doctrine, or "operative ideals."

---

[40] *Ibid.*, p. 318. Both "Der Beruf zur Politik" and "Von Inneren Beruf zur Wissenschaft" were originally delivered as lectures at the University of Munich in 1918.

[41] *Max Weber: Gesammelte Aufsaetze zur Wissenschaftslehre* (Tuebingen, Mohr, 1951), p. 158.

PART III ❧ THE SAVING REMNANT: THE SURVIVAL OF THE THEORETICAL PERSPECTIVE IN THE AGE OF IDEOLOGY AND POSITIVISM

FIVE: PHILOSOPHICAL CURRENTS OF RESISTANCE TO THE POSITIVIST ASCENDANCY

While the period from the latter decades of the nineteenth century until the end of World War II was a bleak one for political theory, this does not mean that currents of resistance to the twin domination of ideology and neopositivism were entirely absent. Indeed, in philosophy there were profound attempts to challenge the narrow empiricism and sensationalism implicit in the new science and to recover metaphysics and ontology as legitimate and indeed central fields of inquiry. Beginning with Kierkegaard and continuing with Bergson, Scheler, Jaspers, Hartmann, Whitehead, and others, one can detect a shift in philosophy from system-building to the concrete person, from experiential reductionism to the rediscovery of the multidimensionality of experience, from dogmatism to openness.

Most of the philosophers who weathered the age of ideology were only tangentially interested in political theory proper, however. They only occasionally drew out the implications of their teaching for the life of man in society, being more directly interested in metaphysical or ontological problems. Some of them did elaborate concepts of major significance for political theory, and even those who failed to do so contributed indirectly to the revival of political theory in our time for the simple reason that political theory does not exist in a vacuum and its fate is related to developments in philosophy as a whole.

Having granted the above, it is still true to say that over this period a harmful division of labor tended to prevail between those thinkers who collectively worked to keep alive the flame of theoretical criticism of man and society. The wholeness of great political theory, combining as it does normative and empirical considerations, was lost; thus, a philosopher like Bergson failed to draw out sufficiently the implications of his teaching for an ordered society, while a thinker like Mosca, who brilliantly described the power realities that lay behind the ideological rhetoric of society, dealt inadequately with the basic questions of philosophical anthropology. With this grasp of the weaknesses characterizing the thought of this period, we are prepared to examine the major contributions which were made from the perspective of political theory and which continue to bear fruit in the post-World War II revival of that tradition of inquiry.

Benedetto Croce

One of the principal figures of the period 1870–1940 was Benedetto Croce whose influence both within and without Italy has been of major proportions. When Croce began writing, a very considerable segment of the intelligentsia of the new Italian nation was under the sway of a rather crude positivism and materialism. Almost single handedly, Croce reversed the trend of Italian lay thought and gathered numerous and influential adherents to his idealistic philosophy which showed strong Hegelian leanings.[1]

[1] For an excellent account of Croce's impact on the Italian intellectual scene in the late nineteenth century, see A. C. Jemolo, *Chiesa e Stato in Italia negli ultimi cento anni,* 3rd ed. (Turin, 1952), *passim.*

From the perspective of the recovery of political theory, Croce's main contribution was his emphatic distinction between theoretical analysis and partisan political advocacy. In his *Elementi di Politica*, he argued that every political party "develops an ideology or theory, or rather a pseudo-theory" which enables it to claim "Truth, Reason, Philosophy, Science, and History as its allies."[2] Although some of the theories put forward in a given party program taken by themselves might be true, the claim made by the parties that the propositions justify only their programs and are their exclusive property is false. An ideology is in the domain of "political will," while a theory is independent of party and aims at an adequate comprehension of reality. It is not valid to insist on a forced relation between a theory and a particular party. A major task of the genuine political theorist is precisely that of pointing out the intellectual distortions and falsehoods in party pronouncements. The goal of political philosophy is to understand political reality, and the purpose of political practice is to take action adequate to that reality. The reality itself is "neither radical nor socialist nor conservative nor liberal."[3]

Although Croce distinguishes sharply between the spheres of theory and practice, of contemplation and action, he never ceases to affirm in his writings or to demonstrate in his own life that theory had an influence on practice. In his major work the *Filosofia dello spirito*, he noted that "theoretical error in ultimate moral principles can have, and always in some manner does have, an effect on practical life."[4] And he insisted in *Elementi di Politica* that Aristotle, "the father of political science," was right in emphasizing that reflection is also a form of action and that "contemplation, which has its origin and end in itself, by educating the mind, prepares one for *eupraxia*," or right action in the world of practice.[5]

Although Croce often spoke of "transcendence," he meant by it a horizontal rather than a vertical transcendence. Reality is a seamless web which analysis can and must divide into parts, or "moments." Thus, although he conceived a reality only in world-

[2] Benedetto Croce, *Elementi di Politica* (Bari, 1925), p. 42.

[3] *Ibid.*, p. 56.

[4] Benedetto Croce, *Filosofia dello spirito*, 3 vols. (Bari, Laterza), vol. I, p. 62.

[5] Croce, *Elementi di Politica, op. cit.*, p. 58.

immanent terms, he did see this reality as comprising diverse modes and moments. Similarly, he opposed the reductionist materialism of Tracy and Marx. Croce is interesting for our study in that he demonstrates how it is possible even from a perspective of radical immanentism to affirm the multidimensionality of human experience.

To illustrate his conception of the relationship between theory and practice, Croce speaks of "the circle of reality and life"; the circle itself was divided into semicircles representing theoretical and practical activity respectively. It is as senseless to speak of the primacy of either the active or the contemplative life, of the thinker or the man of action, as it is to ask which of the semicircles that compose a circle is to be accorded primacy. Theory which does not serve life is superfluous and dangerous, but life without knowledge is blind. Instead, a reciprocal relationship prevails: life serves knowledge and knowledge life. "The contemplative life, if it is to avoid the fate of becoming isolated and otiose, must come to fruition in the active life, while the active life, if it is to avoid being reduced to an irrational and sterile tumult, must fulfill itself in contemplative existence."[6]

The chief defect of a merely empirical approach to the study of politics is that it mistakes the factual raw material for the substance of the activity itself. Empiricism, which seeks to "reduce to types and classes the innumerable facts of history and from these classifications to develop so-called empirical laws," is not wrong so much as it is insufficient. Such an approach "divides the indivisible" and "separates the inseparable." It attains only surface understanding, failing to view the facts in relation to experience as a whole. Thus, the facts are taken only in their abstract content. If, following the positivists, we pretend to go directly to the facts, eschewing philosophical speculation, the result will hardly be a science purified of ethical and metaphysical assumptions. With specific reference to his contemporary, the political sociologist Vilfredo Pareto, Croce remarks that the "professed abhorrence of philosophy . . . only serves to prepare us for the surreptitious introduction of a vulgar or very poor philosophy. . . ."[7]

For Croce, the true model of science is not natural science but

[6] Croce, *Filosofia dello spirito*, vol. III, p. 196.

[7] Croce, *Elementi di Politica, op. cit.*, pp. 49 ff.

philosophy. Natural science is an "impure science, mixed with extraneous elements of a practical origin." Its domain and its authority are severely limited. "Science, true science . . . can be none other than the science of the spirit, or of that which is universal in reality: it can be none other than philosophy." The natural sciences are complexes of knowledge which are "arbitrarily extracted and fixed."[8]

Because he invested political theory with a certain autonomy vis-à-vis political practice and was always careful to distinguish philosophy and ideology, Croce possessed the intellectual basis for his courageous resistance to the Fascist dictatorship. He never permitted himself to become a tool of the powers that be regardless of how irrational and demonic their actions and policies were. In this sense he stands in striking contrast to his former pupil and collaborator Giovanni Gentile who after 1924 became a blatant apologist and spokesman for Mussolini's dictatorship. Living in interior exile from the society of which he was physically a part, Croce was able to demonstrate that the spirit cannot be contained in the vessels of raw power and fact. Nor should it be assumed that, because of his exceptional international reputation, Croce was immune from physical danger. His house was on at least one occasion ransacked by Fascist terrorists. His personal movements were always carefully watched by the secret police. His example could not have failed to give heart to others less famous and, perhaps, less courageous.

In an essay comparing Croce and the French fascistic writer, Charles Maurras, Luigi Salvatorelli has given us a vivid picture of the contrast between a theorist and a propagandist.[9] Croce labored to construct an authentic theory of politics; his goal was to determine, *sine ira et studio*, the character of political activity and its relation to the other forms of activity of the human spirit. The resultant teaching was not in the service of any party or any state. "Croce personally was politically active, and as such may be judged liberal or conservative. But Croce as a philosopher was neither conservative nor liberal nor socialist." For Maurras, a given practical line of action was the beginning and end of his theory of politics; he was not a philosopher but was exclusively "an advocate, or an orator, or a

[8] Croce, *Filosofia dello spirito, op. cit.*, vol. I, pp. 35-36.

[9] "Croce e Maurras" in F. Flora, ed., *Benedetto Croce* (Milan, Malfasi, 1953), pp. 399-415.

preacher."[10] He did not seek the truth but rather engaged in a campaign of calculated lying ("*menzogna pianificata*").[11] One could add to Salvatorelli's comparison of Croce with Maurras a second comparison between the Neapolitan philosopher and his own countryman, the Nationalist intellectual, Enrico Corradini. Corradini complained in one of his speeches that he objected to being called a "theorist," because by theorist is generally meant one "who abstracts himself from his time and from his country, and in perfect solitude weaves his thread between his mind and the universe. . . ." His own theory was a "most practical thing": it was nothing else than a "weapon of combat."[12] Corradini was greatly influenced by Georges Sorel's view of ideas as myths to inspire action rather than as representatives of truth.

Despite his openness, his heroic striving for critical standards, his independence of the gusts of political passion which swirled around him and his fundamental integrity, Croce's political thought was inadequate on many counts. He easily lapsed into vagueness of terminology at crucial points in his argument, and although he made intelligent evaluations of contemporary political movements, rejecting all totalitarian ideologies, he did not always relate these judgments explicitly to his theoretical foundations. Furthermore, he only imperfectly overcame the two chief defects of nineteenth-century political and social thought: immanentism and a mania for the construction of intellectual systems.[13] At best we can say that Croce achieved a partial opening of the closed systems of the nineteenth century. Reality remains for Croce an enclosed circle, although the circle is now divided into distinct parts, with practical activity being limited to only one area of total experience.

In concluding his *Philosophy of the Spirit*, Croce wrote the following passage which reveals that despite his passion for construct-

[10] *Ibid.*, p. 410.

[11] *Ibid.*, pp. 410-411.

[12] Enrico Corradini, *Discorsi politici* (Florence, 1925), pp. 7-8.

[13] "A particularly characteristic feature of the nineteenth century is the uncommonly strong tendency to system-building: synthesis prevailed over analysis"; the most noteworthy feature of twentieth-century philosophy on the other hand is the reemergence of "personalistic pluralism." I. M. Bochenski, *Europaeische Philosophie der Gegenwart*, 2nd ed. (Bern and Munich, Francke Verlag, 1951), p. 20.

ing systems he was cognizant of the limits to human knowledge and the fallibility of all systems:

> Because philosophy no less than art is conditioned by life, no particular philosophical system is ever able to close within itself all that can be philosophized [tutto il filosofabile]: no philosophical system is definitive, because life itself is never definitive. A philosophical system resolves a group of historically given problems, and prepares the conditions for the posing of other problems, that is for new systems. So it has always been, and so it will always be.[14]

The transcendental ground of being is obscured in the Crocean teaching, and, as has been noted, he gains at best only an awareness of horizontal as opposed to vertical transcendence. As one close student of his thought has written, Croce conceived of immanence and transcendence as only "distinct grades of a single and indivisible reality." Croce's position was essentially one of "reasonable immanentism," which accepted the dialectic of distinct moments within world-immanent reality.[15]

Croce was unable to recover the truth of classical and Christian philosophy that Being escapes all systems and that the essence of human personality was the capacity to open the psyche toward the world-transcendent God. Thus, although he rescued spirit from the subjugation to matter to which the Marxists had consigned it, in Croce's teaching the life of the spirit remains impoverished and the content of its experience truncated. "There is no Truth, but only thought that thinks, no Good, but only moral will, no Beauty but only artistic activity,"[16] he wrote in Elementi di Politica.

Despite its advances relative to ideological and positivist reductionism, Croce's political teaching remains encumbered to the end by

[14] Croce, Filosofia dello spirito, op. cit., vol. III, p. 390.

[15] Giorgio E. Ferrari, "Metafisica dell'immanenza nello storicismo crociano" in F. Flora, op. cit., pp. 131-132.

[16] Croce, Elementi di Politica, op. cit., p. 12. He adds, much more correctly, that "there is no State, but only political actions." The notion that the state is the central object of theoretical reflection about politics is another fiction which must be dispensed with in the contemporary revival of political theory. Strictly speaking, the state does not exist in political thought until the advent of Jean Bodin in the sixteenth century. Politics is much broader and much more concrete than the state.

the twin nineteenth-century intellectual accomplishments: the decapitation of Being and the murder of God. While Croce, to his credit, rejected the fanatical anticlericalism prevailing among his most progressive contemporaries and made a positive evaluation of the religious contribution to human culture, he always thought of religion as "inferior and imperfect knowledge"[17] to be superseded by philosophy in the minds of the intellectual elite. Indeed, he declared bluntly, "the old God has been killed," and the job had been done by the philosophers themselves.[18] We are with Croce still a long way from Marcus Aurelius' philosopher, who is "the servant of the gods."

Henri Bergson and the Open Society

Like Croce, Bergson's philosophy is burdened with certain deficiencies all too characteristic of nineteenth-century thought. Even more than Croce, however, he deserves to be singled out as one of the leading figures responsible for the recovery of the theoretical perspective in our time. With Bergson's philosophy we can see the beginnings of a radical break with the prevailing immanentism of his time.

Beginning in 1889 with his *Essai sur les donnés immediates de la conscience*, Bergson wrote many books, the most famous one being his *L'évolution creatrice* of 1907.[19] For our purposes, however, it is his last major work, *Les deux sources de la morale et de la religion*,[20] first published in 1932, that is worthy of particular attention.

Bergson held that metaphysics was possible, that its language and mode of proceeding were qualitatively different from that employed in the analysis of the phenomenal world, and that "life"—the total experience of the human person—could not be confined within the bounds of material existence. These are hardly novel theses in the history of philosophy, but they were expounded and elaborated in a powerful and original way. Bergson had a decisive impact on his

[17] Croce, *Filosofia dello spirito, op. cit.*, vol I, p. 70.

[18] *Ibid.*, p. 178. Philosophy has circumscribed the "fantasies" of religion and, as a result, "killed" the "old God." This is a gentler execution than that described by Nietzsche in *Zarathustra*.

[19] Translated by Arthur Mitchell as *Creative Evolution* (New York, Holt, Rinehart and Winston, 1924).

[20] Translated by R. A. Audra and C. Brereton as *The Two Sources of Morality and Religion* (New York, Holt, Rinehart and Winston, 1935).

times, and his influence has extended far beyond the confines of his native France.

Bergson nowhere explains the core of his epistemology and metaphysics more lucidly and succinctly than in his brief volume *An Introduction to Metaphysics*.[21] Metaphysics, in contradistinction to "analysis," is a grasping from within. The theme of man as a partner of Being, as a participant in the reality which confronts him, is extensively developed by Bergson. Whereas analysis "moves around the object," metaphysics "enters into it." Whereas analysis looks at the object from a particular point of view and expresses itself in symbols, metaphysics "neither depends on a point of view nor relies on any symbol." The method by which metaphysics apprehends reality is called "intuition." "By intuition is meant the kind of intellectual sympathy by which one places oneself within an object in order to coincide with what is unique in it and consequently inexpressible."

For Bergson, philosophy is less a body of doctrine than it is a way of life or a mode of existence. The language of metaphysics, precisely because it deals with realities that ultimately defy simple description and which are known in a radically different manner from objects in sense experience, is inevitably unequal to its task. The goal of metaphysics is to indicate to us the truth about ultimate reality by means of the least inadequate concepts of which the mind of man is capable.

In his stress on the limitations of our habitual, customary language and modes of thinking for the representation of ultimate reality, Bergson is reminiscent of the intellectual humility of classical and Christian philosophy. He places himself firmly in opposition to the gnostic ideologists who claimed to have attained certain knowledge respecting the human condition. So-called philosophical "systems" are to him only combinations of abstract concepts, concepts which impose an unreal rigidity and uniformity on the object they are supposed to represent. Metaphysics, writes Bergson,

> is only truly itself when it goes beyond the concept, or at least when it frees himself from rigid and ready-made concepts in order to create a kind very different from that which we habitually use; I mean supple, mobile, and almost fluid representations, always ready to mold themselves on the fleeting forms of intuition.[22]

[21] Translated by T. E. Hulme (New York, Putman's, 1912).

[22] *Ibid.*, p. 21.

Metaphysics is concrete where analysis is abstract, and, in fact, the "true empiricism is the true metaphysics."[23] It presupposes a reversal of the ordinary, practical, utilitarian role of thought. "Thinking usually consists in passing from concepts to things, and not from things to concepts."[24] Metaphysics, on the other hand, "can only be a laborious, and even painful, effort to remount the natural slope of the work of thought," in order to achieve "a passage from reality to concepts and no longer from concepts to reality."[25] The "normal work of the intellect" as it has been fashioned by and has adapted itself to nature "is far from being disinterested. We do not aim generally at knowledge for the sake of knowledge, but in order to take sides, to draw profit—in short to satisfy an interest." This entails "fitting a concept on an object" and asking "what we can do with the object and what it can do for us." In this sense there can be as many theories as there are practical interests. If "all knowledge of things is a practical knowledge aimed at the profit to be drawn from them," then metaphysics is impossible.[26]

According to Bergson, prior to the decisive breakthrough in the life of the spirit achieved by the mystic philosophers and Christianity, man was a denizen of the "closed society," and was subject to a "closed morality." Closed morality, which was typical of the ancient Babylonian and Egyptian civilizations but also, at the popular level, of Greece and Rome, had the function of curbing the destructive and egoistic potentialities of men's intellects by reminding them of their social duties. Closed morality is based on man's "fabulatory" or "myth-making" capacity. Taken in the literal sense, the myths are falsifications of reality; they are the work of "infrarational" as opposed to "suprarational" intuition.[27] The morality of the closed society is hostile to the freedom of the spirit in that it always gives social necessities priority over the requirements of the person. In fact, the individual is trapped in the closed circle of society; society's laws are

[23] Ibid., p. 36.

[24] Ibid., p. 40.

[25] Ibid.

[26] Ibid., pp. 40-41.

[27] These terms are employed in the interesting essay by Ellis Sandoz, "Myth and Society in the Philosophy of Bergson," Social Research, XXX (Summer, 1963), 171-202 at 192.

identical with those of nature and of god. The closed morality inevitably applies only to a circumscribed group and is incapable of arriving at an experience of the universal community, the essential brotherhood of men. Closed morality is harsh, unreflective, rigid, unspontaneous, and joyless. It is the morality of the letter rather than the spirit. It rests on fear rather than love, on necessary obligation rather than on the voluntary acceptance of duty.

The "open morality," which is the discovery of the great mystics, and above all of Christianity, is grounded on the suprarational experience of the transcendent God who is beyond nature and society and whose essence is love. The open morality is not derived from the necessity of practical existence in society but from the interior experience of the mystic who discovers for all mankind a new height and depth, a new freedom of spiritual movement for human personality. The transition from the closed to the open society is the decisive event in the history of the human spirit.

In the *Two Sources of Morality and Religion*, Bergson is plagued with a fundamental ambiguity. He never makes fully clear whether he regards the transition from the closed to the open society as a change *within* existence or a change *of* existence. At times he writes as if the mystic "heroes," of which Christ is the supreme example, constitute a wholly new race of men. The notion of the constancy of human nature, which is proclaimed in his earlier works, seems to give way to the idea that there is not only a change in human experience but also in human nature. He is at this point in danger of derailing into a metastatic as opposed to a metanoetic conception of existence (See Chapter Two).

As one commentator has expressed Bergson's dilemma: "Even in the face of a proof and the repeated assertion of the immutability of human nature, Bergson falls victim of a progressivist fallacy which he consistently derides. He has man raise himself from natural man to mystic and, by so doing, create a new species. Two essentially different theories of the nature of man are thereby postulated when a single theory of greater generality would have been sufficient to account for the experiential sources of both instinctive and mystical morality. The roots of this inconsistency lie in Bergson's persistent biologism. In considering life as the essence of being, Bergson fixed upon a facet of being insufficient to account for the profundity of human experience. In metaphysical terms, this criticism may be phrased in the following language: Bergson mistook pure being as endless becoming, the *élan vital*."[28]

Thus Bergson endangers the very discovery of transcendence that he found to lie at the core of the experience of the mystic heroes by implying at key points of the argument that man himself by his own effort has transcended nature and created a new reality. His concluding sentence of the work on *The Two Sources* states that the universe is a "machine for the making of gods." Bergson seems in considerable danger of falling into the messianic humanist fallacy of seeking to immanentize the transcendent. The promised trans-figuration of existence beyond time of Christianity is near to being perverted into an inner-worldly *eschaton*. The biologism and progres-sivism implicit in his earlier work on evolution came back to haunt him in his last work. It will require further theoretical labor to elucidate the full implication of his rediscovery of the open society. But the rediscovery remains his and, given the ideological pressures of his time, it was an achievement of no mean proportions.

Bergson meant by the open society something far different from the use of the term today. Since his time the term has come to mean something akin to a plural society which encourages the widest possi-ble freedom of expression and association. The open society in this sense—and this is essentially the interpretation of Karl Popper[29]—is equated with secular liberal democracy.

From Bergson's perspective, the difficulty with this latter-day interpretation of the open society is that it concentrates on form instead of substance. While Bergson was clearly an advocate of democratic *procedures*, it was above all the *content*, the *quality* of life that an open society made possible that was of crucial importance to him. A society might be open in the technical procedural sense (of permitting a substantial degree of freedom of discussion, etc.) but closed in the qualitative sense. If the principal participants in the public debate failed through their speech to evoke images that draw men on toward goals beyond those of necessity and the material conquest of nature, then we would still be living in a closed society. If Bergson makes any sense at all, he must mean that the open

---

[28] *Ibid.*, p. 195.

[29] Karl Popper, *The Open Society and Its Enemies*, 2 vols. (New York, Harper & Row, 1962). Strangely enough, Bergson emerges as an "irrationalist" enemy of the open society for Popper.

society is one in which the freedom of the spirit in existence under the world-transcendent God is experienced, if not by the whole people, at least by the predominant part thereof. The source of this experience must be continuously reexplicated by an inevitably small number of mystic philosophers and presumably transmitted by ritual and dogma through institutions such as churches.

Bergson, who has been pictured by such writers as Popper, William McGovern, and W. Y. Elliott as an "irrationalist" precursor of Fascism, was in truth neither irrational nor a Fascist precursor. He worked very carefully with reason in illustrating its limits and did not advocate an uncontrolled intuition but always presupposed the experiential basis of the existing human person. He was also a proponent of democracy—a fact which was recognized by the Italian Fascist intellectual, Enrico Leone, in his attack on Bergson written in 1923.[30] Indeed, it has even been argued that Bergson was out to create a new myth of democracy. Bergson made clear that he regarded democracy as the only possible vehicle for the realization of the open society in the modern age. By democracy, however, he understood something more than a set of techniques and procedures; these were only the necessary preconditions for the realization of freedom of the spirit. Bergson's "democracy" moreover, was hardly the equivalent of mass society, or the society of mediocrities. It was not the Benthamite democracy of the greatest happiness of the greatest number. Democracy was an aspiration, a strenuous affair, a striving for excellence and a spiritually rich existence. Democracy, he wrote, "takes for its matter an ideal man, who respects others as he does himself, inserting himself into obligations which he holds to be absolute. . . ." This is the opposite of the herd society, the society of mediocrity.[31]

Other Developments in Philosophy Contributing to the Contemporary Recovery of Political Theory

Of the various thinkers, in addition to Croce and Bergson, who offered intellectual resistance to positivist and ideological reductionism, only a few individuals who are of particular interest to the student

---

[30] Enrico Leone, the Fascist intellectual who was a onetime exponent of syndicalism, wrote a book attacking Bergson as the archphilosopher of democracy: *Anti-Bergson* (Naples, Luce, 1923).

[31] Audra and Brereton, *op. cit.*, p. 270, ftn. 4.

of the present-day revival of political theory need be mentioned here. Their existence serves to illustrate that, even at the point of the maximum influence of the antimetaphysical persuasion, there were significant thinkers and philosophical schools outside the explicitly theological *ambiente*, whether Catholic or Protestant, that were in opposition to the fact-value separation and the increasing exaltation of practical-productive activity over other dimensions of human experience.

Julien Benda

Julien Benda was in his time one of the most uncompromising and hostile critics of the transformation of the disinterested intellectual into a fanatical partisan. His book *La trahison des clercs*, which first appeared in 1927, was an eloquent exposition of the thesis that civilization is possible "only if humanity consents to a division of functions, if side by side with those who carry out the lay passions and extol the virtues serviceable to them there exists a class of men who depreciate these passions and glorify the advantages which are beyond the natural."[32] The effect of his argument is to affirm and even to champion the division of labor into practical and theoretical activity which Marx had described as the product of an alienated and perverted social order. Benda found that intellectuals such as Treitschke, Barrés, Maurras, D'Annunzio, and numerous others, had committed treason to their calling by serving "lay passion" at the expense of truth and justice. Their attitude was characterized by the

> tendency to action, the thirst for immediate results, the exclusive preoccupation with the desired end, the scorn for argument, the excess, the hatred, the fixed ideas. The modern "clerk" has entirely ceased to let the layman alone descend to the market place. The modern clerk . . . is filled with . . . contempt for the man who shuts himself up with art or science and takes no interest in the passions of the state.[33]

The intellectual, the modern equivalent to the "clerk" of the middle ages, must not be defiled through submission to popular passions, the most dominant of which he found to be xenophobia. Those

[32] Translated as *The Betrayal of the Intellectuals* (Boston, Beacon Press, 1955), p. 111.

[33] *Ibid.*, pp. 32-33.

who indulge in political fanaticism and extol violence betray their duty "which is precisely to set up a corporation whose sole cult is that of justice and of truth," as distinguished from the injustice to which the majority are committed by virtue of their "religions of this earth."[34]

Benda's reaction to the intellectual turned ideologist is perhaps excessive, and his case is not expressed in sufficiently careful language. He often sounds like a proponent of complete withdrawal from politics to the utter disregard of his clerks' social duties and responsibilities. He sounds in places as if he were advocating a kind of apolitical universalism typical of the ancient Cynic school. What he is apparently trying to say, however, is that the intellectual best fulfills his responsibility to society precisely by extricating himself from the tumult of the marketplace. And he did not deny that on occasion the intellectual should in fact speak out in behalf of a cause, provided that he did so as a representative of the interest of humanity and not "for the purpose of securing the triumph of a realist passion, whether of class, race, or nation."[35] In such an eventuality he is going against the current of dominant lay opinion and can expect to be reviled by the laymen.

Although one can scarcely expect to derive a political theory from such a position as that maintained by Benda, nonetheless we do encounter here a partial vindication of the political theorist and his critical function vis-à-vis society. While Benda's authentic intellectuals would have little that is positive to say about the ordering of society, they would courageously and uncompromisingly attack the worst excesses of ideological thought and practice. But their interest in politics would be only peripheral to their main intellectual pursuits, in which they could engage in the spirit of *l'art pour l'art*. From time to time a particularly grievous occurrence in the political world would call forth their expression of moral outrage. His position smacks of a moralism that may have little relevance for the ambiguities of politics, and it seems to ignore the continuous moral responsibility of at least some portion of Benda's *clercs* to point the way toward a possible reordering of society so that these excesses might in fact be curtailed. It is doubtful whether any participant of modern industrial society—

[34] *Ibid.*, pp. 41-42.

[35] *Ibid.*, p. 36. He cites as examples of valid interventions by "clercs" in political affairs Gerson's denunciation of the murder of Louis d'Orleans and Spinoza's outcry against the liquidation of de Witts.

and all who live in it are inevitably participants, including the clercs —could afford to enjoy the feeling of moral superiority and perfectionism envisaged for them by Benda. For all his limitations however, and despite the vagaries of his later political positions which seemed blatantly to contradict his earlier teaching,[36] Benda rendered a signal service to the recovery of political theory through the writing of his eloquent little volume *La trahison des clercs*.

Max Scheler and the Phenomenological School

Max Scheler's importance for the contemporary revival of political theory is the result of his originality and the fact that he anticipated in many respects the work of Eric Voegelin, who is perhaps the leading representative of that revival. Scheler, who was a professor at Cologne during the last decade of his life, was the most well-known follower, excluding the aberrant Heidegger, of Edmund Husserl, the founder of the phenomenological school of philosophy. Scheler went beyond Husserl in many respects; he was no mere disciple but stands as a creative thinker in his own right. Toward the end of his life, Scheler abandoned his earlier teaching, with its decisively theocentric orientation, in favor of an immanentism reminiscent of Nietzsche. This phase of his thought, terminated by his early death, was too brief to be developed sufficiently, however, and it is to Scheler's writings prior to the last phase of his life, beginning about 1926, that we refer here.

Scheler agreed with the main points of Husserl's teaching. Husserl had rejected all forms of Kantian subjectivism as inadequate, insisting that reality possesses a structure independent of our conceptualization of it, and that consciousness was consciousness *of something*. He also condemned positivism for concentrating on only the "surface dimension" of experience to the neglect of the "depth dimension." The reality which man sees is more than the world of external relationships to be grasped by sense experience. In addition to the "factual sciences" there were the "eidetic sciences," whose task was to explicate the essence of the thing being observed by "bracketing" everything that was not relevant to it.

Husserl insisted that the phenomenological method was highly

---

[36] He became philo-Communist in his last years. See Robert J. Niess, *Julien Benda* (Ann Arbor, University of Michigan Press, 1956) for a full intellectual biography. Another peculiarity of Benda was his all-consuming hatred of Bergson's teaching and influence.

rigorous and concrete, concentrating on the "immanent act of observing and the immanent 'something' being observed."[37] Although he discovered in experience a greater depth than the surface empiricism of positivism had allowed it, he still did not achieve a breakthrough to transcendence. Scheler went beyond him in this respect and argued for an extension of our observation of experience to include objective values and the world-transcendent God. Nonetheless it should be said that Husserl shares with Scheler the rediscovery of the concrete person in the totality of his experience as the center of proper philosophizing about man and the reality in which he participates.

Scheler taught that true metaphysics is based on philosophical anthropology which has as its task the consideration of the question "What is man?" Man, Scheler answers, is the living being who is aware of the realm of values. These values have objective reality and are as real to the apprehending subject as are colors to our vision. "Not values themselves, but only our knowledge of values is relative."[38] Values are experienced directly as being a component of reality; they cannot be treated as epiphenomena, as reflections of transient historical conditions or psychological states. There are positive and negative values: man as person seeks the former and avoids the latter. Values are not equal but arrange themselves in a hierarchy beginning with sensory and vital experience and feeling and ascending to the values of the spirit (beauty, right, the knowledge of truth) and finally to the values of the realm of the "holy."

To be a person means to be capable of inwardly perceiving the entire range of values and of according priority to the higher over the lower ones. To be a person means to be capable of responsible action in accordance with the highest values. Scheler did not think that all men were persons in the full sense of the word. Personality involves much more than intelligence and cleverness in problem-solving; it reveals itself in spiritual openness and concrete ethical acts resulting from that openness. Each person is a unique individual, but he also participates in various forms of communal life the highest of which are the nation and church, which are the spheres for the actualization of the sacred (holy) and spiritual-intellectual values.

---

[37] Arnold Brecht, *Political Theory: The Foundations of Twentieth-Century Political Thought* (Princeton, Princeton University Press, 1959), p. 379.

[38] I. M. Bochenski, *op. cit.*, p. 155. I have relied heavily on this excellent treatment of Scheler's philosophy.

Man as person is much more than *homo naturalis*. *Homo naturalis* is qualitatively on a par with the animal world. He has neither dignity nor greatness. *Homo naturalis* is the Comtean or Marxian man. Man, authentic man, is the God-seeker, the being who has achieved a breakthrough from the sphere of the natural and the material to an encounter with the source of all existing things. The awareness of God is the fundamental experience of the human consciousness. Man as person recognizes God as the living God, "the Person of all persons." Man is "theomorph"—the creature who in the fullness of his being reflects a likeness to God, in whose image he is formed. The true humanism is that which recognizes that it is only in his relationship to God that we can understand man. To Scheler, metaphysics depends on theology, not theology on metaphysics. Metaphysics cannot prove, but can only take as its basis, the reality of God as the ground of being. It is this original experience of God which is the necessary presupposition for all valid metaphysics. All men believe in an ultimate: if it is not God then it is an idolatrous substitute such as History or Humanity.

From the encounter with God the person learns the meaning of love, learns to love the world through God's love of the world. Love is to be distinguished from altruism and sentimental fellow-feeling. So-called love of humanity is anything but authentic love. Humanity is an abstraction, but love is experienced only between persons. "Love of humanity" [sentimental humanitarianism] is actually an expression of hatred of God, of "resentment" against the fact of man's dependence on God. Love of humanity is thus the opposite of humility; it is an expression of collective *hybris* that would erect a society in which man as person would be destroyed. Modern altruism, the zeal of self-sacrifice for humanity, has as its root the hatred of higher values and, above all, of God. It is the typical spiritual expression of a condition of spiritual death. It is the destruction of love because it excludes the ultimate source of love, which is God.

Scheler left an unfinished philosophy. He did not deal sufficiently with man's existence in society. On occasion his anthropology came close to denying the essential equality of all men, who are persons in the essential sense even if only a small minority realizes this essence faithfully. On balance, however, he has to be reckoned as one of the most significant architects of the new philosophical anthropology that has flourished in our time.

The Reemergence of Metaphysics

Scheler was not alone in advocating, against positivism and related movements, the restoration of metaphysics to the central place in philosophical inquiry. Nicolai Hartmann in Germany and Alfred North Whitehead in Great Britain were other key thinkers who cooperated in this venture. All of these men were in agreement with Scheler that metaphysics is an experiential, as opposed to an experimental, science. Hartmann, who developed an ontology which identified the various "layers" or "strata" of being—inorganic matter, organic life, the psychic sphere, spirit, community, and history,—is reminiscent of both Scheler and Voegelin in his emphatic rejection of system-building and his conception of philosophy as the analysis of specific problems or *topoi*. Again, like Scheler and Voegelin, Hartmann stressed the inevitable limitations of our knowledge, stating that only a "side of being" is turned toward man for his understanding. Ultimate reality inevitably escapes our system and attests to the inadequacy of our symbols and concepts. The intellectual humility that had been implicit in classical and Christian philosophy is reasserted by Hartmann against any hint of pretension by philosophy to have arrived at complete and certain *gnosis*.

Like Hartmann, who insisted that all knowledge involves the "apprehension of something that was prior to and independent of all knowledge,"[39] Whitehead denied every form of conceptualism and subjectivism. Man discovers himself to be part of a world that extends beyond himself in time and space and which points to a transcendent source. Metaphysics is a descriptive science, although it differs from the modern natural sciences in that it employs "speculative" instead of "methodic" reason and inevitably achieves a knowledge that is of a different order from that of the natural world.

In an essay, "The Function of Reason," Whitehead reaffirmed the distinction of classical philosophy between neotic and pragmatic, or substantive and instrumental, reason. "There is Reason, asserting itself as above the world and there is Reason as one of many factors within the world. The Greeks have bequeathed to us two figures whose real or mythical lives conform to these two notions—Plato and

[39] Quoted in A. Verdross, *Abendlaendische Rechtsphilosophie* (Vienna, 1958), p. 185. Our consciousness must "emerge from itself insofar as it is a knowing consciousness."

Ulysses. The one shares Reason with the Gods, the other shares it with the foxes."[40] The former is reason as "seeking a complete understanding" versus reason as "an immediate method of action."

Speculative reason, according to Whitehead, is "in its essence untrammelled by method. Its function is to pierce into the general reasons beyond limited reasons, to understand all methods as coordinated in a nature of things only to be grasped by transcending all method."[41] The distinctive characteristic of modern scientific thought is its discarding of the speculative reason and its attempt to confine itself exclusively to the employment of methodic reason. The separation of science and speculation has been achieved at the price of ignoring the philosophical assumptions (that the universe is ordered in some fashion, etc.) at the base of Science itself. A harmful general result of the concentration on methodic reason to the neglect of speculative reason in modern thought has been to encourage irrationality with respect to ends as we increase our rationality with respect to means. We thus become shrewder instead of better.

Whitehead prepares the ground for the later criticisms in political science (by Strauss and others) of the practice of the neopositivists in allowing method to determine the content of a science of man. Methodic reason can tell us next to nothing about the ends of human action. But this is precisely the kind of question with which a critical political science, or political theory, needs to be concerned.

Other writers of the period under discussion could be listed as having contributed significantly to the survival of philosophical reflection. Both T. H. Green, at the beginning, and R. G. Collingwood at the end of the period (1870–1940) are excellent examples of such thinkers. Green is well-known among students of the history of political thought, while Collingwood, whose *Autobiography*, *Speculum Mentis*, and *New Leviathan* are works of great interest, is undeservedly neglected. (Collingwood is also important for this study as an influence on Michael Oakeshott.)

In the following chapter emphasis will be placed on the contribution of certain members of the "elitist" school of political sociology to the survival of the theoretical perspective in the age of ideology.

---

[40] Alfred North Whitehead, *The Function of Reason* (Princeton, Princeton University Press, 1929), p. 7.

[41] *Ibid.*, p. 50.

Just as the thinkers discussed in the present chapter tended to neglect the "empirical" dimension of political existence, so the elitists were not sufficiently articulate as philosophers of the person. Nonetheless, when both strands are taken together, one can make out the background for the contemporary reemergence of a coherent and unified political theory embracing both aspects of existence.

SIX: THE PARTIAL SURVIVAL OF POLITICAL THEORY IN THE ELITIST SCHOOL

Among the unsung heroes of the history of political theory in this century have been certain writers who rediscovered the crucial importance of elites in any body politic. Because of the exigencies of the political struggle in our time, their contribution has been and remains even today obscured. "Elite" and "elitist" have become taboo words in the Western political vocabulary, being associated with Fascist and Nazi ideologies. One of the tasks of contemporary political theory is to recover the elite concept for political science. Actually, "elite" is a neutral word; there can be open as well as closed elites. Concepts in theory must be sharply distinguished from symbols in the ideological struggle. Political science, understood as being synonymous with political theory, cannot dispense with a theory of elites. The question is not whether political science shall embrace an elite theory or not, but whether it is to employ a scientifically valid or an ideologically debased elite theory.

The credit for recovering the study of elites as a central concept for political science must go to the Italian-Swiss triumvirate Gaetano Mosca, Vilfredo Pareto, and Roberto Michels. To these names should be added a fourth: that of Guido Dorso, an undeservedly obscure Neapolitan whose untimely death in 1947 brought to an end his noteworthy attempt to demonstrate that elite theory is not on principle inimical to the existence of a democratic polity.

The great achievements of the Italian school were its refusal to confuse the democratic rhetoric with political science and its determination to view even the democratic polity from a critical distance. These men wrote at a time when the eloquent Lincolnian definition of democracy as the "government of the people, by the people and for the people" was widely accepted as a description of fact. What the elite theorists sought to do was to show that democracy in the literal sense of government of and by the people was a myth, a realistic impossibility.

As Maurice Duverger expressed the matter in his book on *Political Parties*, Lincoln's eloquent formula will have to be rewritten by a critical political science to read that democracy is "government for the people by an elite sprung from the people."

Accordingly, the elite school found that the differences between political regimes lay not in whether they were ruled by minorities (for all polities were), but in the quality, mode of selection and replenishment, social composition, and openness to permeation from below, of the various ruling and political classes. Not constitutional forms but the men who made them work emerged as the key considerations for a critical political science.

For this discovery—or rediscovery, for Plato, Aristotle and Machiavelli were aware of the crucial importance of elites, even if they did not use this precise term—the elitist school has received little thanks and much vilification. More often than not, Mosca, Pareto, and Michels have been labelled as precursors of Fascism. There is little or no evidence to suggest that these men had even an unintentional influence on the development of Fascist ideology, and so far as their personal political views were concerned, Mosca and Pareto were opposed to Italian Fascism. Only Michels remains suspect as a sympathizer of Mussolini. Pareto can be considered a liberal who was fiercely opposed to any censorship of the press.

Mosca, who with Dorso made the most profound contribution to political theory of the group, was an open and even courageous opponent of Fascism. In what proved to be a farewell speech as Senator on December 19, 1925, Mosca was the only member of that body to oppose a Fascist law to make the Head of the Government unaccountable to parliament. He rendered homage to the parliamentary regime, observing that he never would have believed he would be the only man in the Italian parliament to eulogize it. Indeed, as early as 1904, Mosca had made clear that he was antidemocratic only if democracy were understood in the abstract ideological sense of a headless people ruling itself from below. But, he went on to say,

> the fact that the abstract theory of democracy is mistaken does not signify that the practice of democracy is necessarily to be condemned. In fact, democracy has substituted for one method of choosing the political class another method of choice: and one cannot say that the substitution has been a bad thing . . . We owe to democracy, at least in part, the regime of discussion in which we live; we owe it the principal modern liberties: those of thought, press and association. And the regime of free discussion is the only one which permits the ruling class to renew itself . . . which eliminates that class quasi-automatically when it no longer corresponds to the interests of the country.[1]

As Norberto Bobbio has pointed out in a prescient essay, Mosca's most prominent disciples in Italy, far from being supporters of Fascism, were actually dedicated opponents of the dictatorship. If one were to locate such men as Guido Dorso, Piero Gobetti, and Filippo Burzio on the conventional left-right political spectrum, they would all have to be classified as members of the democratic left![2] The point is that the elite concept should be viewed as a contribution to political theory rather than as a tool of ideology. Like any genuinely theoretical concept, it is neither left-wing nor right-wing, but seeks to contribute to our understanding of political reality. When properly employed, elite theory seeks neither to denigrate nor to glorify in an uncritical fashion the parliamentary democratic system.

In varying degrees, Mosca, Pareto, and Michels were burdened with positivistic terminology. Only Dorso may be said to have remained uninfluenced by the positivistic orientation. Pareto even fell prey to an extreme and crude form of reductionism in his doctrine of irrational "residues" as determining human behavior. Yet, somehow, a basic common sense, an ironic quality of mind, and a feel for the pulse of actual political life kept these men from derailing into either the peculiar abstractness or quasiutopian scientism char-

[1] Gaetano Mosca, "Aristocrazia e democrazia" in G. Mosca, *Partiti e Sindacati nella crisi del regime parlamentare* (Bari, Laterza, 1949), pp. 334-335.

[2] N. Bobbio, "La teoria della classe politica negli scrittori democratici in Italia," in *Le élites politiche* (Bari, Laterza, 1961), pp. 54-58.

acteristic of so much of positivist political science. Mosca in particular had an extensive knowledge of the history of political thought and an even more impressive knowledge of the history of institutions. This recognition of the profound importance of the historical dimension to political reality served him in good stead, giving to his empiricism a breadth and depth so often lacking in recent empirical political research.

In this chapter, attention will be focused on Guido Dorso's formulation of elite theory both because it is the most advanced and sophisticated form of that theory to come out of the Italian school and also because, outside Italy, Dorso's work remains virtually unknown. Mosca, Pareto, and Michels laid the groundwork for Dorso's achievement through their rediscovery of the fact that all societies, whatever their outward political form (that is, whether they are described and describe themselves as monarchies, aristocracies, democracies, or dictatorships) are ruled by a minority of the total population. Consequently, the most significant questions for political science are not those relating to constitutional form but those relating to the quality, composition, and method of replenishment of the ruling strata or elites. As Mosca summarized the basic premise of elite theory:

> In all regularly constituted societies in which something called a government exists, we find that all authority is being exercised in the name of the entire people, or of an aristocracy, or of a single sovereign . . . but besides that fact we find unfailingly another: the ruling class or rather those who hold and exercise the public power, will always be a minority, and below them we find a numerous class of persons who do never, in any real sense, participate in government but merely submit to it: these may be called the ruled class.[3]

Mosca, Pareto, and Michels were concerned with demythologizing the prevailing political rhetoric of their day which spoke of popular sovereignty, the people's will, etc., as if rule in a democracy were really conducted from the bottom up. They found that, empirically speaking, "the people" did not exist and that universal suffrage, whatever its symbolic significance, did not insure the effective participation of the majority in the making of basic decisions. Mosca

[3] Quoted in James Meisel, *The Myth of the Ruling Class* (Ann Arbor, University of Michigan Press, 1958), pp. 32-33.

commented acidly that "it is a lie to argue that the masses of the people are represented through electors." He found the cardinal assumption of representative democracy, viz., that "the representative is chosen by the majority of voters," to be a falsehood if taken literally:

> Whoever took part in an election knows perfectly well that the representative is not elected by the voters but . . . has himself elected by them. Or, if that sounds too unpleasant . . . his friends have him elected. In any case, a candidacy is always the work of a group of people united for a common purpose, an organized minority which inevitably forces its will upon the disorganized majority.[4]

Michels, in his study of the German Social Democratic Party, was so impressed by the comparative formlessness of the mass that he propounded his famous "iron law of oligarchy," which held that both because of the technical requirements attendant on the operation of large-scale organizations and because of the psychological need in the rank and file for leadership, the masses were condemned to a condition of "eternal tutelage," and "must be content to constitute the pedestal of an oligarchy."

A major weakness in the argument put forth by the early elite theorists, such perceptive critics as C. J. Friedrich, Robert Dahl, and others have pointed out, is the proposition that the ruling minority even in a representative democracy possesses organizational unity and cohesiveness. As Friedrich has shown in Man and His Government,[5] it is impossible to speak of elites in a democratic regime as "cohesive cliques" or conspiracies. The merit of Dorso's analysis is that it recognizes the fact that political struggle always leads to divisions within the ruling and political class, and that in a democratic regime this competition is blessed with legitimacy. Thus, in the crucial respect, Dorso revises the Mosca-Pareto-Michels formulation.

Norberto Bobbio has described the Dorso revision of elite theory in the following terms:

> The fulcrum of Mosca's doctrine was the notion of the organized minority. In the writers examined [Dorso, Gobetti, and Burzio] the notion of a minority has remained, but the idea of organi-

[4] Quoted in Ibid., p. 106.

[5] C. J. Friedrich, Man and His Government (New York, McGraw-Hill, 1964).

zation has become so attenuated as virtually to disappear. . . .
When Dorso admits the distinction between a governing and an
opposition political class, the idea that the political class is nec-
essarily a monolithic bloc is definitively superseded.[6]

Guido Dorso's Political Teaching

Although it is primarily within the context of elite theory that
Dorso is important, it should be observed that he came close to creating a political theory in a more comprehensive sense. One definitely
finds in his works promising beginnings of a full-fledged philosophical
anthropology. That Dorso possessed the theoretical temperament, or
style of thought, is unquestionable. As one writer has noted, even
those who vehemently disagreed with his conclusions admired Dorso's
"critical spirit." He was possessed of a "passion for reality" and an
"anti-rhetorical temperament" which led him to pierce "the veil
of ideological formulas" and ascend from illusion to reality. In those
respects, Dorso is reminiscent of Mosca and Machiavelli.[7]

His writings, including the better essays on the corruption of
the southern political class, even though written for partisan newspapers were critical analyses instead of "programmatic declarations
for immediate action." He was the very opposite of Mussolini who,
as Dorso himself had pointed out, was always the partisan and
"never battled for the truth, but only for the triumph of his 'part.' "[8]
Dorso's theoretical stance is also made apparent when one compares
him to his contemporary, Antonio Gramsci, who was Italy's most
gifted and influential Communist intellectual. Gramsci, in full agreement with Lenin, felt that all thought was a tool for action; the problem was not to understand the world but to create a monolithic
organization—the party—capable of razing the old decadent culture to
the ground and erecting a new Communist society oriented to production and the complete mastery of the human and natural environment.
"Everything is politics, including philosophy and philosophies, and
the only 'philosophy' is history in the making, that is, life itself,"

---

[6] Bobbio, *op. cit.*, p. 58.

[7] G. Macera, Introduction to "Lettere a Guido Dorso," in *Realtá del Mezzogiorno*, II (June-July, 1962), 697-707 at 699.

[8] G. Dorso, *Mussolini alla conquista del potere* (Turin, Einaudi, 1949), p. 76.

wrote Gramsci. To the Sardinian revolutionary, the so-called philosopher or theorist was nothing else than "political man, that is, active man who modifies the environment." With Gramsci, we witness, as with Marx and Lenin, the inversion of the primacy accorded to the *vita contemplativa* over the *vita activa* in Greek, Stoic, and Christian philosophy.

Because so little is known about Dorso, a few facts about his life are in order. He was born at Avellino in southern Italy on May 30, 1892. He received his degree in jurisprudence from the University of Naples, but at first turned to the practice of journalism rather than law. In 1923 he founded his own weekly paper which, because it was highly critical of Fascism, was suppressed after January 3, 1925. He became well known in Italy through his penetrating analyses of the ruling class in the *Mezzogiorno*, or Italian south, although his objectivity did not make his contributions completely acceptable to the leftist paper in which they were published (Gobetti's *Rivoluzione Liberale*). From 1925 onward, Dorso never ceased to have contact with clandestine anti-Fascist movements, including the *Guistizia e Libertá*, and his house was under special surveillance by the Fascist police. Around 1938 Dorso began work on his study, undertaken in secrecy, of Mussolini's rise to power. After the victory of the allies he played a leading role in the left-of-center Action Party. He found that he disagreed with some of its policies and resigned his party membership and the editorship of its southern newspaper on December 31, 1945. Although appointed to Italy's Constituent Assembly, the body assigned the task of drawing up a new Constitution for Italy, he spent the remaining year of his life primarily in his study where he continued his researches on political theory. He died on January 5, 1947, at the age of 54.[9]

Dorso's main works are *La rivoluzione meridionale*,[10] *Mussolini alla conquesta del potere*[11] and *Dittatura, Classe Politica, e Classe Dirigente*.[12] The latter is a collection of essays, the most important

[9] Biographical details in Carlo Muscetta's preface to *Ibid.*, pp. xi-xiii.

[10] Guido Dorso, *La rivoluzione meridionale*, 3rd ed. (Turin, Einauldi, 1955).

[11] Guido Dorso, *Mussolini alla conquesta del potere* (Turin, Einaudi, 1949).

[12] Guido Dorso, *Dittatura, Classe Politica, e Classe Dirigente*, 2nd ed. (Turin. Einaudi, 1955).

of which is entitled "Classe politica e classe dirigente."[13] This masterful essay contains the core of Dorso's political teaching and constitutes the basis of the following exposition of his thought.

Dorso's Terminology

Three terms are basic to Dorso's analysis: ruled class (*classe diretta*), ruling class (*classe dirigente*), and political class (*classe politica*). Dorso lays great stress on the third element in this enumeration, i.e., the political class, criticizing his teacher Mosca for not having differentiated the political class, from the ruling class proper.[14] The ruling class[15] in its widest connotation is the segment of society which "has the political, intellectual, and material direction" of that society. As such, the ruling class "includes the political class properly speaking," or to put it another way, the political class is a "specialized sub-section" of the ruling class.

Dorso is well aware that his concepts are in some respects imprecise and yet he is not deterred from using them obviously having imbibed the Aristotelian wisdom that one may not legitimately demand greater precision than the subject matter inherently affords. He concedes that the ruling class is a "spontaneous formation" and its relations with the ruled class are difficult to specify. "By terminological and scientific necessity we must draw a line between the two great classes in society, but it is not possible to say where one begins and the other ends." Income, the most obvious and measurable criterion for determining the precise boundaries between ruling and ruled elements, is unsatisfactory as a measure because it excludes from the ruling class people who have "great moral and intellectual influence"

---

[13] *Ibid.*, pp. 121-184. All quotations from Dorso in the following pages are from this essay.

[14] Dorso gives Pareto credit for distinguishing between a "governmental elite" (*classe eletta di governo*) and a "nongovernmental elite" (*classe eletta non di governo*), but observes that he does not really develop this distinction.

[15] It is difficult to give a precise translation of *classe dirigente* and *classe diretta* in English. "Directing class" and "directed class" or "governing class" and "governed class" are other possible renditions. I continue to employ "ruling class" because of its general use in connection with Mosca, whose *Elementi di scienze politiche* was translated into English as *The Ruling Class*. "Ruling" sounds a shade more heavy-handed and "authoritarian" than *"dirigente"* does in Italian, however.

but low incomes. Nor will other such factors as education and occupation afford us an infallible criterion.[16] It is, therefore, necessary "to distinguish the two classes without pretending to separate them neatly," and to consider them as "inter-communicating." There exists "an intermediate or grey zone" which cannot be determined with certainty to be in either the ruled or the ruling class but "oscillates continuously, perhaps in a disturbing fashion."

Historically, recruitment of elements of the ruled class into the ruling class has occurred principally by co-optation. With the advent of elections and political parties, co-optation remains a significant although less noticeable method of selection, but designation has also assumed importance (the electorate designating one of the candidates offered by the political class). Of course, another method of renewing the ruling class has been revolution, or the forcible overthrow of the old ruling class (or rather of a part of it, for even the most extreme revolutions never succeeded in entirely replacing the previous ruling class). Whether by co-optation, revolution, or designation, the fact remains that "in all times there has been a continuous exchange between the two social classes, and new elements are added to the ruling class, renewing it, while old elements are detached from it, sinking into the masses."

Revolutions have in general resulted when an energetic populace is subjected to domination by a privileged oligarchy which fails to open its ranks to able elements in the masses. A "decadent ruling class" is one which has failed to "renew itself" by co-opting "the free formations of the ruled class," and which has fallen into a "legalism that is slowly transformed into a tissue of privileges." This results in the formation of an alienated counter-elite outside the system which awaits the opportunity to seize political power.

One of the primary tasks of political theory—by which term Dorso understands "critical political science"—is to study the processes by which societies in the past have elaborated their ruling and

[16] As Roberto Michels, citing Pareto with approval, observed, to deny the existence of class stratification in a society on the grounds that it is difficult to draw the precise boundaries between them and because an intermediate area exists between the classes "would be exactly like denying that there is high-priced and low-priced merchandise. 'Because it is a fact that we insensibly go from one class of objects to another, the existence of choices is not less real.'" A. De Grazia, ed., *Roberto Michels. First Lectures on Political Sociology* (Minneapolis, University of Minnesota Press, 1949), p. 21.

political classes. This will throw light on the contemporary situation, for it is extremely difficult to describe accurately significant events taking place close at hand. We lack both the historical perspective and the necessary documentation to analyze adequately the formation of elites in contemporary society.

An optimal relationship between the ruling and ruled class is held by Dorso to be one in which (1) there is frequent and constant exchange of elements in each class, with the most able and energetic forces in the masses being co-opted into ruling positions, and (2) the ruling class takes seriously its obligation to rule on behalf of the entire society instead of its own particular interests.

Dorso refuses to accept the Marxist view that the ruling class of a society inevitably exploits the mass of the people. When it does do so it is, quite simply, corrupt, and unless the entire society is in a condition of decadence so that the mass is incapable of elaborating new elites to challenge it, such a ruling class courts its own removal from power. When a ruling class is occupied exclusively or primarily with the cultivation of its own interests to the detriment of the community, then the privilege which it enjoys "appears in full light, deprived of its justification." This will probably result in the eventual "declassation" (*declassazione*) of the ruling class. The imperfections of human nature, Dorso goes on to say, make oligarchies an inescapable necessity in social life. "Oligarchies rule politics, economics, and the whole realm of human culture." They "ought to be supported . . . as long as they perform their social function, that is, as long as their policies coincide with the interest of the collectivity and contribute to collective well-being." It is scarcely surprising that the "material and moral advantages" enjoyed by elites are "often the object of envy on the part of the masses; but these advantages are the payment for onerous and difficult duties, which the masses are not able directly to perform and which one finds implicitly delegated to the men at the summit of the social structure."

In stressing the onerous duties of the principal elites in a society and their inevitability, Dorso sounds a different note from that of C. Wright Mills in his widely read book, *The Power Elite*. Dorso may be judged to have had a more subtle and theoretically adequate grasp of the elite phenomenon than Mills.

The political class, according to Dorso, is "selected from the interior of the ruling class, of which it constitutes a specialized subsection." As is the case with the relations between the ruling and ruled classes, so also between the ruling and political classes there is a continuous exchange of elements. If a political class damages the interests of the collectivity, it should be replaced by the ruling class, on the predominance of whose support the power of the political class rests. If the ruling class does not respond in the appropriate manner, then this means that the corruption of the political class extends to the ruling class as a whole, and what is demanded for the health of the body politic is a change in the entire ruling class. If, despite the normal functioning of the circulation of elites from the masses to the ruling and political classes, a defective political class is nonetheless elaborated, then "the entire society is sick and has entered a period of decadence." It is in this sense that Dorso finds the ruling class of a society ordinarily to be the mirror of the whole people; the ruling class represents, or reflects, the entire society and is that society *in nuce*. The entire process of exchange between ruled, ruling, and political classes is complicated, but only a "mature" people can elaborate an adequate ruling class. The qualitative greatness of a society is not therefore solely the result of the determination and activity of its elite elements; these elements themselves must find a response in and be elaborated out of the entire people. Only a great people can produce a great ruling class.

Dorso finds, contrary to Michels and Pareto and in part even to Mosca, that a valid theory must have its "democratic" aspect; it cannot leave out of consideration the people at the base of the power structure. On the other hand, he continues to emphasize that leaders are indispensable and that even the most mature populace cannot rule itself but must elaborate a ruling class.

The Latitudinal Differentiation of Modern Society

In his essay, Dorso next discusses the social structure of modern industrial societies. The details of his presentation will be omitted here, attention being focused on the main points. According to Dorso, every society is composed of numerous classes or "social groups." At any given moment it is possible as it were to photograph the class structure of a society, and such a static picture is useful for political analysis. On the other hand, the dynamic dimension of social reality must not be neglected, and it must be understood that the social field is constantly in motion, with new social formations coming into being and others disappearing over time. Dorso's notion of class is an extremely fluid one. He explicitly rejects the Marxist notion of society as an eternal struggle between clearly differentiated classes. Rather, Dorso insists that class lines continually shift, with new classes and subdivisions of classes perpetually being articulated. These social formations are numerous and are always breaking up into factions even to the detriment of their interests. Members of a society identify themselves with a particular group; they tend to share its beliefs, habits and interests. These levels, or longitudinal divisions, in society are "the fruit of our mind" and the boundaries between them "are not rigid and recognizable at first sight. But it is indubitable that they exist and that they are not the consequences of mere arbitrariness."

Dorso found modern industrial society in Italy and western Europe to be composed of four principal strata, within which he made numerous subdivisions. The four principal classes were (1) upper class (including the "defeudalized nobility" and upper bourgeoisie), (2) the middle bourgeoisie, (3) the lower bourgeoisie, and (4) the "mass of the people" (including peasants, factory workers, artisans, and servants). The detail of his class analysis, which he assumed to have a basic validity for industrial societies in general, need not concern us here.

His remarks on the status and role of intellectuals, however, do bear repeating in this context. Intellectuals (under which category he subsumed doctors, lawyers, professors, writers, journalists, architects, scientists, engineers, and some managerial personnel) are today divided into two sectors, one "technical" and the other "humanistic." This division is of relatively recent origin and is due to the industrialization process; down to the beginning of the nineteenth century most intellectuals in a society had shared a common humanistic culture. Today, on the other hand, "a great many lawyers work for banks and corporations and read the commercial code more than the Pandects; many intellectuals . . . understand economics better than Latin and Greek." Within the scientific world there is the division between the "pure" and "applied" disciplines. The humanistic intelligentsia, "from which is recruited a notable portion of the political class," is found primarily in the ranks of the middle and lower bourgeoisie, with a preponderance of members in the latter category. In the past, lower bourgeois humanistic intellectuals have been attracted to a species of "enlightenment" political thinking and have fallen prey at certain moments of history to "vague romantic aspirations." The lower humanistic bourgeoisie has often sided with revolutionary movements. Its members are to be found frequently in the leadership of opposition political forces. This social group has tended to over-simplification and abstract thinking in the political realm.

The Lotta politica and the "Fission" of the Ruling and Political Classes

At this stage of the analysis Dorso introduces further distinctions and clarifications. "Up to this point," he remarks, "both the political class and the ruling class have been considered as a unity." This characterization has been necessary "to lay the groundwork for a theory of politics." It must not be thought, however, that either the political class or ruling class is a monolithic block which preserves its internal unity at all costs in order to minimize the dangers of being overthrown by the ruled class. Such an attitude, which is fre-quently held, is in effect an "ideological blindfold" which it will be necessary to remove if we are to "take hold of reality." In fact, in the process of forming the political class, complex sociopolitical phe-nomena occur that result in the "fracturing" (*frazione*) of the ruling class and, concomitantly, of the political class. This process need not destroy the basic unity of the ruling and political classes toward the governed classes because, if the exchange mechanism is working satisfactorily, the more proficient elements in those classes are con-stantly absorbed into the ruling and/or political class, thus "bleeding" the ruled classes of those leaders which could bring about the over-throw of the existing order.

The first fracture or split within the political class is that between the "governing" and "opposition" elements (the *classe politica gov-ernante* and the *classe politica di opposizione*). Between these two factions of the same elite formation "the political struggle [*la lotta politica*], which constitutes the supreme guarantee of the governed classes, is established." The continuous fission of the ruling *cum* political classes into factions is the indispensable condition for the development of the *lotta politica*, which in turn is the "condition of legitimacy for the power of the political class considered as a unity." Dictatorships, which attempt to repress the *lotta politica* and establish a "fictitious unity" in the political and ruling classes, do not possess legitimacy and, indeed, are "irrational" and "anti-historical" phenomena.

The schism of the political class into government and opposition wings happens as a result of the "composition and decomposition of sub-groups of the ruling class." The *classe politica di governo* has its roots in the *classe dirigente di governo*, that is, in the "more or less homogeneous constellation of social subgroups, interested in the realization of a given governmental program." The "remaining part of the political class" either organizes itself into a unified opposition, sustained by the remaining social subgroups, or it fragments into several oppositions, each sustained by some social subgroup or groups and all held together by the prospect of taking power from the government. The *lotta politica* is waged by the opposition with the objective of taking away support of enough social subgroups formerly adhering to the governing political class to bring about a situation in which it can itself become the governing political class. Under optimal conditions, in societies which enjoy a "perfect exchange" (*ricambia perfetto*) between elements within the ruling and political classes, the governing political class guarantees the status of the opposition and does not impede its function. Full acceptance of the legitimacy of the opposition and public acknowledgment of its loyalty is however more the exception than the rule. If opposition elements are systematically prevented from taking power peacefully and from acquiring the necessary social support thereto, this may well result in alienating the opposition groups from the system itself. They may then go underground and seek to effect political change by violence.

The Lotta politica and the Development of Political Parties

Dorso cites Mosca in support of his view that the "impulse for struggle with other men" is one of the key constants of human nature. In addition to the agonistic or competitive side of his nature, man is also cooperative. Thus "man is constrained to satisfy concomitantly two contradictory but equally essential inclinations: one for human solidarity, and the other for human conflict." The first drives him to associate with others in a "nucleus"; the second is fulfilled by the struggle of rival nuclei with each other.

However desirable it might be to have the "combative inclination" eliminated from human nature (we should recognize, however, that without it historical existence would be "dull"), "any conception that foresees the end of the struggle either through the thaumaturgic intervention of some new divinity or through the modification of human nature," deserves to be rejected as "utopian."

Dorso's stress on the inevitability of struggle between men should not be interpreted to mean that he is a proponent of some variety of social Darwinism. *Lotta* between men is qualitatively distinct from *lotta* between beasts in the jungle. Man possesses an "ideational capacity," and the *lotta* itself is primarily "ideological"[17] rather than "biological" in character. To ideologize, or to form and project ideas, is a "compulsion" for human beings.

Parties and the Longitudinal Differentiation of Society

To Dorso, the key institution for the conduct of the *lotta politica* in modern industrial society is the political party. It is to his credit that he placed this phenomenon at the center of his analysis, for neither Mosca nor Pareto did it justice and Michels was largely concerned with providing an (excessively simplistic) account of the power relations within a given political party for him adequately to grasp the role of parties as such in the political process. In a sense, Dorso writes, parties have always existed—witness the plebes and patricians in the Roman Republic or the Guelfs and Ghibellines in late medieval and renaissance Italy—but it is only comparatively recently that "these delicate instruments for the conquest of power have become refined." Essentially, parties are "inter-classist organizations" founded on the basis of the "ideological struggle." Parties are composed of fractions of the political, ruling, and ruled classes, and indeed of all the classes into which society latitudinally divides itself.

Here, Dorso introduces a distinction between the latitudinal and

---

[17] Dorso uses the term "ideological" as equivalent to "ideational"; that is, he does not use it in the reductionist manner of Tracy, Marx, etc. Dorso is aware of the role of ideas as more than the reflection of economic interests or irrational drives. In this respect, his position appears to be close to that of Max Weber in *The Protestant Ethic and the Spirit of Capitalism*.

longitudinal differentiation of society. On the one hand, it is possible to view human society in terms of its stratification (*stratigrafica-mente*), and here one speaks of social classes. But this same society "also segments itself longitudinally, giving way to other solidarities and other animosities which cannot be attributed to the class struggle in the strict sense." The "party struggle" is thus quite distinct from the "class struggle"; fractions of the same socioeconomic class will oppose each other in the *lotta dei partiti*.

In one sense, the "end of parties is the conquest of power." Another primary objective, however, is to propagate a doctrine. Actually, the struggle for power and *ideologomachia* (battle for an idea) are intermingled in the *lotta dei partiti*, just as the antagonistic and cooperative impulses are intermingled in individual men. It is possible to view the ideational aspect of the political struggle as "only the justificatory apparatus for the hunger after power; but he who has a profound knowledge of human nature knows by experience that the ideological struggle also embodies a need of our psychology, and that many men sacrifice not only their careers but also their lives" to ideal objectives. Human psychology is in fact a "marvelous texture" in which the strands of altruism and egotism are intermixed.

On the basis of his anthropology, which supplies a much-needed corrective to the Hobbesian concept of man as *homo homini lupus* without any sacrifice of "realism," Dorso concludes that political parties are neither simply "instruments of the economic and political struggle" nor "ideological academies"; rather "as institutions *sui generis*" they "satisfy in an integral manner contradictory aspirations in the human psyche and succeed in organizing into great voluntary and necessary associations individuals belonging to all social groups." Aside from their role in mitigating the acerbity of the class struggle in society (as a result of their interclassist character and the establishment of a longitudinal societal differentiation), parties have the function in modern democratic regimes of elaborating the greater part of the political class. Dorso is aware that in every regime the political class is partially comprised of "unconfessed politicians" (high civil servants, military leaders, "*ministeri di tecnici*"), but in democratic regimes the initiative and controlling influence lie with those elements elaborated directly from the party struggle.

To Dorso the modern political party is the instrument of democracy par excellence—and this despite the fact that parties, like every other vast human organization, are oligarchically structured. The party is the instrument of democracy because, when functioning optimally, it continually selects "from the masses the men who have the greatest capacity for governing the country." This ceaseless selection process results in the bleeding (*anemizzazione*) of the ruled class, which is regularly and systematically deprived of those leaders who are capable of leading a revolution that would overthrow the ruling class itself. There is, however, nothing diabolical or conspiratorial or unjust about this process; it is an unmodifiable reality of human social existence that the ruled class is incapable of ruling itself. "Direct democracy in the absolute sense" is an impossibility; but "direct democracy in the historical sense, that is, an organization in which the least possible number of obstacles is placed in the way of the double exchange [*duplice ricambio*] between ruled class and ruling class and ruling class and political class" is a reality in some societies and may become so in others.

In the strict sense, then, even in a democratic regime, it is the political class, and not the whole people, which governs. And yet its rule is not arbitrary; there are many factors that inhibit the *merum arbitrium*. In any but the most perverted regimes, the political class is much more than a mere executive committee of the ruling class; rather it not infrequently governs on behalf of the collectivity. Furthermore, in a democratic regime, the political parties make possible the extremely rapid rise of able elements from the ruled classes. It is true that a preponderance of the members of the political class comes from those who are not newcomers to the ruling class. But in such a society

> no one chooses the members of either the ruled class or the political class. There are no examinations or civil service competitions to choose these two oligarchies. They are born as a result of rather complicated social processes, into which only gradually the student is initiated. If it continuously happens that the political parties abound with the elements of the ruling class, it is because the ruling class is richer in elements adapted to the political struggle. But elements of the ruled class, by means of the parties, also make extremely rapid ascension into the political class and, consequently, into the ruling class.

Thus, Dorso arrives at the conclusion—surprising if one adopts the perspective of popular rhetoric—that the genuinely democratic societies are at the same time the most conservative ones. This is because the supremely efficient operation of the exchange mechanism among ruling, ruled, and political classes prevents the accumulation of "new cells" in the ruled class and thereby insures against the formation of revolutionary counterelites from the masses who seek the destruction of the political system itself. "The most securely conservative countries are the democratic ones," he observes.

Therefore, writes Dorso, those who "accuse parties of all the evils of politics" are not conservatives, but rather "reactionaries." Parties deserve praise, for in actuality they are "the only instruments through which the political struggle can organize itself in a stable way" under modern conditions. Both "conservative" and "popular" parties contribute to this "intelligent conservatism." Anticipating Robert McKenzie's study of the Conservative and Labour parties in Great Britain, Dorso noted that the two types of parties resemble each other in large measure, the conservative parties being more "democratic" than their opponents will give them credit for being and popular parties being more "oligarchical" in structure than they are wont to admit.

Toward the end of his essay, Dorso deals briefly with the "political formula" and the problem of an alienated, or revolutionary, opposition. In order for the vast majority of the politically active population to be committed to the democratic political formula (which endorses peaceful competition for the command posts in the governmental structure), obstacles must not be placed in the way of the free formation of political parties, and elections must not be tampered with through the use of devices designed to keep the governing political class in power even after it has lost its preponderance of support. If the competitive process is interfered with, then the opposition elements will become disenchanted with the democratic political formula itself and will be encouraged to seek, through violent means if necessary, a change of the system rather than merely a change within the system. Alienated opposition elements are those which fight not only for the conquest of governmental power but for the transformation of the political formula itself, which in a viable polity should be supported by a consensus of the major competing parties and social forces.

Dorso recognizes, however, that not all the ills of a democratic regime are attributable to the malfunctioning of the circulation of elites. There is also the problem of ideological fixation, and he points out that some "malcontents regarding human nature" would be opposed to the democratic political formula even if the exchange mechanism between ruled, ruling, and political classes functioned perfectly. Men of a utopian mentality, the "pure idéologues" are impatient with the cumbersome process of bargaining and compromise inherent in competitive politics. These *ideologi puri* are "very bad politicians" because they lack the "sense of reality and possibility."

For purpose of illustration, a diagram is enclosed concerning Dorso's key analytical concepts. Both parts of the diagram have been simplified and abbreviated; in particular, only a simple two-party system is represented whereas, of course, his analysis applies with equal weight to a multiparty system.

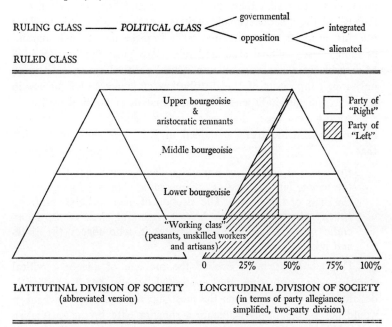

RULING CLASS ——— *POLITICAL CLASS* < governmental / opposition < integrated / alienated

RULED CLASS

LATITUTINAL DIVISION OF SOCIETY
(abbreviated version)

LONGITUDINAL DIVISION OF SOCIETY
(in terms of party allegiance;
simplified, two-party division)

It should be observed that Dorso rejected the view that the "ruling class" of a society necessarily coincided with its "social class" divisions. Especially in a democratic society—and principally by means of the political party—elements low on the class scale could indeed be members of the political and, therefore, of the ruling class. Correspondingly, an "upper class" social position did not inevitably carry with it membership in the ruling class.

Dorso's Achievement

Dorso's essay is a noteworthy contribution to the recovery of a critical political science and, therewith, political theory. Although some of his concepts need further elaboration, the seeds of a genuine political theory may be found in his work. Beginning with a common sense knowledge of political reality, he refines this knowledge conceptually, making acute distinctions and clarifications which appear faithfully to reflect the complexities of that reality. Dorso has made a very substantial advance on the road to the necessary demythologizing of popular democratic rhetoric without in any way falling prey to a wholesale and reactionary condemnation of democracy. He brings us far closer to reality than do the models and "developmental constructs" of the archbehavioralist writers. At the heart of his teaching was his awareness that the inevitable imprecision of such notions as ruling class, political class, and ruled class must not be permitted to prevent their employment by a critical political science. Although only rough indicators of the distribution of power and influence in a society, they are indispensable to any analysis of political reality.

At the very least, their employment facilitates the recognition of the fundamental truth contained in Eric Voegelin's observation that

> the essential problem of a working democracy is not the vote of the people but the type of the governing elite and its relation to the mass of the people. The election of men and the voting on issues is the last and relatively least important phase of the democratic process. The decisive question is, who shapes the issues and who presents the men?[18]

Dorso only began to explore the problem of adequate critical standards for evaluating the existential reality he so brilliantly described. He knew that even the most superior exchange mechanism would not automatically elaborate a superior elite in the qualitative sense. His insistence upon the importance of the internalized commitment of the ruling and political classes to the public interest as well as of the need for principled rejection of ideological fixation demonstrated that he was aware of the crucial Platonic distinction between the power elite and the character elite. Membership in the power elite did not automatically guarantee that one also could be

[18] Eric Voegelin, "Extended Strategy," *Journal of Politics*, II (May, 1940), 180-200 at 193-194.

classed with the character elite, and only in the best regime in the absolute sense would the two elites precisely coincide. He also appeared to grasp the potential role of political education in furthering the development of a society's character elite.

But Dorso never managed to break through to the recovery of the paradigmatic society as a central theme for political theory, just as he never achieved a complete anthropology of the various character types crowned by the *spoudaios* or mature man. His analysis of the dual (cooperative-antagonistic) nature of man failed to include— although it did not deny—the possibility of transcendent experience, together with the fact that the *amor sui* (whether of self or of group) must be supplemented and corrected by the Augustinian *amor dei*. As a result, his critical standards were more implicit than explicit, and his focus on existential reality was not adequately balanced by a metaphysics and a consideration of essential reality. Nonetheless, as shall be pointed out in the last chapter, Dorso opened up many areas of exploration for contemporary political theory. With a truly Aristotelian (and Machiavellian) sense of the existential givens of politics, he helps to underscore the genuine empiricism of all authentic political theory which is poles apart from any supposedly abstract, deductive, and idealistic understanding of man and society.[19]

[19] As is evident from Norberto Bobbio's interesting writings and the proceedings of the 1960 meeting of an international gathering of political sociologists held in Italy—published as *Le elites politiche* (Bari, Laterza, 1961)—elite studies after the manner of Mosca and Dorso continue to be the subject of scholarly attention. In this connection, the writings of Giovanni Sartori of the University of Florence should be mentioned. In *Il Parlamento Italiano: 1946-1963* (Naples, ESI, 1963), Sartori attempted a further revision and elaboration of elite theory terminology. Sartori retains the concept of ruling class (*classe dirigente*) by which he means "all ruling minorities— political, economic, social, religious, intellectual, technological, military, and bureaucratic." With Dorso, he then distinguishes the political class (*classe politica*) as a subsection of the ruling class, or as "that part of the ruling class which concerns itself with political power." Elites to Sartori are those at the highest level of the political and ruling class—those who have the last word. Within the political elite he distinguishes between a political elite exercising rule (*una elite politica dirigente*) and a political elite exerting influence (*una elite politica influente*). Of the overall political elite there are at least three subgroups: the extra-party elite, party elites, and elective elites. He recognizes as a special problem, of course, the possible lack of correspondence between the de jure and de facto ruling political elite. Mention should also be made of Sartori's excellent book (first published in Italy as *Democrazia e definizione*) *Democratic Theory* (New York, Praeger, 1965).

PART IV ❧ THE REVIVAL OF POLITICAL THEORY

SEVEN: THE CONTEMPORARY REVIVAL OF POLITICAL THEORY: OAKESHOTT, ARENDT, JOUVENEL, AND STRAUSS

The period since the end of World War II has been the occasion for a significant turning point in the fortunes of political theory. From today's vantage point it is clear that the apex of the positivist ascendancy was in the 1930s; since that time significant advances have been made in the recovery of a critical political theory by a number of highly gifted and creative thinkers. Among this sizeable group of present-day scholars five individuals stand out as particularly worthy of attention: Michael Oakeshott, Hannah Arendt, Bertrand de Jouvenel, Leo Strauss, and Eric Voegelin. The first four of these important writers will be discussed in the present chapter, while Voegelin, whom later generations may well acclaim as the greatest political theorist of our time, will be considered in Chapter 8.

All of these contributors to the revival of political theory in our time reject political messianism and utopianism in politics. They are all centrally concerned with the phenomenon of totalitarianism, and their voices are being increasingly heard in the postideological age in the West. None of them offers neat solutions to the complex problems of human existence; as Jouvenel has suggested, political problems differ from mathematical ones precisely in the sense that there may be no solution for them, in which eventuality it will be the mark of wisdom to recognize that fact. However, they are all engaged in the search for principles of order and in the application of these principles and criteria to our contemporary situation.

Michael Oakeshott

Michael Oakeshott's contribution to the contemporary effort to recover political theory as a tradition of inquiry is considerable, although it is frequently overlooked by people who regard him as essentially a spokesman for the neoconservative intellectual movement or even for the Tory party in Great Britain.[1] That Oakeshott is a conservative in both the lower and upper case sense is true, but it is his least interesting characteristic in evaluating his work as a scholar. All of the figures who have been or will be cited as significant in the revival of political theory have taken stands on specific contemporary issues and some might be classified—on the basis of these opinions— as more leftist or rightist than others. But what unites them is more important than what divides them. This uniting factor is the objective of regaining the possibility of a critical, theoretical analysis of politics in our time.

Oakeshott's principal theoretical achievement is a philosophical analysis of experience which seeks to rediscover the multidimensionality that had been denied to experience by the ideological and positivist reductionists whom we have previously discussed. According to Oakeshott, experience is a concrete whole within which it is possible to distinguish various "modes." The modes constitute "arrests" in experience and only from the standpoint of philosophy, whose task is to identify each mode and define its relationship to other worlds of experience, can we hope to see experience as a whole. Oakeshott has distinguished between four principal modes of or arrests in experience: practice, science, history, and poetry.[2]

[1] Thus, Bernard Crick has argued—in a book that otherwise has much to commend it—that Oakeshott's inaugural essay at the London School of Economics on Political Education (Cambridge, Bowes and Bowes, 1951) is an exposition of Tory political doctrine rather than a critical analysis of the character which the academic teaching of politics ought to assume. See Crick's *In Defence of Politics* (London, Penguin, 1964).

[2] Michael Oakeshott, *Experience and Its Modes* (London, Cambridge University Press, 1933)—the most important but the least known of Oakeshott's works—concerns itself only with practice, science, and history. Poetry is

Practice has to do with the activity of desiring and obtaining and of tending to the arrangements necessary for such activity in society. Science is essentially preoccupied with inquiry that results in measurement and predictability. It views the environment as a field of objects which can be classified and whose relations can be measured and quantified. History is the activity of understanding "past conduct and happening in a manner in which they were never understood at the time," and the task of the historian is to "translate action and event from the practical idiom to the historical idiom."[3]

Oakeshott is a superb writer, and nowhere is his distinguished style more admirably displayed than in his essay on poetic activity. While practice is the world of desiring and science that of understanding, poetry is the activity of "contemplating and delighting." Poetry thus becomes "the activity of making images of a certain kind and moving about them in a manner appropriate to their character."[4] Poetry, given here a broader meaning than that ordinarily assigned to it, is essentially aesthetic experience. It is not concerned with truth or utility but with the creation of aesthetically satisfying images whether in words, paintings, sculpture, or buildings. Poetry is its own reward: one delights in engaging in it.

In his essay on poetry Oakeshott refers to the "conversation of mankind," and to the activities of practice, science, history, and poetry as comparable to four different "voices" in the conversation. Particularly in the recent past there has been a danger that the voices of practice and science will drown out those of poetry and history, to say nothing of philosophy. To Oakeshott, philosophy does not contribute to the conversation, but rather listens to it; philosophy has the task of distinguishing and identifying the nature and character of each of the voices. With regard to history, Oakeshott has observed that "the practical idiom has imposed itself for so long

---

treated in the lengthy and brilliant essay, "The Voice of Poetry in the Conversation of Mankind," published separately in 1959 and reprinted along with other essays in *Rationalism in Politics* (New York, Basic Books, 1962).

[3] Michael Oakeshott, "The Activity of Being an Historian," in *Historical Studies* (London, Proceedings of the Second Irish Conference of Historians, 1958), pp. 1-19 at p. 17.

[4] Michael Oakeshott, *The Voice of Poetry in the Conversation of Mankind* (Chester Springs, Pa., Dufour, 1959), p. 31.

upon all inquiry into the past that its hold cannot readily be loosened." Because of its "addiction to practice" our intellectual world is "hostile to history."[5] If men forget how to speak in the idiom of the other voices, then the conversation will become boring, or to put it differently, human existence in all its richness is lost sight of. The truncation of experience, its reduction to the two modes of practice and science, can only mean diminution of the human spirit. "Poetry," Oakeshott maintains, "is a sort of truancy, a dream within the dream of life, a wild flower planted among our wheat."[6]

Oakeshott nowhere actually defines philosophy, but rather indicates that it is the sort of activity that one undertakes in discoursing upon experience and its modes. When we philosophize we leave the tight model islands of incomplete experience for the "open sea of experience." Oakeshott obviously writes in praise of philosophy but, consistently with his basic skepticism, he is modest in the claims he makes for it. Philosophy, for example, cannot serve as a guide for practical life, for it is not the "clear-sighted, not those who are fashioned for thought and the ardours of thought, who can lead the world. Great achievements are accomplished in the mental fog of practical experience. What is farthest from our needs is that kings should be philosophers."[7]

Philosophy serves truth at the expense of life; in practical life we inevitably proceed on the level of "arrested" experience. Rather pessimistically, he concludes *Experience and Its Modes* with the observation that there may be "something decadent, something even depraved in an attempt to achieve a completely coherent world of experience." However, it is true that the particular modes of experience—including above all practical life—afford one only "the empty kisses of abstraction." But "if these give but little satisfaction, and give that little not for long, it is at least a tangible and certain satisfaction while it lasts and one not to be despised."[8]

---

[5] Michael Oakeshott, "The Activity of Being an Historian," in *op. cit.*, p. 18. It is "not only the recent past that is difficult to see historically; it is any period or situation that provokes a practical interest. . . ." (p. 16). Oakeshott gives the middle ages as a prime example. *Ibid.*

[6] Oakeshott, *The Voice of Poetry*, *op. cit.*, p. 63.

[7] Oakeshott, *Experience and Its Modes*, *op. cit.*, pp. 320-321.

[8] *Ibid.*, p. 356 (concluding sentence of the work).

Whereas Oakeshott mainly talks about what philosophy is by indirection and intimation, he is quite direct and definite on the question of what philosophy is not. Philosophy is not determined by its historical setting. While it is correct to say that every philosophy has its place and time,

> the admission of this truth does not make relevant an appeal to this aspect of its character. . . . What we must ask about a philosophy is, Can it maintain what it asserts? And its setting will certainly not help us to answer this question. . . . Place and time are, indeed, as irrelevant to a philosophical theory as they are to a scientific investigation.[9]

And yet the similarity between science and philosophy in this respect should not obscure the fact that philosophy and science are basically different kinds of activities and it is illicit to attempt to transfer the methods and concerns of the one to the other. "The notion that philosophy has anything to learn from the methods of scientific thought," or that its conclusions must be in harmony with those of the special sciences "is altogether false."[10] Philosophy is not practice, nor does it serve the demands of the practical world. It must be sought for its own sake and must "maintain its independence from all extraneous interests, and in particular from the practical interest."[11] Philosophy is not the preaching of a doctrine, although all philosophers generally have something of the preacher in them. "But we must learn not to follow the philosophers upon these holiday excursions."[12] Philosophy consists "not in persuading others, but in making our own minds clear."[13] Philosophy cannot if it remains true to itself be a popular enterprise, for to popularize philosophy "is at once to debase it: a general demand for philosophy is at once a general demand for its degradation."[14] Finally, philosophy is not the search for a universal system within which full knowledge is contained about every aspect of reality. The philosopher does not seek to

[9] *Ibid.*, p. 349.

[10] *Ibid.*, p. 354.

[11] *Ibid.*, p. 3.

[12] *Ibid.*, p. 1.

[13] *Ibid.*, p. 3.

[14] *Ibid.*

compile information, but to see things steady and see them whole (to paraphrase Matthew Arnold). The philosopher must "resign what is merely encyclopaedic. The *savant* as such is not a philosopher; there is little or nothing in common between the philosopher and the *philosophe*." The philosopher seeks "valid knowledge," not "universal knowledge."[15]

Oakeshott's conception of the nature of *political* philosophy— or, as he would prefer to put it, of the activity of philosophizing about politics—must also be gleaned primarily by indirection and negation. To begin with, political philosophy is not philosophy in the full sense because of its anchorage in the world of practice. What is true of moral philosophy is also true of political philosophy: It attempts to "see one particular mode of experience—practical experience—from the standpoint of the totality of experience."[16] Political philosophy is not full-fledged philosophy because it involves an arrest in experience; neither is it one of the abstract modes or levels of experience because the arrest on which it is grounded is indeterminate rather than being determinate and homogeneous.[17] Political philosophy would appear to inhabit a domain of "indeterminate location" between the incompleteness of the world of practice and the coherence of philosophic experience.

In his famed Introduction to Hobbes's *Leviathan*[18] Oakeshott distinguished between several levels of reflection about political life:

> Reflection about political life may take place at a variety of levels. It may remain on the level of the determination of means, or it may strike out for the consideration of ends. Its inspiration may be directly practical, the modification of the arrangements of a political order in accordance with the perception of an immediate benefit; or it may be practical, but less directly so, guided by general ideas. Or again, springing from an experience of political life, it may seek a generalization of that experience in a doctrine. And reflection is apt to flow from one level to another. . . . Political philosophy may be understood to be what occurs when

[15] *Ibid.*, p. 1.

[16] *Ibid.*, p. 345.

[17] *Ibid.*, p. 335.

[18] Michael Oakeshott, Introduction to Thomas Hobbes, *Leviathan* (London, Blackwell, 1957).

this movement of reflection takes a certain direction and achieves a certain level, its characteristic being the relation of political life . . . to the entire conception of the world that belongs to a civilization. That is to say, at all other levels of reflection on political life we have before us the single world of political activity . . . but in political philosophy we have in our minds that world and another world, and our endeavor is to explore the coherence of the two worlds together.[19]

Toward the conclusion of the essay on Hobbes, Oakeshott returns to the question about the character of political philosophy, declaring it to be "the consideration of the relation between politics and eternity."[20] It is in the context of this discussion that Oakeshott's emphatic rejection of ideology is to be understood. For authentic political philosophy, as represented in Plato, Aristotle, Augustine, Aquinas, Hobbes, and Hegel, has never promised that salvation of man from his existential predicament can come through political activity alone. The "great political philosophers" are in agreement that "politics is contributory to the fulfillment of an end which it cannot itself bring about."[21] Ideology, on the other hand, offers escape into a "bogus eternity." Ideology is perpetually in danger of "making civil society a hell by conceiving of it as a heaven."[22]

In his inaugural lecture (upon, ironically enough, succeeding to the chair Harold Laski had held) on Political Education delivered at the London School of Economics, Oakeshott maintained that the purpose of political philosophy is "to consider the place of political activity itself on the map of our total experience." As a tradition of inquiry, it has uncovered a variety of problems which each generation reconsiders. It is not a " 'progressive' science, accumulating solid results and reaching conclusions upon which further research may be based with confidence. . . ." The noncumulative nature of political philosophy means that "its history is especially important: indeed, in a sense it has nothing but a history, which is a history of the problem philosophers have detected and the manner of solution they have proposed, rather than a history of doctrines. . . ." The advantages

[19] *Ibid.*, p. ix.

[20] *Ibid.*, p. lxiv.

[21] *Ibid.*

[22] *Ibid.*, p. lxv.

that a student of politics can expect to derive from its study are not practical: "Political philosophy cannot be expected to increase our ability to be successful in political activity." The advantages to be derived from its study are not to be despised however, that is, the straightening of crooked thinking and the correction of a simplistic, doctrinaire approach. A careful student of political philosophy will avoid being cheated by ambiguous statements and irrelevant arguments. For all these reasons, political philosophy should comprise a major segment of the academic study of politics.[23]

In contrast to political philosophy, ideology to Oakeshott is "an abstract principle, or set of related abstract principles," which has been premeditated independently of any settled tradition of behavior. Ideologies are typically expressed in catechismic form for the widest possible dissemination. Ideologies select from the multiplicity and variety of political life a single abstract goal which they insist on imposing upon practice. Typically, they also inform their followers of the specific techniques for implementing these goals.[24]

In his concept of ideology, Oakeshott casts his net far and wide; Locke's *Second Treatise*, the Declaration of the Rights of Man as Citizen, Liberalism, Democracy, and the Atlantic Charter—all of these are included as examples of ideology. He cites Freedom, Equality, Maximum Productivity, Racial Purity, and Happiness as abstract ideas which comprise the "simplest sort of political ideology." Ideology is thus essentially any abridgement or simplification of a political tradition or tendency. Within the world of ideologies, however, he distinguishes between some that are more appropriate and useful than others. The inappropriate ones, of which Marxism is a good example, instead of abstracting from a political tradition of a society, model themselves after "some other manner of activity—war or the conduct of industry for example. And here the model we are shown is not only abstract, but is also misleading on account of the irrelevance of the activity from which it has been abstracted."[25] Politics is essentially the activity of tending to the "general arrangements" of a society; the soundest kind of political education is one which teaches its practitioners to acquire a feel for and a sympathy with

[23] Michael Oakeshott, *Political Education* (Cambridge, 1951), pp. 26-27.

[24] *Ibid.*, pp. 12-13.

[25] *Ibid.*, p. 17.

the multifaceted yet inwardly coherent tradition of behavior that characterizes a given society. Ideologies, which abridge and distort that tradition, if they do not lose touch with it altogether, must be seen for what they are and their influence as determinants of actual concrete decisions must be contained as far as possible.

Michael Oakeshott scarcely qualifies as a complete political theorist. His fundamental skepticism, which prevents him from holding that philosophy has anything of substance to teach mankind, has severely restricted his creative role as a political theorist. And yet he is an important figure in preparing the way for the work of constructive political theory. Essentially he is an "underlaborer" (if we may borrow this term from Locke) in the service of the new theory of politics. With his brilliant and trenchant style, he has helped point the way to a renaissance of political theory.

Perhaps his principal service has been his supremely articulate resistance to the tyranny of the practical attitude. Although Oakeshott cannot bring himself to affirm that a hierarchy exists among the various realms of experience and is therefore unable to reassert the Aristotelian-Thomistic claim of the superiority of the *vita contemplativa* to the *vita activa*, nonetheless he is extremely effective in the negative sense of challenging the widespread fallacy that the world of practice is self-contained and self-fulfilling. Practical life is a mistress who affords only "the empty kisses of abstraction," or, alternatively, she is a tiresome and homely housemaid who can only plod dully through the routine of the day. In the rediscovery of the inherent insufficiency of practice and world-immanent external activity, Oakeshott has prepared the way for the rediscovery of transcendence. But he himself has not been able to cross over to that discovery. Oakeshott is a true skeptic—one who is open and searching. He continues—perhaps thanks to the idealist inheritance via Bradley with which he began—to speak in the language of immanence. But like Croce there is in Oakeshott a horizontal transcendence, a transcendence within immanence which is closer than he might admit to the reopening of the psyche toward the divine measure of right order.

Hannah Arendt

One of the brightest stars in the firmament of contemporary political theory is Hannah Arendt. A person of enormous erudition, she has published extensively on the major problems of political theory in the postwar era. A thinker of exceptional originality, she reveals in all her writings a keen awareness that a new era of political thought has begun, an era which promises to carry us beyond ideology to a conception of man and society based on greater experiential openness. A theme which looms large in all of Arendt's writings is the uniqueness and responsibility of the individual human person. In her study, *The Origins of Totalitarianism,* which has already become a classic, and her brilliant and provocative reflections on the Eichmann trial, she casts the searchlight of reason on the "cog mentality" which to an increasing extent has permeated contemporary social thought. Her principal objection to behavioralist social science is precisely the fact that, in its search for uniformities in human behavior, it will itself contribute to the making of a uniform, stereotyped "man."

> The unfortunate truth about behaviorism and the validity of its "laws" is that the more people there are, the more likely they are to behave and the less likely to tolerate nonbehavior. Statistically, this will be shown in the leveling out of fluctuation. In reality, deeds will have less and less chance to stem the tide of behavior, and events will more and more lose their significance, that is, their capacity to illuminate historical time. Statistical uniformity is by no means a harmless scientific ideal; it is the no longer secret political ideal of a society which, entirely submerged in the routine of everyday living, is at peace with the scientific outlook inherent in its very existence.[26]

Eichmann, the "perfectly normal man," as Arendt described him, the man who turned himself into a tool for use by higher authorities, the transportation expert who was just doing his job of making the trains to Auschwitz with their human cargo run on schedule, is the most revealing manifestation of the "banality of evil" inherent in the system-thinking of our time. Eichmann was a creature who knew how to "behave" efficiently, but who had suppressed entirely the knowledge of how to *act* responsibly. Arendt tirelessly and uncompromisingly exposes the prevalent fallacy of viewing history in terms of the operation of silent, anonymous forces that inexorably plow their

[26] Hannah Arendt, *The Human Condition* (Garden City, N.Y., Doubleday, 1959), p. 40.

way through time. The actors of history are individual men in positions of authority, not "bureaucracies," "states," "churches," and other collectivities.

Arendt shares with the other leading figures in the revival of political theory an understanding of the basic incompatibility between political theory and ideology. Ideologies, defined by Arendt as "isms which to the satisfaction of their adherents can explain everything and every occurrence by deducing it from a single premise,"[27] only developed as a significant force in recent history. The nineteenth century saw the proliferation of ideologies, but their lethal potentialities were not fully recognized until the rise to power of Hitler and Stalin.

Commencing with a single master idea, such as race or class, ideologies consist of unbroken and completely consistent chains of reasonings. "You can't say A without saying B and C and so on, down to the end of the murderous alphabet."[28] Whereas any authentic political *theory* will encounter *aporiai*, difficulties and even inconsistencies at either the logical or experiential level, ideologies have ironed out all such irregularities and kinks. The result is a foolproof system which bears very little resemblance to reality, to existence and its concrete limitations and problems.

Ideologies, and in particular the totalitarian regimes which take them seriously enough to put them into practice, ignore the inevitable discrepancy that must exist between legality and justice. In nonideological thinking it was inconceivable that this discrepancy could ever be bridged "because the standards of right and wrong into which positive law translates its own source of authority . . . are necessarily general and must be valid for a countless and unpredictable number of cases, so that each concrete individual case with its unrepeatable set of circumstances somehow escapes it."[29]

"An ideology," Arendt has written, "is quite literally what its name indicates: it is the logic of an idea. . . . The ideology treats the course of events as though it followed the same 'law' as the logical exposition of the 'idea.' Ideologies pretend to know the

---

[27] Hannah Arendt, "*Ideology and Terror: A Novel Form of Government*," reprinted in *The Origins of Totalitarianism*, 2nd ed. (New York, 1962), pp. 460-479 at 468.

[28] *Ibid.*, p. 472.

[29] *Ibid.*, p. 462.

mysteries of the whole historical process—the secrets of the past, the intricacies of the present, the uncertainties of the future—because of the logic inherent in their respective ideas."[30]

For all Hannah Arendt's brilliance, erudition, and insight, she has defects as a constructive political theorist. Her writings are not always well-organized, and her style tends to be on the obscure side. She appears to be groping for a new humanism, but she sometimes writes as if the great political theory of the past can give us little assistance in constructing it. The crisis of our times, which indubitably exists, has assumed such vast proportions in her mind as to make necessary a totally new beginning in political thought. And yet she does not offer, the only possible reason being that she has not formed, clear guidelines for a new political theory.

Notwithstanding her limitations, the fundamental attributes of the theorist shine forth in Arendt's works. She thinks for herself rather than for any movement, and she has the integrity to take unpopular and unfashionable political stands if these seem to be called for by the evidence at hand.[31] She has a keen awareness of the theorist's critical function, which inevitably involves resistance to corrupting trends in contemporary societal life, while at the same time refusing to permit oneself the easy path of blanket and indiscriminate rejection and attack. Arendt often engages in controversy, but her writings are always luminous with reason, they never degenerate into shrill polemics. It is not so much the substance as the style of her thought that has had and continues to have a profound effect on the political thought of our time. One can say of her what Urs von Balthasar has written about Karl Barth: she combines "passion and objectivity." In her teaching, lecturing, and writing at various institutions in the United States and Europe, she has left her mark on the political education of the coming generation.

[30] *Ibid.*, p. 469.

[31] She also possesses the humility and wisdom to revise positions in the light of new knowledge and experience. Thus, in a conversation with the author in 1964, she indicated that she had reversed her stand on racial integration of the public schools in the United States; in a controversial article she had once argued that education is in the private realm so that discrimination on the basis of race, however evil, could not properly be legislated out of existence by the public authorities. See "Reflections on Little Rock," *Dissent* (Winter, 1959).

Arendt on Modernity

Arendt has grasped as fully as anyone the dangers which certain trends in modern industrialized society present to the life of the spirit, and she is aware that the possibilities exist for what C. S. Lewis called the "abolition of man." These dangers are nowhere better summarized than in her major work *The Human Condition*:

> If we compare the modern world with that of the past, the loss of human experience . . . is extraordinarily striking. It is not only and not even primarily contemplation which has become an entirely meaningless experience. Thought itself, when it became "reckoning with consequences," became a function of the brain, with the result that electronic instruments are found to fulfill these functions much better than we ever could. Action was soon and still is almost exclusively understood in terms of making and fabricating, only that making, because of its worldliness and inherent indifference to life, was now regarded as but another form of laboring, a more complicated but not a more mysterious function of the life process.
>
> Meanwhile, we have proved ingenious enough to find ways to ease the toil and trouble of living to the point where an elimination of laboring from the range of human activities can no longer be regarded as utopian. For even now, laboring is too lofty, too ambitious a word for what we are doing, or think we are doing, in the world we have come to live in. The last stage of the laboring society, the society of jobholders, demands of its members a sheer automatic functioning, as though individual life had actually been submerged in the over-all life process of the species and the only active decision still required of the individual were to let go, so to speak, to abandon his individuality, the still individually sensed pain and trouble of living, and acquiesce in a dazed, "tranquilized," functional type of behavior. The trouble with modern theories of behaviorism is not that they are wrong but that they could become true, that they actually are the best possible conceptualization of certain obvious trends in modern society. It is quite conceivable that the modern age—which began with such an unprecedented and promising outburst of human activity—may end in the deadliest, most sterile passivity history has ever known.[32]

[32] Arendt, *The Human Condition, op. cit.,* pp. 294-295.

Only the naively optimistic or the ideologically mesmerized can avoid facing the obvious fact that Arendt is right when she says that the freedom of the spirit is gravely threatened today. Yet Arendt is no prophet of inevitable *Untergang*. Man remains man, with the capacity for responsible action instead of automatic "behaving." Arendt's own work is a testimony that a recovery of the sense of dignity and responsible freedom in human action is not only a possibility in our time but may actually already be underway. This, indeed, is what the recovery of political theory is all about.[33]

Bertrand de Jouvenel

Hannah Arendt and Bertrand de Jouvenel are alike in their resistance to the modern tendency to transform politics into administration, thereby losing the potentiality which politics could have for creative activity in the public realm of our existence. Their teachings also resemble each other in that they both conceive of politics as a competitive process and are concerned to correct the bias of the majority of the great political theorists of the past on the subject of the legitimacy of factions and factional struggle. Again, there are similarities in that both thinkers have been through and experienced deeply the ordeal of twentieth-century totalitarianism and are concerned with discovering the intellectual and moral roots of this momentous phenomenon.

Furthermore, Jouvenel and Arendt speak with one voice in condemning the terrible simplifications of ideological sloganeering and the pipe dreams of utopian schemes for social salvation. They have reappropriated for political thought the Platonic discovery that institutions are not made of wood and rock, but are extensions of the personalities of those who make them work. Politics is preeminently

[33] A prolific writer, Arendt continues to publish at an extraordinary rate. In addition to the volumes cited above, she is the author of *Between Past and Future: Six Exercises in Political Thought* (New York, Viking, 1961), which contains brilliant essays on "Freedom" and "Authority"; *Eichmann in Jerusalem: A Report on the Banality of Evil* (New York, Viking, 1962); *On Revolution* (New York, Viking, 1963); and at least thirty-five major articles. The report on the Eichmann trial brought her much abuse and misunderstanding, with some reviewers actually attributing to her the incredible thesis that the Jews—rather than the Nazis—were the authors of their own destruction!

the sphere of moral choice in our relations with our fellowmen. "It is impossible to establish a just social order," Jouvenel has written, although by this statement he emphatically did not mean to rule out the possibility of working through political education to bring into being, over time, a social order *permeated with justice*: "Justice is a quality, not of social arrangements but of the human will. . . . Therefore, what we should be concerned with is that the whole ceaseless process of change would be permeated by the quality of justice in our individual wills."[34]

Jouvenel is more reticent about making evaluations than is Arendt, and there is an air of serenity about his writing that reminds one of Oakeshott. Jouvenel is acutely conscious of the realism and even empiricism present in the works of the great political theorists of the past, and especially in Rousseau of whom he has made a close study.[35] His works are offered as *descriptions* of political reality, and they abound with examples drawn from history and contemporary social life. At the same time it is clear that he is opposed to any conception of political science as value-free. The political theorist must isolate and describe key developments in political life, but he must offer criteria for evaluating these developments as well. As he points out in *Sovereignty*, political theorists, "who for so long devoted themselves to the question of what was right for the public authority to do, are now concerned only to consider what is the right manner of its formation. In the result, the only judgments now formed are on whether public authorities have a good title to act, not on whether they act well."[36] These judgments, however, cannot be uncritical opinions and emotive preferences, but must be based on the critical clarification of human moral experience. Such experience is more than a private affair, and there exists in the tradition of political theory itself the public record of the efforts of men in a variety of epochs and environments to elucidate regulative principles of society. This tradition, although it is not to be imitated in a sterile fashion, cannot but be of relevance to contemporary life.

[34] Bertrand de Jouvenel, *Sovereignty: An Inquiry into the Political Good* (Cambridge, 1957), pp. 164-165.

[35] See his brilliant introduction to Rousseau, "Essai sur la politique de Rousseau" in *Du Contrat Social de Jean-Jacques Rousseau* (Geneva, Editions du Cheval Oilé, 1947), pp. 13-160.

[36] Jouvenel, *Sovereignty, op. cit.*, p. xii.

Jouvenel's interpretation of his role as a political theorist is stated most explicitly and succinctly in the preface to his book, *Sovereignty*, which as he explains, is a sequel to his book, *Power* published ten years earlier. The purpose of the *Power* volume, he informs us, was two-fold: (1) to describe the stages in the growth of public authority in the western nation-states, and (2) to note an "attendant phenomenon," viz., the "moral emancipation" of the same public authority. He hoped thereby to demonstrate how "the idea of the legitimate origin of Power has suppressed and driven out its natural fellow, that of the legitimate use of Power, and to drive home the loss thereby inflicted."[37]

However, he adds, "what was the good of noting and emphasizing this loss if no attempt was made to repair it? So it was that my original purpose drew me on to a search for the criteria applicable in our own day to the conduct of public authorities."[38] Jouvenel modestly adds at the conclusion of his preface that what he offers in *Sovereignty* are only "the exploratory workings of a questing spirit." And, indeed, his works are essentially exploratory in this regard, for he does not do much more than intimate what the criteria are by which we measure the legitimate use of power.

One possibility would be a revival of natural law thinking, a position with which Jouvenel obviously has considerable sympathy as is manifested in the following passage:

> The absence in Society of any concrete authorities capable of restraining power does not matter if Power itself makes humble submission before the abstract force of the Natural Law. The idea of the limitation of Power by such a law puts no trust in material makeweights, which in their nature are egoist and may as often hinder Power's beneficent action as check its malignant use; rather it calls into being a spiritual process to take the place of a mechanical.[39]

However, Jouvenel fails to develop and clarify his support of a natural law position perhaps out of a belief, similar to that entertained by Arendt, that the vocabulary of traditional political theory is no longer adequate to contemporary realities. Like Arendt, Jouvenel

[37] *Ibid.*, pp. xi-xii.

[38] *Ibid.*

[39] *Ibid.*, p. 256.

appears to be in search of a surrogate for natural law, although, also like her, it is only intimated what the surrogate is. Both thinkers, however, attest to the experiential reality of inner moral restraints on the use of power, even if they fail to arrive at or articulate clearly substitute symbols for the natural law. Both of them see vividly the bankruptcy of positivist social science, and they call for a new beginning in political thought.

In one of his most brilliant analyses, Jouvenel discusses the essence of politics. From this portrayal, Jouvenel clearly maintains that it is possible to derive certain norms for the good society. Politics has a "nature" or essence which is actualized more fully in some societies than others.

Jouvenel gives politics a much wider meaning than is customary today, for he defines it "as an activity that builds, consolidates, and keeps in being aggregates of men." The building of aggregates is the work of men whom he refers to as *duces*. Jouvenel finds it more plausible to conceive of society as resting ultimately on authority rather than on either force or spontaneous consent (the "social contract"). If we look around us at organizations formed in our midst we will see that they come into being as the result of the activity of one man, the founder, with a small minority of assistants. "The man who leads into action a stream of wills . . . is *dux*, the conductor or leader." The *dux* possesses *vis politica*, which is "the causative force of every social formation or company of men." He is the Initiator or Promoter. "The process of formation gets into gear through the initiative of a single man, who sows among others the seed of his purpose; some of them, in whom it rises, turn into a small group of apostles for the scheme, and these form the nucleus that preaches and recruits." Thus, consent does not arise spontaneously as in the Lockean social contract, but has to be promoted and aroused by men who possess authority—who are *auctors*—and who are the social magnets around whom men organize for action.

The distinguishing mark of a "progressive society" according to Jouvenel is the "great proliferation of action groups of all sizes and natures; they die and are born. Teams of action are seen now working together and now in conflict; it is a process of increasing movement in the course of which no state of things is stable. . . . It is in the nature of things that the multiplication of initiatives should multiply friction and tensions."

Jouvenel's central preoccupation is with the problem of authority —a theme which also looms large in Arendt's reflections. Jouvenel and Arendt independently arrive at the conclusion that authority is to be sharply distinguished from force, and that, in fact, to the extent that force has to be threatened or applied, authority is absent. Authority is essentially voluntarily elicited assent to leadership. In any social formation some men are found to possess and exercise more aggregative capacity than others. Unless the public authority preempts the field of action and, as, for example, in totalitarian dictatorship, represses authoritative initiatives exercised independently of it, the normal condition of the social field is to be "strewn with hubs of authority." In this condition, "man is conscious of being affected by the action of several hubs."

The task of government is conceived by Jouvenel to lie more in the domain of regulation than of initiation. He distinguishes between two types of authority: that of the *dux* and the *rex*. "The man who leads into action a stream of wills . . . is *dux*—conductor or leader. The man who institutionalizes co-operation is *rex*, the man who regularizes or rules." The *rex* is the "rectifier," the "adjustor," the "stabilizer." The task of government, as the highest and most comprehensive regulative authority in a society, is to maintain the predictability of the milieu—the network of rules and regular procedures within whose framework individual and group initiatives may operate.[40]

From his observations of human beings in the social context, Jouvenel concludes that politics is a far more pervasive activity than it is often taken to be in the modern period. Leadership and allegiance are pervasive factors throughout society as such, and government, if it does not seek to repress politics altogether, cannot be seen as occupying the whole political field. Thus, political science in Jouvenel's view opens itself again to consider the entire social existence of man, as it had done with Plato and Aristotle.

Jouvenel returns to the classical conception of education in moral responsibility as the only firm basis of an ordered polity and the only conceivable focal point of a true political science. Power is used by men and they will exercise it with restraint only if they know and experience moral limits to action. A good government cannot produce

[40] For the discussion of the *rex-dux* distinction, see Jouvenel, *Sovereignty, op. cit.*, pp. 20 ff.

a good society, but a good society—a society with a good political class in the larger Jouvenelian concept of politics—will produce a good government.

The idea that the domain of the political is something far wider and more general than commonly noted "took such hold on me," Jouvenel has written,

> that in the end I came to picture the entire movement of society as an unceasing flow of authoritative initiatives; each of them comports a moral responsibility, whether consciously felt or not, and in them may be found more forms of authority at work than that represented by the public ordinances. This last is the highest in one sense but the lowest in another as being the most dependent on the force of intimidation.[41]

What for Jouvenel is the source of moral norms, of the justice that is to "permeate individual wills?" As we have indicated, he does not really answer this question. There is a touch of the skepticism of Oakeshott (or Montaigne?) in him that leads him to be reticent. What he does is to return again and again to indicate the decisive and central importance of this question for political theory today as in the past. This is no small service, nor is his reticence to be condemned. Out of the integrity, the openness, of thinkers like Oakeshott, Arendt, and Jouvenel can come the recovery of a comprehensive *epistēmē politikē* for our time, a recovery that will at once be a restoration and a new beginning.

Leo Strauss

One of the most influential figures in the contemporary resistance movement to positivist political and social science is Professor Leo Strauss of the University of Chicago. Strauss is best known for his works on major political philosophers, such as Machiavelli and Hobbes, and for his lectures on *Natural Right and History*. Equally important has been his role as a teacher. Strauss's impact on American philosophy and political science has been one of almost astonishing proportions. More than any of the other leading figures in the contemporary revival of political theory, it may be said that Strauss has disciples and a school. However, insofar as I can determine, the

[41] Jouvenel, *ibid.*, p. xiii.

"Straussians" do not share a definite body of doctrine. What seems to unite Strauss and those who have learned from him is a determination to take the teaching of major political theorists seriously and to attempt to understand that teaching on its own terms, as free as possible from ideological glosses and anachronistic interpretations. Strauss and his followers also share a strong interest in Greek political philosophy, especially that of Plato and Aristotle. They do not possess this interest out of mere antiquarianism, however. As Strauss himself has put it: "It is not self-forgetting and pain-loving antiquarianism nor self-forgetting and intoxicating romanticism which induces us to turn with passionate interest, with unqualified willingness to learn, toward the political thought of classical antiquity. We are impelled to do so by the crisis of our time, by the crisis of the West."[42]

The crisis of our time, Strauss maintains, has given us an unparalleled opportunity to arrive at a much fuller understanding of the political theory of the past, and especially classical political theory:

> It is then necessary to study the political philosophies as they were understood by their originators in contradistinction to the way in which they were understood by their adherents . . . but also by their adversaries and even by detached or indifferent bystanders or historians. For indifference does not offer a sufficient protection against the danger that one identifies the view of the originator with a compromise between the views of his adherents and those of his adversaries. The genuine understanding of the political philosophies which is . . . necessary, may be said to have been rendered possible by the shaking of all traditions; the crisis of our time may have the accidental advantage of enabling us to understand in an untraditional or fresh manner what was hitherto understood only in a traditional or derivative manner. This may apply especially to classical political philosophy which has been seen for a considerable time only through the lenses of modern political philosophy and its various successors.[43]

The determination to recapture, within the limits of human capabilities, the original intention and meaning of the great political writers of the past inevitably leads Strauss to question the predominant assumptions of positivist social science and especially the fact-value dichotomy. For the dichotomy itself was unknown to political

[42] Leo Strauss, *The City and Man* (Chicago, Rand McNally, 1964), p. 1.
[43] *Ibid.*, p. 9.

theory until recent times, and to look at the history of political theory through the lenses of the fact-value separation would mean fundamentally to distort our interpretation.

Strauss is also led to doubt the contention that all political theory is ideological in character, reflecting a given socioeconomic interest. He rather discovers that among political thinkers, some men are philosophers, and as such aim primarily at the truth rather than the usefulness or practical efficacy of their teachings: "A political thinker who is not a philosopher is primarily interested in, or attached to, a specific order or policy; the political philosopher is primarily interested in, or attached to, the truth."[44] What, at least since Karl Mannheim, has been referred to as the "sociology of knowledge" has in fact committed a grievous error: it has "failed to consider the possibility that all philosophers form a class by themselves, or that what unites all genuine philosophers is more important than what unites a given philosopher with a particular group of non-philosophers."[45] This mistake was made in the main because the proponents of the sociology of knowledge limited themselves to a study of nineteenth and twentieth-century political thought, which is to say the period when philosophy was at its nadir and ideology was in its ascendancy.

The thread which binds together all political philosophers is the reasoned conviction that there is a possibility of discovering the principles of right order in social existence. "The whole galaxy of political philosophers from Plato to Hegel . . . assumed that the fundamental political problem is susceptible of a final solution. This assumption ultimately rests on the . . . answer to the question of how man ought to live."[46]

The method which Strauss employs for the interpretation of the great political thinkers of the past is to begin by assuming a tight coherence and consistency to their work. This consistency is rarely if ever on the surface, but has to be extracted with diligence (and, it might be added, ingenuity) from between the lines. If a thinker of the first rank makes obvious and elementary mistakes in fact, or is

[44] Leo Strauss, *What is Political Philosophy?* (New York, Free Press, 1959), p. 12.

[45] Leo Strauss, *Persecution and the Art of Writing* (New York, Free Press, 1952), pp. 7-8.

[46] Leo Strauss, *Natural Right and History* (Chicago, University of Chicago Press, 1953), pp. 35-36.

caught in a blatant inconsistency, it should be taken for granted that this "error" was deliberate, part of a covert design which if discovered would yield to us the true, esoteric meaning of the work. As Strauss formulates this cardinal principle of interpretation in his *Thoughts on Machiavelli,* "it is safer to believe that he has given careful thought to every word he uses than to make allowance for human weakness."[47] The authors of the classics of political theory are held to be decisively superior to the ordinary mortals who interpret them, not only in their genius but in the extraordinary carefulness with which they wrote. Contemporary interpreters of these great thinkers, who have perhaps lost the art of writing and who in any case do not have to contend with the threat of persecution for heterodox opinions, find it difficult to understand precisely how they took pains to compose a work of art in which each sentence, indeed each word, had its place and role. Thus, for Strauss such matters as the numbering and location of chapters and the frequency of use of certain expressions assume a vital significance as clues for the understanding of the author's meaning.

Although Strauss's determination to understand the great minds of the past on their own terms is wholly admirable, and although his insistence on digging out of the major works the consistency at the root of apparent contradictions is a much-needed corrective to the widespread habit of lazily ascribing to the thinker under scrutiny an eclectic attitude which the interpreter himself might favor, nonetheless Strauss's method is subject to abuse. On occasion, as in the interpretation of Machiavelli as a "teacher of evil," he appears to have gone so far as to impose a straitjacket of consistency upon a man who surely saw his own inner tension too clearly to come up with a doctrine free of self-contradiction.[48] Another caveat which needs to be observed in reading Strauss has to do with his propensity to attribute a covert atheism to most of the major modern thinkers.

[47] Leo Strauss, *Thoughts on Machiavelli* (New York, Free Press, 1958), p. 47.

[48] Cf. my article "Second Thoughts on Leo Strauss's Machiavelli," in *The Journal of Politics,* XXVIII (November, 1966), 794-817, for elaboration of this point. I incline to agree with Felix Raab that Machiavelli "is a diffuse writer; inconsistent and often self-contradictory. There are many tensions in him, the strongest of which is that between the political technician and the passionate republican." *The English Face of Machiavelli* (London, 1964), p. 255.

It is arguable whether even Hobbes was an atheist; not until the nineteenth century does a radical and consistent atheism become the basis of a significant movement in the history of political thought.

Having noted these important reservations, it remains true that Strauss has left a brilliant legacy in his reinterpretations of the political teaching of Plato, Aristotle, Thucydides, Machiavelli, Hobbes, and Locke. Because he works independently, with the fewest possible intermediaries between himself and the text, and because he examines the text itself with unprecedented minuteness, he has given us many fresh insights into the great political writers. By reading Strauss, one always gains a new dimension of understanding with respect to the particular writer he has examined.

In various places in his works, Strauss modestly disclaims the title of political philosopher and claims to see himself as being principally an historian whose chief objective is to present the political thought of the past as its authors intended it to be understood.[49] Thereby he is furthering the cause of present-day political theory by giving it an accurate interpretation of previous political philosophy, but he is not actually constructing a philosophy himself. There is a sense in which this self-portrait is correct; possibly Strauss is of the opinion that the "decay of political philosophy into ideology"[50] has gone so far that extensive labors which are wholly preparatory in nature are necessary before the actual rebirth of political theory can take place.

However, anyone who has read through his historical works will recognize at once that in addition to an exposition of the thinker's meaning, they contain Strauss's own reflections on matters of basic importance to political theory. For Strauss not only expounds, he also evaluates. It is quite clear, for example, that he regards the "modern project" of the conquest of nature and the ultimate "manipulation of human nature" as perverse and misconceived, and he gives solidly reasoned explanations for this view.

At the least, it can be said that Strauss is opposed to an unthink-

---

[49] In this context, see, for example, Strauss's essay "The Literary Character of the *Guide for the Perplexed*," in Wittmayer Baron, ed., *Essays on Maimonides* (New York, Columbia University Press, 1941), pp. 37-92; and the introduction of *On Tyranny: An Interpretation of Xenophon's Hiero* (New York, Free Press, 1948).

[50] Strauss, *The City and Man, op. cit.*, p. 7.

ing rejection of classical or premodern political philosophy. He regards the all-too-prevalent attitude toward the classical writers as "out-dated" and hopelessly irrelevant to our contemporary situation as "a dogmatic assumption whose hidden basis is the belief in progress or in the rationality of the historical process."[51] It is quite clear that, in his sober and restrained way and not without reticence, Strauss comes down on the side of premodern political philosophy, and particularly that of Plato and Aristotle, as more likely to lead us to an understanding of political things than is the political theory of the modern period.

In his "Epilogue" to a volume devoted to an analysis of behavioralist political science written by four of his former students, Strauss examines the intentions, methods, and results of the "new" political science and concludes that it is woefully defective when measured against the classical *epistēmē politikē*.[52] After commencing with a brief account of the emergence of positivist political science in the twentieth century and a description of the present tripartite division within the discipline,[53] Strauss proceeds to contrast the new political science with the classical, or more specifically, Aristotelian, conception.

"For Aristotle, political science is identical with political philosophy because science is identical with philosophy."[54] Science (or

[51] *Ibid.*, p. 11.

[52] Herbert J. Storing, ed., *Essays on the Scientific Study of Politics* (New York, Holt, Rinehart and Winston, 1962). For Strauss's Epilogue see pp. 307-327. The other essays are by Storing (on Herbert Simon), Leo Weinstein (on Arthur Bentley), Robert Horwitz (on Harold Lasswell), and Walter Berns (on various recent contributions to voting studies).

[53] "If we look around us, we may observe that the political science profession contains a strong minority of the right, consisting of the strict adherents of the new political science or the 'behavioralists,' a small minority of the left, consisting of those who reject the new political science root and branch, and a center composed of old-fashioned political scientists, men who are concerned with understanding political things without being much concerned with 'methodological' questions but many of whom seem to have given custody of their 'methodological' conscience to the strict adherents of the new political science and thus continue their old-fashioned practice with a somewhat uneasy conscience." *Ibid.*, p. 308. Strauss explains that he puts the behavioralists on the right because they are the new orthodoxy, and "the natural place of an orthodoxy is on the right." *Ibid.*

[54] *Ibid.*, pp. 307-308.

philosophy) is of two kinds: theoretical and "practical or political." The theoretical sciences are mathematics, physics, and metaphysics; the practical sciences are ethics, economics (household management), and politics. Political science, as the master science, includes all of these. Practical, or political, science is based on the awareness of the principles of action which are the "natural ends of man." "Practical science, in contradistinction to practical wisdom itself, sets forth coherently the principles of action and the general rules of prudence. . . ."[55]

In the Aristotelian scheme the political scientist or political philosopher strives to attain an impartial perspective among the various contending political forces in the marketplace: he seeks to "become the umpire, the impartial judge; his perspective encompasses the partisan perspectives because he possesses a more comprehensive and clearer grasp of man's natural ends and their natural order than do the partisans."[56] Other characteristics of Aristotelian political science are that it "necessarily evaluates political things," that it defends the autonomy of prudence in practical matters, and that it views man, "the beast with red cheeks," as qualitatively superior to other living beings in that he possesses reason, language, and the sense of shame. This means that political action is ethical action, and that the sphere of the political reflects the highest that is within man.

Behavioralist political science denies all these premises of the "old" political science. It separates political philosophy from political science, which itself loses the status of a master science, being essentially on a parity with the newly independent social sciences, especially economics and sociology. It replaces the distinction between the theoretical and practical sciences with that between the theoretical and applied sciences, the applied sciences being directly derivative from the theoretical sciences in a way not contemplated under the old dispensation.

The new political science "views human beings as an engineer would view material for building bridges"; it tends to be a productive science which imputes purpose to the human raw material rather than a practical science which takes the ends as given in human nature itself. It "conceives of the principles of action as 'values'

55 *Ibid.*, p. 319.
56 *Ibid.*, p. 310.

which are merely 'subjective'; the knowledge it conveys has the character of prediction and only secondarily that of hypothetical advice."[57] Instead of understanding other human activities in terms of political activity, which is the highest, most distinctively human, type of practical activity, the new political science deals with the political as a function of the subpolitical. It denies any qualitative distinction between man and beasts, and seeks the understanding of what is complex in human activity by comparison to that which is simplest and most animal-like.

The emergence of behavioral political science may be explained in part as a reaction against the excessive formalism and legalism of a good part of American political science in an earlier period. Although this legalism—"which, for example, took the written constitution of the USSR very seriously"—was very much in need of correction, it should be added "immediately that the error had been corrected, as it were in advance, by an older political science," that of "Montesquieu, of Machiavelli or of Aristotle himself."[58] As for behavioral political science itself, one may wonder whether it has "brought to light anything of political importance which intelligent political practitioners with a deep knowledge of history, nay, intelligent and educated journalists, to say nothing of the old political science at its best, did not know at least as well beforehand."[59]

Although it is true with the development of nuclear weapons, we live in an unprecedented situation, it remains a "political situation," and therefore it may be doubted that the old political science is entirely outmoded. It may further be doubted that what is required for the unprecedented situation is an "unprecedented political science" grounded on "a judicious mating of dialectical materialism and psychoanalysis to be consummated on a bed supplied by logical positivism."[60] The new political science is founded at least in part on the hope that it will be able to predict political behavior more accurately than has been done in the past; yet in the decisive respect of the so-called unprecedented situation for which it was formed, it must admit that it is "as unable to predict the outcome of the

[57] *Ibid.*

[58] *Ibid.*, p. 311.

[59] *Ibid.*, p. 312.

[60] *Ibid.*

unprecedented conflict peculiar to our age" as were "the crudest soothsayers of the most benighted tribe."[61]

Strauss is convinced that the positivist separation of fact and value and the taboo on including values in the realm of science is at once based on a philosophical position that cannot be sustained and that has had a disastrous effect on contemporary political and social science. "According to our social science," he has written elsewhere,

> we can be or become wise in all matters of secondary importance, but we have to be resigned to utter ignorance in the most important respect: we cannot have any knowledge regarding the ultimate principles of our choices, i.e., regarding their soundness or unsoundness; our ultimate principles have no other support than our arbitrary and hence blind prejudices.[62]

Along with other political scientists in the resistance movement to the positivist predominance in the profession, Strauss regards the rise of totalitarianism as the key event which revealed the bankruptcy of the positivist teaching, demonstrating that, for all its accumulation of certain kinds of factual information, positivist political science was helpless when it came to the crucial matter of providing standards for distinguishing between just and tyrannical regimes.

Toward the end of his "Epilogue" to the volume on the scientific study of politics, Strauss confronts the question of "whether the distinction between facts and values, or the assertion that no Ought can be derived from an Is, is well founded."[63] His conclusion is, contrary to the protestations of the positivists, that, far from being illegitimate, it is not possible to do anything but derive an Ought from an Is. When we look at man "empirically," we see a being who has a latitude of positing and choosing between various values, and, furthermore, "this latitude, this possibility, has the character of the fact." However, one must distinguish, again on sheer empirical grounds, between a desire and a value. "The fact that someone desires something does not yet make that something his value; he may successfully fight his desire or if his desire overpowers him he may blame himself for this as a failure on his part; only choice, in contradistinction to mere desire, makes something a man's value."

[61] *Ibid.*, p. 313.

[62] Strauss, *What Is Political Philosophy?, op. cit.*, p. 4.

[63] Storing, *op. cit.*, p. 325.

The distinctive characteristic of man is that he posits ends, or if you like, "values," and "this positing—is . . . a fact." The new political science may, without contradicting itself, deny that there are natural ends, objectively given, for our choice but it cannot deny that "the choice of ends, the positing of ends, or rather of values," is itself a fact, an Is, even the most "pertinent Is."

> The view that the pertinent Is is our positing of values, in contradistinction to the yielding to mere desires, necessarily leads to Oughts of a radically different character from the so-called Oughts corresponding to mere desires. We conclude that the "relativism" accepted by the new political science according to which values are nothing but objects of desire is based on an insufficient analysis of the Is, that is, of the pertinent Is; and, furthermore, that one's opinion regarding the character of the Is settles one's opinion regarding the character of the Ought. We must leave it open here whether a more adequate analysis of the pertinent Is, that is, of the nature of man, does not lead to a more adequate determination of the Ought. . . .[64]

Behavioralist political science, Strauss concludes, while proclaiming itself as value-neutral, is actually committed, when consistent with its basic premises, to "dogmatic atheism" and "permissive egalitarianism." "The new science uses sociological or psychological theories regarding religion which exclude, without considering, the possibility that religion rests ultimately on God's revealing Himself to man. . . . The new science rests on a dogmatic atheism," which, although presenting itself as merely "methodological or hypothetical" is actually an attitude of "unreasoned unbelief." Just as "our opponents refuse to accept unreasoned belief, we on our part, with at least equal right, must refuse respect to unreasoned unbelief; honesty with oneself regarding one's unbelief is in itself not more than unreasoned unbelief probably accompanied by a vague confidence that the issue of unbelief versus belief has long since been settled once and for all."[65] A corollary of the new science's "dogmatic exclusion of religious awareness proper" is that this exclusion "renders questionable all long-range predictions concerning the future of societies."

The new science, Strauss insists, is congenitally unable to understand on its own terms thought which took place before the revelation of the fact-value dichotomy. "The traditional value systems antedate

[64] *Ibid.*

[65] *Ibid.*, p. 322.

the awareness of the difference between facts and values"; indeed, "they claimed to be derived from facts—from Divine Revelation or from similar sources, in general from superior or perfect beings which as such unite in themselves fact and value." The claim to have separated fact and value is in truth the claim to have destroyed these traditional value systems, for they cannot "be divorced from what present themselves as their factual bases."[66]

Behavioralist political science is committed to an implicit value-judgment in favor of a society grounded on "permissive egalitarianism." The "difference between facts and values" means to its proponents that

> men can live without ideology: they can adopt, posit, or proclaim values without making the illegitimate attempt to derive their values from facts or without relying on false or at least inevident assertions regarding what is. One thus arrives at the notion of the rational society or of the non-ideological regime: a society that is based on the understanding of the character of values. Since this understanding implies that before the tribunal of reason all values are equal, the rational society will be egalitarian or democratic and permissive and liberal: the rational doctrine regarding the difference between facts and values rationally justifies the preference for liberal democracy—contrary to what is intended by that distinction itself.[67]

Behavioralist social science, while claiming to be value-neutral and objective, is actually the promoter of a creed which can be called "democratism." This more or less hidden preference for democracy in the Benthamite sense is uncritically accepted. Man, as such, is "tacitly identified with democratic man." The new political science "puts a premium on observations which can be made with the utmost frequency, and therefore by people of the meanest capacities. Thus it frequently culminates in observations made by people who are not intelligent about people who are not intelligent." While the new political science cannot view democracy in critical perspective or "hold a mirror to democracy," it "ever more reflects the most dangerous proclivities of democracy. It even strengthens those proclivities."[68] By teaching the equality of all desires, it destroys man's possibility for both self-contempt and self-respect. By denying that there is "an

[66] *Ibid.*, p. 324.

[67] *Ibid.*

[68] *Ibid.*, p. 326.

essential difference between men and brutes," it "contributes to the victory of the gutter."

Yet it would be false, Professor Strauss notes in concluding his indictment, to "call the new political science diabolic: it has no attributes peculiar to fallen angels. . . . Nor is it Neronian. Nevertheless one may say of it that it fiddles while Rome burns. It is excused by two facts: it does not know that it fiddles and it does not know that Rome burns."[69]

In this essay Strauss pinpoints the crucial fact that, in the name of methodology, positivist social science smuggles in a whole counter-theology to that presupposed by the classical, Jewish, and Christian writers of the Great Tradition of Western political thought. He thereby raises the entire question of the relationship of theology to a new political science that would be based on a recovery of this tradition. But although he raises the question, and although his writings attest profoundly to an openness on his part to religious awareness, he nowhere shows how theology and political philosophy can be related in a new political science properly understood. Indeed, in his essay "What is Political Philosophy," he explicitly distinguishes between political philosophy, which is based on reason, and political theology, which is based on revelation. Insofar as it is possible to ascertain from his writings, Strauss adheres to a form of Latin Averroism that presupposes the radical separation, not of fact and value, but of reason and faith. This "separationist" approach even mars his interpretations of Plato and Aristotle, for he nowhere makes clear the dependence of their political theories on their experience of transcendence or their religious awareness.

Implicit in Strauss's teaching is the recovery of the authority of the theorist as *spoudaios* to measure the relative validity of conflicting conceptions of the nature of the *summum bonum* for man. He and not the mass man is the "measure of everything." But Strauss nowhere makes explicit the Platonic-Aristotelian corollary to this teaching: the *spoudaios-philosophos* is the measure precisely because he measures himself by divine Being. This is the ground of his claim to speak with authority.

Despite the limitations and deficiencies of his position, Strauss must be judged a most significant contributor to the recovery of political theory in our time. He combines intransigence in the service

---

[69] *Ibid.*, p. 327 end.

of truth with a philosophic openness that is incompatible with dogmatism. He calls a spade a spade in the dispute with positivism, but he never loses his temper or indulges in bombast or petty polemics. His great virtue is that he will never permit a mushy desire for accommodation to blunt his recognition of real and basic disagreements. And he recognizes that we have come to the point where, to go forward, we need initially to go back. For the elaboration of a new science of politics in the true sense can come only as a result of building on the old science of politics at its best. As he has summarized the issue with characteristic acuteness of vision and economy of style:

> The return to classical political philosophy is both necessary and tentative or experimental. . . . We cannot reasonably expect that a fresh understanding of classical political philosophy will supply us with recipes for today's use. For the relative success of modern political philosophy has brought into being a kind of society to which the classical principles as stated and elaborated by the classics are not immediately applicable. Only we living today can possibly find a solution to the problems of today. But an adequate understanding of the principles as elaborated by the classics may be the indispensable starting point for an adequate analysis, to be achieved by us, of present-day society in its peculiar character, and for the wise application, to be achieved by us, of these principles to our tasks.[70]

EIGHT: ERIC VOEGELIN'S CONTRIBUTION TO CONTEMPORARY POLITICAL THEORY

Some fifty years ago, Douglas Ainslie wrote of Benedetto Croce: "I can lay no claim to having discovered an America, but I do claim to have discovered a Columbus."[1] Eric Voegelin, today at the height

[70] Strauss, *The City and Man, op. cit.*, p. 11.

[1] Introduction to Croce's *Aesthetics* (London, 1909), p. xv.

of his career as a political philosopher, scarcely needs to be discovered; he is regarded as a Columbus in the realm of the spirit by many concerned with the theoretical analysis of politics.[2] But in the political science profession he has been more often ignored or systematically misunderstood than read for what he has to teach. Among those according an indifferent or hostile reception to Voegelin are many who, bewailing the recent "decline" of political theory, might have been expected to welcome the appearance of a thinker meticulously pointing the way to the recovery of political theory as a tradition of inquiry. The basic reasons for this curious reception will be referred to in the course of this chapter. The major objective, however, is to isolate the key elements in Voegelin's political theory and to give some indication of his general position in contemporary political science. Hopefully, the result will be to further the understanding of his work and the appreciation of his achievement.[3]

Voegelin's erudition is so vast and his impatience with explaining and elaborating certain points which he believes should be clear to

[2] Indeed, at the 1960 convention of the American Political Science Association, a panel was set aside for the discussion of his magnum opus, *Order and History*. This is a rare distinction for a living political philosopher.

[3] The present time is a propitious one to evaluate Voegelin's contribution to contemporary political theory because, although the fourth and final volume of *Order and History* is as yet unpublished, the main themes of his analysis have been expounded and the Voegelin corpus has now attained considerable proportions. His published writings include eleven books and at least fifty-five articles and essays. A bibliography of his works published through 1961 is in H. Arendt and Alois Dempf, *Politische Ordnung and Menschliche Existenz: Festgabe fuer Eric Voegelin* (Munich, 1962).

Voegelin's principal recent writings in German, together with some previously unpublished material from an earlier period, are collected in his *Anamnesis: Zur Theorie der Geschichte und Politik* (Munich, 1966). For a discussion of this volume's contents, see the Bibliographical Notes at the end of this book.

The writer has also been able to consult two hitherto unpublished writings of Professor Voegelin, available at the *Institut fuer Politische Wissenschaft* at the University of Munich. One is a mimeographed copy of a lecture which he delivered at Munich and Notre Dame in 1961 entitled "Debate and Existence." The other is the typescript of a small treatise entitled *The Nature of Law*. In addition, during the 1961 summer term at Munich, I had the opportunity to hold a number of valuable conversations with Professor Voegelin and to hear his lectures and seminar presentations. I am most indebted to him for these courtesies.

all students of political thought so marked that reading him is quite difficult. But so it is with many philosophers. Once the necessary effort has been made to learn his terminology and to read some of the literature cited in his footnotes as essential background material, his teaching becomes readily comprehensible. He is well worth the effort required.

To Voegelin, political science and political theory are inseparably bound together. The object of the critical reflection induced by the activity of *theōria* is *epistēmē politikē*, or political science. Without an ontologically grounded theory of politics, a fully developed political science is impossible. When political science is fully developed, it will contain a comprehensive inventory of all the relevant problems. Such an inventory can be organized under three headings: ethics, politics proper, and history. Today, for the first time in centuries, the materials are available and the intellectual climate is suitable for great advances in the theoretical analysis of politics. These advances presuppose a recovery of the achievements of the Platonic-Aristotelian *epistēmē*, nearly lost during the period since 1500, a period which has witnessed the triumph of fallacious gnostic symbolizations.

It is essential to recognize that Voegelin conceives of political theory not as an ideology, utopia, or scientific methodology, but as an experiential science of right order in the soul and in society. Since human experience is the control for the propositions elucidated in the course of his theoretical analyses, it would be well to preface an exposition of those propositions with a discussion of Voegelin's highly creative analysis of the structure of experience itself. This "experience" is multidimensional in nature and incapable of being contracted, in the Comtean or logical positivist fashion, to the single plane of physical sensation.

The "Experience of Existence"

The starting point of Voegelin's explorations is the empirical fact of the human person in his awareness of the finiteness of his existence. Man

> discovers his existence as illuminated from within by Intellect or Nous. Intellect is the instrument of self-interpretation as much as it is a part of the structure interpreted. . . . By virtue of the

noetic structure of his existence . . . man discovers himself as being not a world unto himself, but an existent among others; he experiences a world of existents of which he is a part. Moreover, in discovering himself in his limitation as part in a field of existents, he discovers himself as not being the maker of this field of existents or of any part of it. Existence acquires its poignant meaning through the experience of not being self-generated but having its origin outside itself.[4]

In discoursing upon the structure of existence, Voegelin distinguishes between four functions of the *nous*: (1) the "illumination" of the transitory nature of human existence; (2) the apprehension of "transcendence"—of an ultimate ground of all existing things; (3) the formation of an "idea" of the structure of existence ("ideation"); and (4) the rational elaboration of the experience and its components.[5]

It is of particular importance that Voegelin's description of the second phase of the cognitive activity of the *nous* be properly understood. In reflecting upon his finiteness and mortality, man is led to an awareness of the transcendental ground of all existing things, including himself. The cognitive illumination of the structure of existence makes it transparent to him that existing things could not be the origin and end of themselves. That origin and end will not be found by ranging over the field of existing things but must be traced to a something beyond that field.

Voegelin has gone to considerable lengths to emphasize that valid philosophizing about politics must rest upon an adequate symbolization respecting the something that constitutes the ground of being. Above all, to discourse upon the transcendental ground as if it were an object located in the stream of immanent experience must be recognized as a fundamental impropriety. All knowledge of the ground of being is analogical in character, for man in the limitations of his existential situation can only reason from that which is known by immediate experience to that which lies beyond, but is the necessary presupposition of, such experience and is in its essence unknowable. Such knowledge is inevitably fragmentary, uncertain, and intangible, for at the center of his existence man is a mystery to himself.

The knowledge of transcendence is, in Augustinian terms, a

[4] Voegelin, unpublished lecture, "Debate and Existence," p. 13.

[5] *Ibid.*, p. 17.

cognitio fidei, a knowledge of faith. Voegelin employs the term "faith" precisely in the New Testament sense as expounded in Hebrews 11. Faith is the "substance of things hoped for, the evidence of things not seen. . . . By faith we perceive that the universe was fashioned by the word of God, so that the visible came forth from the invisible."[6] Let it be remembered at once that for Voegelin faith is a property of the *nous,* or intellect, and that faith and reason, far from being antithetical, are the necessary complements of each other.[7] It is by the "tenuous bond of faith" that we apprehend the "world-transcendent God" that is the origin and end of all existing things.[8] To experience through faith the transcendental ground is the *conditio sine qua non* for the valid operation of human reason in its articulation of the structure of existence. Experience of the ground of being through faith is what Voegelin calls the *première Erfahrung*: it is the experience which must precede all theorizing about the human condition. Reason must build on faith if its symbolic constructions are to represent adequately the real structure of existence. Without the prior experience of faith, the vital component of transcendence will be left out of the calculations of reason in its attempt to illuminate the structure of existence to the fullest extent possible within the limited capabilities of the *nous.* This will result in a falsification of the symbolic picture—the theory—which reason produces.

As Voegelin has expressed the matter in his important paper "Debate and Existence": "The logical operations of Intellect qua Reason will arrive at widely different results if Reason has cut loose from the *condicio humana.*" Faith is the fragile bond which keeps reason tied to this condition, which is to say, to reality. The rejection

[6] *Hebrews* 11:1-3. I have combined the translations of the King James and New English bibles.

[7] In a profound sense, Voegelin transcends both the "fideist" and "rationalist" positions in contemporary Protestant and Catholic political thought. Cf. my article, "Two Types of Recent Christian Political Thought," *Journal of Politics,* XXI (August, 1959), for a discussion of the two approaches. In no sense can Voegelin properly be termed a "Barthian fideist"; the experience of faith is to prepare the way for the work of reason, and faith that does not issue in rational knowledge (that is, in philosophy) is inadequate. In this connection, the assertion of Jean Meynaud that Voegelin writes from a "purely doctrinal" and "confessional" viewpoint is an absurdity. *Introduction à la science politique* (Paris, 1959), p. 11.

[8] Eric Voegelin, *The New Science of Politics* (Chicago, University of Chicago Press, 1952), p. 122.

of the fragile bond and the pursuit of massively possessive knowledge based on an illusory simplification of human existence through the incorporation of the transcendental ground within the stream of immanent existence have produced the imaginative, gnostic ideological speculations of the modern era.

These speculations, although sometimes possessing an internal, rational coherence, are actually the repudiation of a rational science of politics because they are grounded on an imagined "second reality." They proclaim an illusory self-salvation and self-perfection for man within history. The thinkers of the second reality reject the

> experience of finiteness and creatureliness in our existence, of being creatures of a day as the poets call man, of being born and bound to die, of dissatisfaction with the state experienced as imperfect, of apprehension of a perfection that is not of this world but is a privilege of the gods, of possible fulfillment in a state beyond this world.[9]

They renounce existence in uncertain truth for existence in certain untruth. With such men it is impossible to have rational philosophic communication, for "edifices of reason enacted on the experiential basis of existence in truth" are "useless in a meeting with edifices of reason erected on a different experiential basis."

In metaphysics, Voegelin is to be counted among that group of contemporary philosophers (including thinkers like Alois Dempf and Hans Urs von Balthasar) who seek to expose the defects of system-building in modern philosophy. The term system is often used today to refer to any orderly body of philosophical speculation, and one hears of Thomistic and Aristotelian "systems." Actually, writes Voegelin, systems "are a modern invention, and I doubt that one can properly speak of a 'system' before Descartes." Whereas a work like the Thomistic *Summa Theologica* employs analogical reasoning in discoursing upon the transcendental ground and remains open and necessarily incomplete, moving in the "tension between reason and faith," a systematic construction of a Spinoza or a Hegel derives its propositions from axioms.[10] In its enclosed conversation with itself,

---

[9] Voegelin, "Debate and Existence," *op. cit.*, p. 7.

[10] Voegelin's attack on systems and system-building in philosophy runs through all his writings, but note especially the interesting articles "Philosophie der Politik in Oxford," *Philosophische Rundschau*, I (1953/54), 23 ff., and "Religionsersatz," *Wort and Wahrheit*, XV (1960), 55 ff.

it becomes further and further removed from the reality which it is supposed to be explicating. The system is founded on the illusion that all realms of being are susceptible to being compressed to the point where they can be fully grasped and conceptualized by the finite human mind. System-constructors are ignorant, or pretend to be ignorant, of the basic experience of existence which teaches that there are ultimate realms of being which escape our systems altogether and that at the center of being the source of all that is remains unknowable in its essence.

One of the few modern thinkers to whom Voegelin always refers with admiration is Bergson, and it may be said that the Munich philosopher has sought to follow Bergson in fashioning a metaphysics which passes "from reality to concepts and no longer from concepts to reality."[11] Voegelin is a philosophical realist rather than a nominalist, idealist, or conceptualist in that he holds that reality possesses a structure, or constitution, independent of human thinking and willing. The philosopher must aspire to attune his thinking to that reality (or, more precisely, to recognize his thought as participating in the noetic structure of existence) rather than attempt to force reality to conform to his concepts or ideas. In this sense, Voegelin is the supreme empiricist, although it is the entirety of human experience and not some arbitrarily abstracted segments of it that he takes for his field of observation.

Epistēmē Politikē

Given Voegelin's emphasis upon the inevitable limitations of human knowledge, his scorn for system-building, and his Xenophanesian concern about the impropriety of unseemly symbolization in the realms of metaphysics, one might be led to think that he would attempt no scientific political theory at all, but content himself with admonitions to opinionated ideologists and Wittgenstein-like intimations of inexpressible mysteries. He could possibly have retreated into Pyrrhonist (and Oakeshottian) skepticism. Another measure of Voegelin's achievement is that he has pushed far beyond this tenable but ultimately inadequate position and has driven himself to explicate the vital distinction between illegitimate (because illusory) *gnosis* and valid *epistēmē* regarding the *conditio humana*.

[11] Henri Bergson, *Introduction to Metaphysics* (New York, 1912), p. 40.

For there can be no doubt that to Voegelin an *epistēmē politikē* is possible, and that its objective is to articulate propositions that tell us as much as can be known about the right order of the psyche and of society. Part of that knowledge, indeed the most significant part, will be a knowledge of the limits of knowledge or, better, a knowledge of the distinction between the knowable and the unknowable. Included in this category is the understanding—invaluable for a science of right order in political society—of the phantasy permeating all speculations on politics which assume that existence is something other than it is and that a realm of perfect equality, freedom, and human fulfillment is obtainable within time by virtue of the proper manipulation of the institutional environment.

The constructive aspect of Voegelin's work consists in an attempt to elaborate, after the manner of the classical political theorists, the principles of order in human social existence. What follows will be only an inadequate summary of his positive political theory. As with all thinkers of the first rank, there is no substitute for reading him *in extenso*.

PHILOSOPHICAL ANTHROPOLOGY. As was previously stated, Voegelin's political theory may be most suitably discussed under three headings: ethics, politics, and history, which constitute the *topoi* of the Platonic-Aristotelian *epistēmē politikē*. We begin with ethics, because any genuinely theoretical analysis of politics must rest upon a carefully enunciated doctrine of human nature. Voegelin calls this teaching about human nature "philosophical anthropology."

Much of Voegelin's work in the area of philosophical anthropology has been devoted to the recovery of the classical theorizing with respect to the interpenetration of society and psyche. In his unrivalled critical exegesis of Plato in the third volume of *Order and History*, Voegelin gives an account of Plato's discovery (intimated but not fully articulated in Heraclitus) of the "macro-anthropological principle." In contrast to the "micro-cosmological principle" enunciated in the Egyptian and Babylonian symbolizations, which held society to be a miniature analogue of cosmic rhythms, the macro-anthropological principle describes society as the reflection of the order of the psyche in the ruling character type. Knowledge respecting the different types of societies and their relative worth can be attained only through a knowledge of the different human types and their ranking on a scale of excellence.

A sound philosophical anthropology will teach us that (1) the character of a given society is the reflection of the psyches of its ruling elite; (2) the best society (*aristē politeia*) will reflect in its institutional order the pattern of order in the psyche of the best man; (3) the best man (the *spoudaios*) is the man who measures himself by the highest that is within him; and (4) only because he measures himself by the measure of all being does the best man have authority to claim himself as the measure of the best society.

Voegelin's philosophical anthropology, derived from the Platonic-Aristotelian teaching, is an expression of what, following Maritain, we have termed "theocentric humanism," as opposed to anthropocentric humanism. The Protagorean maxim that "man is the measure of all things" is subjected to the crucial qualification "provided that he takes God, or the ground of being, as his measure." Man is seen to be essentially a "theomorph" (to employ a term also used by Alois Dempf and Romano Guardini, two contemporary colaborers with Voegelin in the vineyards of philosophical anthropology); if he achieves his maximal development as a human being, he will live the life of reason in attunement with the divine measure.

Philosophical anthropology enables us to arrive at a scale of character, beginning with the "representative exemplar" of the human species—the type of man who has come closest to actualizing his distinctively human potentialities—and proceeding downward to the most degenerate and antihuman types, such as the gangsters who made up the ruling elite of the Nazi regime. The representative exemplar is given the name "philosopher" by Plato; Aristotle calls him the *spoudaios*, which can be most accurately translated as the "ripe" or "mature" (that is, most fully developed) man.[12]

---

[12] The term "philosopher" has been and continues to be so ridiculously misused that the Aristotelian word may be preferable. As Voegelin points out, Plato formulated the symbol "philosopher" (or lover of wisdom) in contradistinction to "philodoxer" (or lover of opinion): "We have philosophers in English but no philodoxers. The loss is . . . embarrassing, because we have an abundance of philodoxers in reality, but all of them are referred to as philosophers. . . . [Thus] we call philosophers precisely those persons to whom Plato as a philosopher was in opposition." *Order and History* (Baton Rouge, Louisiana State University Press, 1957), vol. III, p. 65.

Voegelin accepts, in its essentials, the portrait of the *spoudaios* sketched by Aristotle (principally in Books I, IV, and X of the *Nichomachean Ethics*). The *spoudaios* is the man who has his priorities in the proper order, who pursues as the highest good that which is really the highest good and not a good which is only instrumental for the attainment of some further good (and is therefore inherently insufficient). True *eudaimonia* can come only from the *bios theōretikos*, the life of reason devoted to the contemplation of the order of being. Not the life spent in the pursuit of wealth, or power, or honor, but the life of reason is the highest life for man. The *bios theōretikos* is the highest life for man because it is the most self-sufficient and god-like activity for human beings to pursue. Such a life is the fulfillment of the capacities and powers which are most distinctively human and which mark man off from the rest of creation. Such a life is oriented towards following "the highest thing within us"; in leading the life of reason, man discovers the theomorphic element in his constitution, for the *bios theōretikos* "will not be lived in our merely human capacity but in virtue of something divine within us, and so far as this divine particle is superior to man's composite nature, to that extent will its activity be superior to that of the other forms of excellence. . . ."[13]

The theocentric humanism of both Plato and Aristotle, which can be summarized in Plato's dictum in the *Laws*, "God is the measure of all things," has been rediscovered by Voegelin in resistance to basic misinterpretations by certain classical scholars. In particular, the theocentric element in the Aristotelian anthropology has been ignored by certain writers, as if it were possible to turn Aristotle into some kind of contemporary secular intellectual who separates reason from the experience of transcendence. The significance of such misinterpretations for present-day political theory can be grasped when one examines Leo Strauss's writings. As was indicated in the previous chapter, Strauss has made a brilliant and effective contribution to the recovery of the insights of the Platonic-Aristotelian philosophical anthropology in our time. And yet, as another political scientist has appropriately pointed out, Strauss's interpretation is deficient to the extent that he ignores the Platonic qualification to the teaching that man is the measure, thereby skirting "dangerously close to a moralism

---

[13] *Ethics* (J. A. K. Thompson trans.), Book X, p. 7.

which depends simply on approval or disapproval, with authoritative approval resting with the men whose character has been formed by a classical education."[14] Strauss does not adequately explain the basis of the claim by the *spoudaios* to be the measure of everything.

Voegelin's philosophical anthropology has been attacked on the grounds of its supposedly antidemocratic and elitist nature, and we may expect the attacks from certain quarters to continue, even to the point of labelling him as a type of "Fascist idéologue."[15] But such criticisms totally miss the point of both the Voegelinian and the Platonic-Aristotelian teaching. In the first place, the claim to authority by the *philosophos-spoudaios* is a spiritual claim and has nothing to do with the direction of a mass movement for the forcible seizure of power in society. The philosopher performs the function of representing the transcendent truth to society; to the degree that the existential power representatives heed him, then to that degree will his teaching have a pragmatic effect on the operation of the society's public institutions. They are perfectly free not to heed him, in which event he will continue his work of critically elaborating the truth about the right order in society until or unless forced to cease doing so.

The philosopher is no *dux* arousing the forces of civilizational pride for an immanent perfection of society. His task is not to take existential power in society but to labor for the "spiritual ordering

[14] William C. Harvard, "The Method and Results of Political Anthropology in America," *Archiv fuer Rechts-und Sozialphilosophie*, XLVII (1961), 395-415 at 413. Some of Strauss's followers continue to make the same error. Cf. especially Walter Berns, *Freedom, Justice, and the First Amendment* (Baton Rouge, Louisiana State University Press, 1958).

[15] Note the review of *Order and History* by the late Moses Hadas in the *Journal of the History of Ideas*, XIX (1958), 444. The review contains the following sentence: "One wonders whether the 'institution that wishes to remain unnamed' which Professor Voegelin thanks for material aid in each of his Prefaces was aware of the nature of his work, and one remembers a remark attributed to a notable patron of the institution which Professor Voegelin serves [at the time, he was on the faculty of Louisiana State University]: 'Sure, we'll have fascism in this country, but of course we'll call it something else.' Leap in being?" Karl Jaspers also turns into a fascist in the course of the Hadas review. Voegelin is in actuality one of the archresisters to that form of political messianism which is at the root of Fascist ideology. Cf. my article "Italian Fascism in the History of Political Thought," *Midwest Journal of Political Science* (May, 1964), 109-126.

of a disordered world." Philosophy, in its discovery of participation in the *nous* as the criterion of man's essential humanity, can do nothing directly to change society to conform to the new truth. But, indirectly, "the differentiation of the life of the soul in a great number of men in a community may have the effect of changing the mores, and ultimately the institutions of a society, because the hierarchy of purposes for individual action has changed."[16]

Another point which needs to be made against those who cry "elitism"[17] is that for Voegelin the ranks of the *spoudaioi* are open to any man who will form his life in accordance with reason, who will open his soul towards the transcendental ground. No man is excluded on the basis of physical characteristics, wealth, social status, and the like. No man is excluded, but any man may exclude himself from the character elite.

As with Plato, Voegelin recognizes the existence of a wide second stratum in the character elite composed of men who, while they do not consciously and primarily pursue the life of reason, nonetheless possess *orthē doxa*, or true opinion, and sound common sense. These individuals, of sound habits and a practical turn of mind, who know the good, but imperfectly, and who could not give an adequate rational defense of it if pressed to do so by intellectual adversaries (these men are customarily philosophically inarticulate) make up the predominant part of the governing class of any well-ordered society. They are aware of the limitations of political action and act in their decisions on the basis of what Weber called the "ethics of responsibility" (*Verantwortungsethik*). They have absorbed the Machiavellian wisdom that it is the highest irrationality in politics to act out of the supposedly pure motives of conscience without giving proper regard to the foreseeable pragmatic consequences of one's actions.[18] The psyches of these men are capable of being intimately

---

[16] Voegelin, *Order and History, op. cit.*, vol. II, p. 283.

[17] As if there can be any science of politics without a theory of elites! It is not that we shall have either an elite theory or no elite theory; the question is whether we shall have a philosophically sound or an ideologically debased elite theory. Cf. the discussion in Chapter 6.

[18] Cf. Voegelin's article "Machiavelli's Prince: Background and Formation," in the *Review of Politics*, XIII (May, 1951), for some keen insights into the thought of the much-maligned Florentine. In his unpublished treatise on *The Nature of Law*, Voegelin has written of conscience: "Conscience . . .

touched by the philosopher's teaching, and, insofar as he devotes himself to political education, the philosopher labors to reach these men and hopes for the increase of their numbers and influence in society.[19]

As one moves down the character scale, one moves away from the freely formed psyche open to communion with the transcendental ground, to the psyche which relies predominantly on habitual obedience and external formulae. Here we encounter the rank and file in a society who lack leadership qualities themselves but whose instinct for order leads them to reject demagogic appeals by counterelites bent upon wreaking disorder in the society. The "ordering spirit" must work through a "variety of character types," and only exceptional persons can "translate the order of the spirit into the practice of conduct without institutional support and pressure."[20] This means that, for survival in the world, "the order of the spirit has to rely on a blind belief in the symbols of a creed more often than on the *fides caritate formata* [faith formed by love]—though such reliance, if it becomes socially predominant, is apt to kill the order it is supposed to preserve."[21]

Finally, Voegelin's typology of the representative exemplar of the human species provides him with standards for the measurement of the existences of those masses of men in contemporary society who, being without any firm hierarchy of purposes, flit aimlessly from one object of trivial satisfaction to another in search of the Bentham-

---

can be defined as the act, or acts, by which we judge, approvingly or disapprovingly, our conduct in the light of our rational moral knowledge. Conscience in this sense is not infallible." It can err either because the facts of the matter requiring our action are not sufficiently known, or because conflict of obligations is difficult to resolve, or because "moral obtuseness and spiritual perversion" will produce false judgments.

[19] The philosopher also labors to increase the ranks of those who devote themselves fully to the life of noetic reason—of those who will become philosophers. However, he recognizes the unlikelihood that the *bios theōretikos* will be followed by more than a small minority particularly in a technologically oriented civilization. Hopefully, their impact as members of the cultural elite who contribute to the intellectual formation of those who hold the reins of existential power will be greater than their numbers.

[20] Voegelin, *Order and History, op. cit.,* vol. I, p. 440.

[21] *Ibid.,* p. 337.

ite god, pleasure.[22] These people, together with the sophists, opinionated ideologists, and unprincipled power-seekers who pander to their impulses, deserve to be described as "nihilists," because they demonstrate in their lives the absence of any internalized hierarchy of ends. They constitute the stratum from which have issued the enormous, unparalleled disorders and world crises of the twentieth century. Above all, political theory, by virtue of a sound philosophical anthropology, must resist the ideological pressure that, in the name of democracy, seeks to replace the *spoudaios* with the nihilistic mass man as measure.

THE GOOD SOCIETY. The second key element in Voegelin's political theory is the conceptual representation of the paradigmatic society. Under the terms of the macroanthropological principle enunciated by Plato in the *Republic*, society is the "soul writ large"; from a knowledge of the nature of the good man one can arrive at a knowledge of the good society. "In Heraclitus the idea of an order of the soul begins to form which in Plato unfolds into the perennial principle of political science: that the right order of the soul through philosophy furnishes the standard for the right order of society."[23] An essential part of the work of the political philosopher is, in fact, the elaboration of model projects which serve as the basis for the evaluation of existing regimes. The model project of the paradigmatic regime provides, in broad outline, an indication of how a society organized around the *spoudaios* as its representative, dominant type would appear. Such a sketch is an illustration of scientific principles and is derived from a sound philosophical anthropology. It has nothing whatever to do with the so-called ideal state (a fundamental mistranslation of *aristē politeia*) or "utopia." The sketch of the paradigmatic society is not an indulgence in axiological phantasy; it is not a projection of an individual's value preferences. The paradigmatic society is anchored in ontological reality: it is a picture of how society would look if it were guided by the standards of the human type that is attuned to the order of being.

[22] In "Nietzsche, the Crisis and the War," *Journal of Politics*, VI (May, 1944), Voegelin credits Nietzsche with having made a proper empirical assessment of the nihilistic character of "massy" existence (while rejecting, it need scarcely be added, Nietzsche's solution for "overcoming" the nihilism).

[23] Voegelin, *Order and History, op. cit.*, vol. II, p. 227.

One of Voegelin's most valuable contributions has been to demonstrate that the construction of utopias has nothing to do with scientific political theory. Utopia is to be defined as "the dream of achieving the perfect society through organizing men according to a blueprint instead of forming them in an educational process. . . ."[24] Utopia is the "black magic of politics" and Plato, himself so frequently mislabelled a "utopian thinker," specifically contrasts utopia-construction and the philosophic elaboration of the good society when, in the *Critias*, he sets up a utopia in bad faith. The *Republic* is to be understood as an "intense call for spiritual reform," rather than as a "rational blueprint" for an "ideal state."[25]

In discussing the problem of providing a model project of the paradigmatic society valid for contemporary conditions, Voegelin is careful to warn political theorists against attempts to elaborate its structural features in too minute and detailed a manner. The weight of the philosopher's work lies "in the inquiry into the nature of true order" in the soul and in society; "the model projects, while more than a literary device, have the character of secondary elaborations and must not be taken as rules with autonomous validity."[26] Thus, it may be observed that in Plato's *Laws* the preambles take up much more space than the actual laws, while the *Republic* omits whole areas of law from consideration on grounds that "anybody can elaborate the legal projects if he has understood the essence of order and realized the order within his own life." Aristotle provides only the thinnest sketch of his model in Book VIII of the *Politics*. Voegelin is careful to indicate that the actual model does have its validity, however: it provides men with a definite standard in terms of which they may judge the relative deficiency of the actual society in which they live.

Given his strictures against excessive detailing of the good society's characteristics, we need not expect to find in the Voegelinian corpus an institutional representation along the lines of Maritain's *Man and the State*, to cite an example of another contemporary theorist of the good society. Nevertheless, in a highly significant but regrettably little-known paper delivered several years ago to a gathering

[24] *Ibid.*, vol. III, p. 209.

[25] *Ibid.*, vol. II, p. 187.

[26] Voegelin, *The Nature of Law*, *op. cit.*, p. 82.

of European scholars, Voegelin did offer in brief form certain specific norms for the good society in our time. Such a society rests on two postulates: (1) it is to be as large and prosperous as is necessary to make possible the life of reason for the minority choosing to lead it; and (2) it is organized in such a manner that the "life of reason becomes a soul force in the culture and political affairs of the society."

To these postulates Voegelin adds two corollaries: (1) the good society is not a rigid, a priori conception: "Its construction is extremely elastic and ought to vary with our empirical knowledge of the nature of man and society." That the life of reason be "socially efficacious" is its only firm point. (Significantly, Voegelin nowhere insists on a specific scheme of property relations as mandatory for the good society. Contemporary American right-wing intellectuals who attempt to use Voegelin as a cudgel with which to whip the welfare state would receive short shrift from him. He actually takes for granted that under conditions of industrialization a good deal of public ownership and extensive social services will exist and are necessary. Voegelin is neither left-wing nor right-wing because he is neither a publicist nor an ideologist.) (2) The good society is not to be confused with eternal paradise on earth; in the language of the cyclical theory of history, even if it were realized historically, in due time it would run its course, decay, and disintegrate.[27]

Voegelin recognizes with Plato and Aristotle that there exist many degrees of embodiment of the paradigmatic society, and that in addition to fabricating models of the best regime, he must preoccupy himself with the problem of the "dilution of the paradigm." Historical circumstances will most likely make it necessary to compromise certain principles so that at least some measure of order may be injected into a particular existing society. Thus, we have models of what Aristotle called the "best practicable regime." For instance, under current conditions of industrialization, urbanization, and population saturation, participation by the many in politics will be both necessary and proper. Similarly, the owners of resources and the managers of aggregates on both the labor and the management side of the economy must have an important role in the political process, irrespective of their openness to the life of reason, because of the vast extent of their power. Thus, the paradigm would have to be

[27] Voegelin, "La Société industrielle a la recherche de la raison," in R. Aron, ed., *Colloques de Rheinfelden* (Paris, 1960), pp. 44 ff., 53-54.

diluted to the point where it was transformed into a "mixed constitution," in which the many on grounds of their number, the managers on the ground of their position, and the *spoudaioi* on the grounds of their virtue, would have a share in the selection and composition of the political class and the shaping of public issues and policies.[28]

ORDER AND HISTORY. Even had Voegelin done no more than recapture the meaning and contemporary relevance of the classical *epistēmē politikē* in the areas of ethics and politics, his achievement would have been monumental. As it is, however, he has gone decisively beyond the classical *epistēmē* in the field of history, in the third field of investigation proper to a theory of politics conceived as a science of right order in human society. Voegelin has shown that only in our time, with the unparalleled archaeological discoveries and improvements in the techniques of historical research resulting in the enormous widening of the historical horizon, has it become possible to develop adequately the historical side of the science of politics.

Voegelin calls for nothing less than a joining of a "theory of politics" with a "theory of history." "The existence of man in political society is historical existence; and a theory of politics, if it penetrates to principles, must at the same time be a theory of history. . . . Theory is bound by history. . . . [The theorist is not permitted to] take his position at an Archimedean point outside history."[29] Although at the center of Voegelin's analysis of politics is a philosophy of history, it should be understood that this philosophy of history, in contrast to the constructions of a Hegel or a Marx, will not offer a rounded picture of the final meaning of the historical pattern. For Voegelin's philosophy of history is grounded on the experience of existence, which informs us that at

the center of his existence man is unknown to himself and must remain so, for the part of being that calls itself man could be known fully only if the community of being and its drama in

---

[28] As with individual character types, it is possible to arrange societies on a scale of excellence, and one of the functions of political science is to survey the various types of existing societies and categorize them according to their relative worth vis-à-vis the paradigmatic model. For Voegelin, it is *societies*, not forms of government, that are primary. A well-ordered society will produce a satisfactory form of government, but the reverse cannot happen.

[29] Voegelin, *The New Science of Politics, op. cit.,* pp. 1, 78.

time were known as a whole. Man's participation in being is the essence of his existence, and this essence depends on the whole, of which existence is a part. Knowledge of the whole, however, is precluded by the identity of the knower with the partner, and ignorance of the whole precludes essential knowledge of the part. The situation with regard to the decisive core of human existence is . . . profoundly disturbing, for from the depths of this ultimate ignorance wells up the anxiety of existence.[30]

A philosophy of history will not yield us special gnosis regarding the ultimate meaning of history.

It rather reveals a mankind striving for its order of existence within the world while attuning itself with the truth of being beyond the world, and gaining in the process not a substantially better order within the world but an increased understanding of the gulf that lies between immanent existence and the transcendent truth of being.

The contemporary historian is able to cast a ray of light from the present into the past, but "the light that falls over the past" only "deepens the darkness that surrounds the future. He will shudder before the abysmal mystery of history as the instrument of divine revelation for ultimate purposes that are unknown equally to the men of all ages."[31] Thinkers from Joachim of Flora to Hegel and Marx who claim to have captured for us the *eidos* of history have only succeeded in perpetrating a "swindle."[32] "There is no eidos of history," because the

course of history as a whole is no object of experience; history has no eidos, because the course of history extends into the unknown future. The meaning of history, thus, is an illusion; and this illusionary eidos is created by treating a symbol of faith [the eschaton of Christianity which points towards eventual tran-

---

[30] Voegelin, *Order and History, op. cit.*, vol. I, p. 2.

[31] *Ibid.*, p. 129.

[32] See Voegelin's inaugural lecture at Munich, *Wissenschaft, Politik, und Gnosis* (Munich, Koesel Verlag, 1959), for enlargement upon the theme of gnostic political thinkers as "swindlers." As my remarks on Hegel in Chapter 2 indicate, I do not agree with Voegelin's interpretation of Hegel in some important respects.

scendental fulfillment beyond time] as if it were a proposition concerning an object of immanent experience.[33]

Although an adequately articulated theory, or philosophy, of history will yield man no secrets which his existential situation by its very nature bars him from attaining, it will teach him what man is engaged in doing when he participates in the historical process. It will teach the observer to go beyond the understanding of the "phenomenal regularities,"[34] or the dimension of "objective time in which civilizations run their course," to penetrate to the comprehension of history as the "inner form which constitutes a society."[35]

At its deeper level, then, history appears as a succession of "symbolic forms" which various societies have elaborated in their attempts at self-interpretation. The form of a given society "results from the interpenetration of institutions and experiences of order,"[36] for societal institutions reflect the experiences of order which imbue them with a particular form. Voegelin rejects the portrayal in Spengler and the early Toynbee of history as an infinite—and ultimately senseless—series of "civilizations." He does, however, accept Toynbee's insistence that civilizations, rather than nation-states, are the only "intelligible units of study." Rather, in the unfolding of the various symbolic forms of historical order—from the Babylonian and Egyptian cosmological to the Israelite historical, Greek philosophical, and Christian forms—we discern that "the great societies . . . have created a sequence

---

[33] Voegelin, The New Science of Politics, op. cit., p. 120.

[34] Voegelin does not disparage knowledge of the phenomenal regularities in the sequence of historical events (indeed, he has a knowledge at this level of historical fact equalled only by Toynbee), but rather seeks to put them in their proper light as constituting only one level of the historical process: "The ultimate constants of history cannot be determined by forming type concepts of phenomenal regularities, for historical regularities are no more than manifestations of the constants of human nature in their range of compactness and differentiation." This position is in no way opposed to the "search for the phenomenally typical in the course of civilizations. For inevitably we must start with phenomenal regularities in order to arrive at the constant of human nature, as well as at the structural differentiation of the constant range of experiences; that is at the dynamics of human nature that we call history." Order and History, vol. I, p. 63.

[35] Ibid., p. 127.

[36] Ibid., p. 60.

of order, intelligibly connected with one another as advances toward, or recessions from, an adequate symbolization of truth concerning the order of being of which the order of society is a part."[37]

The decisive advance in man's struggle for an adequate symbolization regarding right order in society occurs in the transition from the "truth of cosmic-divine order to the differentiated experience of transcendent-divine order." Voegelin's term for denoting this qualitative advance in the history of the spirit is a "leap in being"; the leap in being "occurs in a plurality of parallel instances, in Israel and Hellas, in China and in India," but the parallel occurrences are "not of equal rank."[38] When the leap in being occurs, involving what Bergson described as the "opening" of the soul to the transcendent truth, human personality in its freedom of the spirit in existence under God appears. Human existence, having emerged from the Sheol of cosmological servitude, becomes for the first time "consciously historical." We move from the mythological compactness of cosmological truth to the more differentiated symbolism of philosophy and religion. With Greek philosophy and the Christian religion, the various components of human existence are differentiated and given appropriate symbolic referents.

The movement from the early empires to Hellas and Israel and finally to Christianity is in theoretical terms an advance from cosmological to anthropological and finally to soteriological truth about the order of being. In the more differentiated symbolic forms, the visible world, the ordered *cosmion*, is replaced as the analogue of social order by the unseen measure "that can be experienced only by a movement of the soul." Thus, the internal order of the psyche rather than the external order of nature becomes the model "that will furnish symbols for ordering society analogically in its image."[39]

Although the anthropological truth of Greek philosophy and the soteriological truth of Christianity are alike in their opposition to cosmological compactness, "the Platonic-Aristotelian complex of experiences was enlarged by Christianity in a decisive point." Philosophy emphasizes the "human side of the orientation of the soul toward divinity." The soul reaches out to an "inviolably transcendent" God but is met by no "answering movement."

[37] *Ibid.*, p. ix.
[38] *Ibid.*, vol. II, p. 4.
[39] *Ibid.*, vol. I, p. 5.

The experience of mutuality in the relation with God, of the amicitia in the Thomistic sense, of the grace which imposes a supernatural form on the nature of man, is the specific difference of Christian truth. The revelation of this grace in history, through the incarnation of the. Logos in Christ, intelligibly fulfilled the adventitious movement of the spirit in the mystic philosophers. The critical authority over the older truth of society which the soul had gained through its opening and its orientation toward the unseen measure was now confirmed through the revelation of the measure itself.[40]

One of the most important—and controversial—aspects of Voegelin's philosophy of history is his description of modern Western civilization as the expression of the gnostic symbolic form. Gnosticism is a stream of thought with pre-Christian roots,[41] which becomes progressively immanentized until it erupts in the totalitarian mass movements of our time. Enormous and important differences exist between the various gnostic symbolisms that coexist in modernity,[42] but they all have in common the fallacious attempt to transform the uncertainties and ambiguities of the experience of existence into the certainties of one-dimensional, intramundane experience. Out of their anxiety regarding the structure of existence they create a second reality which gives more assurance to them than the apprehension of the ground of being by faith and analogical reasoning affords. In its most radical forms, gnosticism is a messianic, chiliastic creed bent on destroying the soul's openness towards transcendental truth in the name of the unrestrained *libido dominandi* of the gnostic elite. The gnostic elite claims to have the recipe for overcoming the gulf between essence and existence, immanence and transcendence, by creating a new man and a new order of being which will be a marvelous improvement over the old order. The increase of phenomenal power over

[40] Voegelin, *New Science of Politics, op. cit.*, p. 78.

[41] Cf. the relevant works of Hans Leisegang and Hans Jonas on the early history of this much-neglected intellectual phenomenon.

[42] Voegelin has been vigorously attacked by various writers for characterizing liberalism as a manifestation of gnosticism. Actually, he displays a lively appreciation for the *institutional* achievements of modern liberalism (rule of law, elimination of the police state, etc.) and writes optimistically of the appearance of a revised liberalism reinfused with the Christian substance on the continent of Europe today. See his excellent discussion of the problems of defining liberalism in "Der Liberalismus and seine Geschichte," in Karl Forster, ed., *Christentum and Liberalismus* (Munich, 1960), pp. 13-42.

the external world rather than the internal ordering of the soul by the divine measure is regarded as the *summum bonum* by the gnostic creed-movements.

The growth of gnosticism to the point where it became the dominant symbolic form of the modern age marked a momentous theoretical regression from the high point reached by Greek philosophy and Christianity. This regression cannot be interpreted simply as a return to the earlier compactness of the cosmological experience of order.[43] The gnostic symbolic form is *sui generis*. In the myth of the cosmological societies, reason and revelation had not differentiated themselves as sources of authority independent of the existential power structure. But gnostic creed-movements such as Communism and National Socialism "attempt the ordering of society by fusing the normative authority into the authority of power." This "fusion of authorities" makes gnostic society a separate historical type because "deliberate fusion of differentiated components is not the same as primordial compactness."[44]

For Voegelin as for Plato, philosophy has a "diagnostic and therapeutic" function. Philosophy, as the "love of being through the love of divine Being as the source of its order," illuminates for us the "modes of existence in untruth." And the substance of history will be discovered to consist "in the experiences in which man gains the understanding of his humanity and together with it the understanding of its limits."[45] These experiences cannot be ignored by the political theorist, but must be empirically examined and critically evaluated for the light which they shed upon his own search for the truth about order in human society. Theory must be correlated to the "maximal experiential differentiation" and this maximal differentiation was achieved by Greek philosophy and Christianity. "This means concretely that theory is bound to move within the historical horizon of classic and Christian experiences. To recede from the maximum of differentiation is theoretical retrogression."[46]

---

[43] Voegelin states in *Wissenschaft, Politik und Gnosis* that he now holds his earlier analysis of totalitarian movements as political religions—in *Die Politischen Religionen* (Stockholm, 1930)—to be inadequate because he failed to take this fact sufficiently into account.

[44] Voegelin, *The Nature of Law, op. cit.*, p. 108.

[45] Voegelin, *New Science of Politics, op. cit.*, p. 78.

[46] *Ibid.*, p. 79.

Voegelin and the Recovery of Political Theory

Eric Voegelin's contribution to contemporary political theory is to have made a philosophically profound and superbly creative effort to restore the tradition of political theory as an experential science of right order in our time. He should be interpreted as having led, along with such scholars as Maritain, de Jouvenel, Strauss, Arendt, and others, a resistance movement of major proportions against the positivist domination that has held sway in political science circles at least since the end of the nineteenth century. Here, of course, is the source of the difficulties which he has encountered in obtaining a hearing from present-day political scientists. To the degree that the resistance movement is successful, there will occur a major upheaval in the research priorities and methods now pursued in the profession.

Within the positivistic universe of discourse, all propositions must be verified by experience. But the only experience accepted as objective—and therefore in the realm of science—is that observable by the physical senses. Other dimensions of experience, apprehended through the *nous* or eye of the mind instead of the eye of the physical body, are treated as subjective because they are not as universally shared and readily communicable as experiences on the level of physical sensation. It requires laborious formation of character to become a *spoudaios* and so be able to verify in one's own experience the metaphysical propositions of the classical and Christian *epistēmē*, but the vast majority of men are able without comparable effort to verify the propositions of positivist political science. Thus, the "people of the meanest capacities" rather than the *spoudaioi* are, in the positivist scheme of things, made the judges of what constitutes the field of experience to which propositions in political science must refer.[47]

The basic positivist dichotomy (running back to Comte but reiterated, only in a more refined form, by the neopositivist avant-garde of the Vienna Circle) between objective fact apprehended by sense-experience and epiphenomenal, subjective value[48] means that

[47] Cf. Leo Strauss, in J. J. Storing, ed., *Essays on the Scientific Study of Politics* (New York, Holt, Rinehart and Winston, 1962), p. 326.

[48] The term "value-judgment" did not come into the philosophical vocabulary until the late nineteenth century (with the neo-Kantians). Classical ethics always spoke of "the good" which is a very important "fact" or datum confronting the consciousness.

political theory tends to be viewed in one of two ways. Either political theory is a body of sociologically conditioned, nonobjective value-judgments (which political science can study for causative effect on human behavior), or it is essentially methodology, in which event its task is to serve as the handmaiden of research into behavioral regularities on the phenomenal level by producing ideal types, models, and the like. Now if all political theory is judged in terms of this fact-value dichotomy, today accepted as dogma by many Western political scientists, then anyone who conceives of political theory as an experiential science of right order, based on the total experience of the existing human person, will be labelled an "ideologist." His claims to scientific status will be dismissed out of hand, and he will scarcely be noticed at all unless his influence becomes a causative ideational factor in the struggle of the political marketplace. In sum, his work will be incapable of being understood on its own terms.

"Theory," Voegelin has written,

> is not just any opining about human existence in society; it rather is an attempt at formulating the meaning of existence by explicating the content of a definite class of experiences. Its argument is not arbitrary but derives its validity from the aggregate of experiences to which it must permanently refer for empirical control.[49]

In a genuinely theoretical analysis of ethics and politics, we are dealing with the realities of human existence in the various realms of being not with value-judgments which correspond with nothing else but the writer's phantasies concerning how he would prefer the world to be organized or disorganized. Political theory elaborates "empirically and critically, the problems of order which derive from philosophical anthropology as part of a general ontology." As an "explication of certain experiences," theory is "intelligible only to those in whom the explication will stir up parallel experiences as the empirical basis for testing the truth of theory." Theory has no argument against those who feel, or pretend to feel, incapable of meditatively reenacting the experience itself.[50]

Thus, while Voegelin is to be counted in the ranks of those who combat the restriction of political theory to the role of methodological

[49] Voegelin, *New Science of Politics, op cit.,* p. 64.

[50] *Ibid.,* pp. 64-65.

auxiliary to the behavioral social sciences, under no circumstances is he to be viewed as advocating opening the door of political science to wild and uncontrolled utopian speculation. Utopia-building is not yet dead in political theory, and efforts are being made to revive it as a legitimate enterprise. To take only one possible example, comparison of Voegelin's *epistēmē* with the utopianism of a writer like Erich Fromm reveals rather vividly the contrast between the two modes of thinking about political problems.[51]

It is too early to evaluate definitively the success of the restorative movement which Voegelin has helped to initiate. The strength of the opposition currents remains massive, but there are encouraging signs that a new generation of political scientists will be more receptive to the new teaching than the one which presently mans the positions of institutional power. Regardless of the social efficacy of his work, Voegelin will be entitled to say with Richard Hooker: "Posterity may know we have not loosely through silence permitted things to pass away as in a dream."

---

[51] Where Voegelin offers the life of reason in attunement with transcendent being as the paradigmatic existence, Fromm posits the spontaneous, "free activity of the self" as the highest aim of life (spontaneity for what?). Where Voegelin refers to the experience of a possible perfection beyond time by grace, Fromm describes as a sign of mental health the "experience of the self as the subject and agent of one's powers"—that is, he embraces the possibility of man's self-redemption (p. 69). Where Voegelin speaks of transcendence as the symbol which indicates reality qualitatively distinct from intramundane being, Fromm makes transcendence into a power for man "to transcend the role of the creature . . . by becoming a 'creator' " (p. 36). The "role of the creature," moreover, cannot be "transcended"; it is an inescapable aspect of the *conditio humana*. Where Voegelin portrays man as *homo viator*, inevitably separated in the existential situation from the perfect fulfillment of his essence, Fromm holds out the promise of an illusionary end to alienation and the attainment of the "experience of union with another person, with all men, and with nature under the condition of retaining one's sense of integrity and independence" (p. 32). Where Voegelin recognizes the limits of politics, and the impossibility of creating an eternity in time, Fromm argues in the manner of Fourier that by right social organization (the grouping of men into intimate "communities of work") we can end the disparities between rulers and ruled, make man fully autonomous, and so on. All page references in this note are to Fromm's *The Sane Society* (New York, Holt, Rinehart and Winston, 1955).

PART V ❧ POLITICAL THEORY AND THE OPEN SOCIETY

NINE: ᗷEHAVIORALISM AND THE IDEA OF THE CLOSED SOCIETY

The Crisis of Modernity

At the close of his book, *La Trahison des clercs*, Julien Benda discusses in a perceptive paragraph the "imperialism of the species" which is the goal of "the great directors of the modern conscience." Man will be master of the world once all national and cultural divisions have been broken down and the idea of God, exposed as the last enemy of such mastery, will have been expunged from the consciousness as an unworthy superstition.

> Thereafter humanity would be unified in one immense army, one immense factory, would be aware only of heroisms, disciplines, inventions, would denounce all free and disinterested activity, would long cease to situate the good outside the real world, would have no God but itself and its desires, and would achieve great things; by which I mean that it would attain to a really grandiose control over the matter surrounding it, to a really joyous consciousness of its power and its grandeur. And History will smile to think that this is the species for which Socrates and Jesus Christ died.[1]

[1] Translated as *The Betrayal of the Intellectuals* (Boston, Beacon Press, 1955), p. 163.

The easy and fashionable response to Benda's sombre meditation is to accuse him of exaggeration or of being a Cassandra. However, on further reflection it is difficult to escape the conclusion that he has accurately described the conscious goal of a significant segment of contemporary social thought. Even in the relatively open and plural societies which comprise the "free world," the pressures against the life of the spirit, eased to some extent in the thaw of ideologies during the postwar period, remain severe. At the popular level, we encounter in the advanced industrialized countries of the West an exaltation of activism, an assumption that a rise in the material standard of living means a corresponding rise in the quality of life. Knowledge tends to be equated with know-how, and the "conquest of space" (a term which is itself saturated with *hybris*) is glorified as the culmination of the entire history of the human race, the apogee in more than the spatial sense of all human effort. Augustine could have been writing today when he observed: "Here are men going afar to marvel at the heights of mountains, the mighty waves of the sea, the long courses of great rivers, the vastness of the ocean, the movements of the stars, yet leaving themselves unnoticed." We mistake "vain and perishing curiosity" for true knowledge, which is of "God and the soul."

G. P. Grant, a Canadian scholar, in his interesting book *Philosophy in the Mass Age*, has sought to lay bare the pragmatism at the root of so much of the thinking of modern industrial societies, with particular reference to the United States. He chooses William James as representative of the exaltation of the practical mentality. Although James was a complex thinker, and there are other aspects of his teaching which should be considered in making a total assessment, it is undeniable that, through his emphasis on the "cash value" of ideas, and in such statements as "pragmatic philosophy turns towards action and power," "truth in our ideas means their power to work," and "the world stands ready, malleable, waiting to receive the final touches at our hands. . . . Man engenders truth upon it," the spirit of James' teaching has to be reckoned as basically inimical to the cultivation of the *bios theorētikos*.

Grant lays the blame on "Protestant civilization" for inhibiting those activities

> such as day-dreaming, sensuality, art, prayer, theoretical science, and philosophy, which do not directly change the world. . . .

Historically, the artist, the philosopher, the mystic have been outsiders in our Protestant civilization. During the excitement over sputnik, it was suggested that the Americans were deeply depressed by the Russian success. I thought this was a wrong interpretation. Rather, there was a great sigh of relief from the American elites, for now there was an immediate practical objective to be achieved, a new frontier to be conquered—outer space. It provided further excuse not to think about what will make life meaningful when the practical problems are settled; about what people will do when the factories are filled with mechanical robots.[2]

Grant's statement could be substantially improved upon for precision of expression, especially with regard to his choice of the term "Protestant civilization" to connote a society which has succumbed to the tyranny of the practical. It may be doubted that an authentically Protestant civilization would be closed to the experience of transcendence and it should be noted that the greatest Protestant theologians of our time are in the forefront of the resistance movement against the kind of society which Grant describes. Without entering into the complexities of the Weber thesis on the "Protestant ethic" and the rise of capitalism, it must be observed that it is only a vulgarization and even caricature of Protestantism, or more precisely of Calvinism, that can be linked directly to the immanent-activist tendencies of modernity.[3] Nonetheless, despite certain deficiencies in terminology, Grant's words convey much truth. The scientist is prized not for his learning but for his power, and, in general, where it has not been entirely destroyed by vocational education, liberal learning is under constant pressure to justify itself in terms of practical results or cash value.

The crisis of modernity consists in the fact that, while at the phenomenal level a tremendous increase of man's power over the natural environment has occurred which has vastly benefited mankind through the mitigation of physical suffering and rising standards of living, nonetheless at the level of spirit there has been a disturbing tendency to idolize these achievements to the neglect of other activi-

[2] G. P. Grant, *Philosophy in the Mass Age* (New York, Hill and Wang, 1960), pp. 100-101.

[3] Cf. Leo Strauss's comments on the Weber thesis in *Natural Right and History* (Chicago, University of Chicago Press, 1953), pp. 60-61.

ties and forms of knowledge. In some quarters there has been expressed the conviction that man himself is an object of conquest.[4] We have already seen how these tendencies, latent in the modern experiment to glorify world-immanent conquest at the expense of the interior life of the spirit, were brought to the surface and extolled in unqualified fashion by the political messianism of the nineteenth century. The ideologies of the Communist, Nazi, and Italian Fascist regimes showed to what terrifying practical consequences political messianism could lead.

As the discussion of Voegelin's political theory makes clear, the legacy of modernity is an ambiguous one. A key task of a critical political science or political theory in our time is to expose those modern tendencies which, even in the nontotalitarian world, favor the development of a closed society. In pursuing this task, political theory finds itself in conflict with an intellectual force described as behavioralism. The most intrepid exponents of the "behavioral persuasion in politics," far from resisting those trends in modern western culture toward the closed society, actually seem to applaud and enforce those trends. Writers such as B. F. Skinner and Harold Lasswell in effect contend for the establishment of a closed, manipulated, scientistically engineered society. Other scholars in the behavioralist school seldom go as far as Lasswell and Skinner in favoring the closed society with all the Comtean trappings. And yet even a figure like Herbert Simon espouses a concept of society which differs only in degree from that of Lasswell.

Many will object strenuously to any linking of behavioralist political and social science with the closed society. In the attempt to avoid misunderstandings and misinterpretations, let me make the following points relative to the material in this chapter:

1. Behavioralism today has an elusive meaning. I recognize that behavioralist political science is not a monolithic bloc and that numerous and important differences of opinion and orientation occur among those who adhere to the "behavioral persuasion in politics."[5] I am

---

[4] Thus, the social psychologist Hadley Cantril has proclaimed that social science has now reached the stage where we can "bring about the human nature we want." "Don't Blame It on Human Nature," *The New York Times Magazine* (July 6, 1947).

[5] For example, Heinz Eulau's *The Behavioral Persuasion in Politics* (New York, Random House, 1963) is a remarkably moderate exposition. Some of

aware that there are many political scientists often referred to as behavioralists or who count themselves as behavioralists who do not subscribe to many of Lasswell's tenets, for example, and who are more cautious and modest in their claims and aspirations for political science and more appreciative of the work of traditional political theorists than are the men discussed in this chapter. Those qualifications having been noted, I remain convinced that what is today called behavioralist political science, considered as a whole, is a force conducive to the achievement of a closed rather than an open society. To assert this thesis is not to deny that within the coming decade

---

his statements are unexceptionable (e.g., p. 9: "It is the function of science to understand and interpret the world, not to change it," and the objections to an avowedly ideological political science on pp. 136-137), and it is clear that the author strives for disinterested political inquiry. His definition of behavioralism (p. 5: "The behavioral persuasion in politics is concerned with what man does politically and the meanings he attaches to his behavior") is general and undogmatic. Although he calls the "psychology, sociology, and even anthropology" of the great political theorists of the past to be "from the contemporary perspective primitive, underdeveloped, and often mistaken" (p. 7), he is not without respect and sympathy for "the classical tradition in political science" (p. 32). For Eulau, behavioralism is not a revolt against that tradition. "If the behavioral persuasion revolted against anything, it was against the failure of academic political science to use the modern technology in the study of politics, as, I believe, the classical writers would have used it had it been available to them" (p. 32). It may be seriously doubted that the preceding statement is true for behavioralism of the past. But if it is an indication of a changed temper for behavioralism in the future, this is of course to the good. Eulau dedicated this book to Harold Lasswell, but many observations in it, as well as its general tone, are so far removed from Lasswell's teaching that we may possibly already be with Eulau on the road to a revisionist behavioralism. Yet some statements in the volume continue to give one pause as to whether new horizons have been glimpsed as, for example, the following statement on p. 32: "In some quarters, there has been fierce resistance to increasing our knowledge about politics through behavioral analysis. Why such resistance occurs is of interest to the sociologist of knowledge, and how it might be overcome is a task for the psychoanalyst." Eulau also seems unwilling to concede on principle that there are natural limits to the "behavioral analysis of politics, limits that no technological revolution can eradicate" (p. 32). It is rather difficult to see how any computer could ever answer the question of the *summum bonum* for man. The misplaced emphasis on technology in Eulau's book is regrettable, but he is far more cautious in his claims and more aware of the difficulties than are most behavioralist political scientists.

or two changes in the overall picture may occur. A revisionist behavioralism—which still carries the label "behavioralist"—may emerge that consciously rejects the rigid reductionism and scientism characteristic of many of behavioralism's leading exponents in the past. Such a development would be a consummation devoutly to be wished from the viewpoint of those seeking to restore authentic political theory.

2. In no sense should this chapter be interpreted as an *ad hominem* attack upon the individuals discussed or on behavioralists in general as men. This is meant to be a serious discussion of ideas and premises which I and others have detected to be present in the literature of behavioralist political and social science.

3. I do not maintain that the writers herein discussed *intended* to advocate the closed society. It may be that for them what, together with others, I take to be the closed society is actually the open society. In that event, a general theoretical debate could ensue about the nature of the open society. There is no more important topic for political scientists today to be discussing and debating.

4. I am a proponent of empirical investigation in political science. In criticizing behavioralism I am not criticizing empirical research. Every leading political theorist of the past undertook such research; one has only to refer to Aristotle and his 158 constitutions, Machiavelli, and Mosca to make this point sufficiently clear. What I object to is the tendency among the advocates of a so-called scientific as opposed to a philosophical political science to decapitate political science and to argue that only propositions purporting to refer to or describe "empirical"—sensorially observable—facts may be considered part of political science. The neglect of critical standards in terms of which we order and evaluate our data is the principal defect of the new or behavioralist political science. This neglect often leads to the adoption of uncritical standards which do not hold up at all well to theoretical reflection. The rebirth of political theory would not lead to the neglect of empirical research—for example, studies regarding the power structure and authority patterns in a community would, as they do now, have an important place—but to the correction of claims that such studies constitute the whole of political science. Such a rebirth would focus again on the need for elaborating criteria in order to evaluate political behavior, the importance of the paradigm, the crucial question of the highest good and

best society for man as man, the dilution of the paradigm for concrete historical conditions, etc.

Behavioralism in general may be described as that doctrine in recent and contemporary social science which accepts without any apparent critical debate the basic thrust of the modern experiment toward an immanentistic, secularized, production-oriented, functional, scientistic "world culture." Thus, behavioralist research has ordinarily been characterized by a commitment (either latent or overt) to the "modernizing ethos." The modernizing ethos has thus far served as the leading value commitment of behavioral social science. Behavioralists in political science are in agreement that the literature of political studies prior to the "scientific revolution" inspired by logical positivism and related movements is seriously defective both as to scope and method. This means that political theory as it has traditionally been conceived is rejected as part of political science. Behavioralists show a marked predilection for quantification, and employ a variety of opinion survey and interview techniques to obtain data which serve as the basis for their generalizations. They also make frequent use of voting statistics. Behavioralists leave themselves open to the criticism that they choose topics for investigation on the basis of whether they are amenable to quantification rather than on the basis of their significance for political science. The tendency of behavioral research in political science is to stress the contemporary, thereby giving rise to the observation that they neglect the historical dimension.

As a term, behavioralism can be traced to John B. Watson and his narrow type of "behavioristic" psychology. Contemporary behavioralism is not Watson's behaviorism either in experimental psychology or in political science, however. But Watson's basic goal of a science for the conditioning of men continues to be expounded by an important segment of behavioralist social science. To Watson the new psychology was to be an applied science of social engineering, and the expressed goal of the social engineer was "to develop his world of people from birth on, so that their speech and bodily behavior could equally well be exhibited everywhere without running afoul of group standards."[6] Watson, like B. F. Skinner, looked to the establishment of a culture in which antagonism and conflict had been virtually eliminated under the skillful management of an elite of social scientists. All

---

[6] Floyd W. Matson, *The Broken Image* (New York, Braziller, 1964), p. 57.

but an inconsequential number of social deviants would be happily adjusted to group standards, the standards of the cave. However, there was a certain ambivalence over the question of whether these standards emanated from the people themselves or whether they were consciously supplied by the scientistic elite: Many traditional ideas and standards of human behavior cherished by large segments of the society were, in the eyes of the new scientistic elite, irrational and outmoded. It was essentially a question of changing the old standards and then making human behavior conform to them.

George A. Lundberg, also a leading originator and exponent of behavioristic psychology, revealed in his work the basic ambivalence characteristic of this kind of an approach. The new conditioners were benevolent men, and they were believers in democracy understood as rule of the people. Thus in Lundberg's thought a noticeable tension developed between his scientism and his democratism. On the one hand, values, according to the accepted positivist teaching, being subjective and a matter of fiat, are to be determined by majority vote; on the other hand, it was thought that the masses cannot be left alone to determine values but must be psychologically managed and conditioned to affirm healthy, stable, adjusted, productive, and functional values—as understood from the perspective of the new social science, which in itself uncritically imbibed the modernizing ethos referred to above as a kind of implicit political doctrine. As will be apparent in the discussion below, the same kind of tension between democratism and scientism runs through Lasswell and Simon's thought.[7]

The four writers discussed in the remainder of this chapter were selected because they illustrate to an unusual degree the proclivities of behavioralist social and political science to advocate a closed society, in the sense that world-immanent values of the modernizing ethos are asserted to the detriment of the life of the spirit in openness toward transcendence. It is not maintained that the views of these writers are identical with each other. Behavioralism has been aptly described as a mood or tendency rather than a fully coherent body of doctrine.

[7] Thus, social science, "which was to be at the disposal of society, in the end disposes of society. It is the word of the scientists, not the 'voice of the people,' which is to prevail after all." *Ibid.*, p. 91.

The Behavioralist Utopia of B. F. Skinner

Professor B. F. Skinner bids fair to rival Comte in the boundlessness of his faith in the capacities of science to engineer a terrestrial paradise. Skinner's *Walden Two* is all too often dismissed as another publication after the manner of Aldous Huxley's *Brave New World*. The difference lies precisely in the fact that, where Huxley is writing satire, Skinner is not. The Harvard psychologist is deadly serious in this work, which is really a scientistic tract for the times. Because this work is often referred to but seldom discussed explicitly, a recapitulation of its main points as they bear on the problem of the closed society is in order.

Walden Two (named, of course, rather ironically after the *Walden* of Thoreau) is a utopian community organized according to the principles of "cultural engineering." The basic assumption of its founder, "Frazier," is that "right conditions" are all that is necessary to produce the highest human type, a benevolent, integrated, and creative personality. Thus, fundamental to the whole enterprise is the view that a qualitative change in man can occur through the proper manipulation of the social environment by self-appointed scientists of human behavior.

Life at Walden Two begins in the communal nursery where the infants are kept in Skinner boxes until they reach their first birthday. Temperature, noise, and oxygen levels within the boxes are carefully regulated; the children are not irritated and so do little crying, and they are not encumbered with clothing. The babies graduate from the nursery ignorant of "frustration, anxiety, or fear." The absence of mother love is replaced by "father love, everybody's love— community love if you wish."[8] From the ages of one to three, the children are kept in small rooms with furniture and play equipment scaled down to size; the rooms are hermetically sealed like the baby cubicles. The children wear no clothing except diapers. They are not envious or jealous of each other. (Adult members who first came to the community as late as the age of twelve can no longer recall the feeling of jealousy, for it has been engineered out of them. Only the cooperative emotions are encouraged, and anger is no longer possible for them.) The children are trained to bear frustrations; they learn

[8] B. F. Skinner, *Walden Two* (New York, Macmillan, 1948), p. 80.

to have a "right reaction" to denials. The community, which has total control over their environment, completes their "ethical training" by the age of six. The objective is to give them full "peace of mind," which the socal engineers understand to be the point of Jesus's teaching to "love your enemies." Because "ethical training belongs to the community," there is no place for religion and family culture in its development. The older children are graduated to a dormitory where they are given clothes and a bed of their own. No adult supervision is needed, for each child emulates another one slightly older than himself. Education is not formal but is acquired in cooperative activities with a minimum of direction from the teacher. There is no standard course for all, and no college where they obtain higher education. The community library is limited to approximately 3,000 books.[9]

Marriage in Walden Two takes place at age fourteen or fifteen, with each new couple building its dwelling in the community (to satisfy the "nesting instinct"). Procreation of children will be completed within a few years, after which the women are free for creative living. There is a Manager of Marriages who must approve all engagements. What promiscuity there is will not be a serious problem since illegitimate children like all the others will be reared by the community which is everyone's true family. Every adult will be obliged to work about four hours per day in return for which he receives "labor credits."

Walden Two will succeed where other utopian communities have failed because it will be based on scientific psychology rather than on "guess." It will utilize the techniques of "positive reinforcement" and can dispense with force (and authority) from the moment of its inception. "Governments which use force are based upon bad principles of human engineering."[10] Conquest of the "old world" will be peaceful; once established in the midst of an existing society, the first Walden (or, rather, the first Walden Two) will eventually split into two communities, the process of fission continuing until the entire society will be absorbed (the conversion of the United States into a network of Walden Two's is expected to take about thirty

[9] See especially *Ibid.*, chap. 14, pp. 85 ff. for a summary of the principles of behavioral engineering.

[10] *Ibid.*, p. 162.

years). No political authority will be needed in the community, leadership being shared collectively by all concerned.[11] (Mention of the authority of the scientistic elite that carried out and presumably continues to carry out the cultural conditioning of all human beings to make them fit for group living is conveniently omitted.) Like politics, religion will also wither away: religious practices which adult converts bring to the community fall away little by little, along with other "bad" habits such as drinking and smoking. The fears and hopes which nourished religious beliefs are allayed and fulfilled here on earth.

There will be a substitute religion, observed on Sundays, which is a form of group therapy in which psychologists take the place of priests. There is also a set of moral rules—the "Walden Code"—to be fulfilled by all.[12] Life in Walden Two will be future-oriented, so that the study of history will also wither away. "History is honored at Walden Two only as entertainment. It isn't taken seriously as food for thought."[13] Along with the dead past, the dead person is also forgotten in Walden Two.

Walden Two is declared a live possibility rather than a piece of visionary speculation because it rests on the scientific discovery that human nature has no constant structure. Man has no nature, but only behavior. "We have no truck with philosophies of innate goodness—or evil, for that matter. But we can *make* men adequate for group living—to the satisfaction of everybody. That was our faith, but it is now a fact."[14]

The problem of the *summum bonum*, of the good life for man, does not trouble the managers of Walden. This is alternatively assumed as self-evident or as having been discovered by science. In any case the good life is a practical and not a theoretical matter and it has been fully realized within the confines of Walden.

One of the most extravagant expressions of the *libido dominandi* in the literature of political messianism occurs near the end of the book when Skinner has Frazier ascend a nearby hill and exclaim: "I look upon my own work, and behold, it is good." We are then

[11] *Ibid.*, pp. 193 ff.
[12] *Ibid.*, pp. 165, 166.
[13] *Ibid.*, p. 94.
[14] *Ibid.*, p. 163.

treated to a comparison between this benevolent behavioral engineer and Christ.[15]

Against this kind of reasoning, what thoughtful person can doubt that the *philosophia perennis*, true to its name, is as relevant today as it was in the past? What could be more valuable in the face of such a teaching than to remind contemporary man of the Aristotelian and Thomistic distinction between the moral and the productive sciences? While an engineer of bridges or roads can mold his materials in the shapes he wishes them to have and make them fulfill the functions he determines for them, the ends of man are given in his nature. For man, however disappointed the social engineers may be to discover this, has been made already. To attempt to impute to him a new character in conformity with scientific determination as to how he should behave can hardly result in the development of the creature known as man. The terribly simplistic assumptions of the benevolent would-be conditioners must be relentlessly examined by political theorists on behalf of a humanity that would be consigned to the clean, well-lighted dungeons of the closed society.

Herbert Simon and Harold Lasswell

A work like Skinner's *Walden Two* although assertedly based on science, openly claims to be a programmatic declaration and a recommendation for action. What is perhaps more surprising is to find blueprints for the closed society contained within the pages of the allegedly technical and value-neutral writings of certain behavioralist writers who take great pains to state their endorsement of the positivistic dogma regarding the separation of facts and values. Herbert Simon, the leading exponent of a behavioral "science of administration," insists that the "process of validating a factual proposition is quite distinct from the process of validating a value judgment. The former is validated by its agreement with the facts, the latter by human fiat."[16] However, as Herbert J. Storing has effectively demonstrated, this commitment to the positivist dogma does not prohibit Simon from committing the archpositivist heresy of deducing values from facts. He comes out in favor of "democratic institutions" which

[15] *Ibid.*, p. 246.

[16] Herbert A. Simon, *Administrative Behavior*, 2nd ed. (New York, Macmillan, 1957), p. 56.

separate "the factual and ethical elements in decisions." He rejects the view, that "philosopher kings . . . should establish the correct value system for the community" in favor of the "contrary theory" that "the community should decide—by the political processes we call democracy—what values are to be sought, and the administrator should be bound by those values."[17] What Simon chooses to call "democracy" is supported by the positivist fact-value distinction. Because values have no objective basis but are personal and subjective, there is no way of ranking them on the basis of knowledge. He rejects the Aristotelian claim of the *spoudaios* to speak with authority on ethical matters, remarking that there is "no 'scientific' or 'expert' way" of arriving at value-judgments, "hence expertise of whatever kind is no qualification for the performance of this function."[18] This position leads Simon to support—by clear implication rather than by direct statement because the latter would infringe upon his self-proclaimed abstemiousness toward introducing value-judgments into science—a philistine or Benthamite conception of democracy, where the lowest common denominator of mass opinion determines the standard of right and wrong for a society. The implicit argument goes something like this: values are a matter of opinion; the value judgments of citizens are of equal weight; the predominant values to guide a society are those of the numerical majority or its representatives. Bentham had expressed the same view when he wrote that "it is the greatest happiness of the greatest number that is the measure of right and wrong."[19]

[17] Herbert A. Simon, Donald W. Smithburg, and Victor A. Thompson, *Public Administration* (New York, Knopf, 1950), p. 22.

[18] Simon, *Administrative Behavior, op. cit.*, pp. 56-57.

[19] Preface, *A Fragment on Government*. It ought not to be necessary to point out that in rejecting the view that the majority properly determines the *values* of a society (or right is what the majority wills), one is not rejecting the view that under certain conditions, the majority properly determines which team of leaders is to occupy positions of governmental power and which program regarding the *means* of implementing just and reasonable ends is to be accepted. "Values" in this sense are the presuppositions, the foundations of the democratic process, and do not themselves emerge out of that process. To use an extreme but relevant example: no majority however sizeable can properly determine that it is right to exterminate a minority racial or ethnic group. The dignity of the human person is a value beyond the reach of majorities.

The burden of Simon's teaching, then, is to counsel the uncritical acceptance of prevailing opinion as the standard for political and organizational personnel in a society. Inevitably such a position deprives the political scientist of his normative or critical function and reduces him to the status of a technician, the means and methods man of a (hopefully) democratic polity. With Simon we are mired deeply in the confines of the cave; there is no basis or justification for the theorist to exercise his authority in order to challenge the prevailing value consensus. If he does choose to do so, it is only as a citizen whose opinion is no more weighty than that of any other individual, and his effectiveness as a political actor is determined by the quantitative support he can arouse for his own "value commitments."

As with many behavioralists, there is a contradiction in Simon's teaching between his passive democratism and his activist predilection for the engineering of consent. The obvious empirical fact that not all individuals are equally influential in the shaping of values leads him to speculate on techniques by which administrators can induce other people to support their objectives. Inducement, we are told, "operates on the individual's motivations so that he directs himself to behave as planned."[20] Indeed, he defines "knowledge of administration" as "knowledge of how to manipulate other human beings— how to get them to do the things you want done."[21] The only effective barrier to the development of an administrative despotism run by the shrewdest and most knowledgeable social engineers in Simon's system is the pluralism of organizations and manipulators. The de facto existence of multiple organizations and manipulators will result in an internal check and balance system which will prevent any single power-holder or group of power-holders from working its will. In addition, there is always that rather nebulous entity, the "democratic process." The mere fact that organizations survive in a

[20] Simon, *Public Administration, op. cit.*, p. 453.

[21] *Ibid.*, p. 22. Simon and his colleagues go on to admit that at least a certain kind of manipulation of other human beings is at variance with the "dignity of the individual human being" or "one of the most fundamental values in Western Civilization." However, the discussion on pp. 23-24 does little more than reveal once again the tension in Simon's thought between democratism and social engineering. He appears to favor "manipulation" by the "expert" *and* "participation" by the "clientele."

democracy shows that "they are being responsive to the goals and values promoted by the democratic political processes." As individual citizens, we have an opportunity to participate in the "procedures of accountability" established to prevent arbitrary and dictatorial behavior by administrative officials. "As individuals in a democratic society we can criticize surviving, and even flourishing, administrative organizations. Our criticism, if it becomes widespread enough, enters into the survival picture, becomes a part of the political process, and forces changes in administration." Simon concludes his supposedly hard and "realistic" textbook on public administration with a somewhat naive and idealist call for an "alert citizenry":

> If people are lethargic, the administrator may have a wide area of freedom of choice. If they are alert and willing to give some effort to their government, they may bring more of the administrator's decisions within the controls of the political process. If survival is the test of responsibility, an alert citizenry can change the conditions of survival. Today, as always, eternal vigilance is the price of freedom.[22]

By common acknowledgment, Herbert Simon is one of the leading exponents of the "behavioral persuasion" in contemporary political science. He deserves mention in this work because his writings reveal, more clearly than do those of most behavioralists, the bleak and retrogressive view of man and society which is implicit in the behavioralist orientation. The world he describes is that of calculating operators, who seek to maximize their desires for more security, status, and income. Simon's man is essentially the "voluptuary without heart" which Max Weber warned that modern industrialized society might produce. If man were in essence a creature of such shrunken stature, political science would have no alternative but to describe him. But Simon's "administrative" (or, one is tempted to say, "organization") man is a portrait of only one possible human type, and that one rather low on the character scale.

And always, below the banalities about vigilant citizens and the democratic process, one detects the whir of computers, ready to do more successfully than man can do himself the problem-solving which is assertedly the main function of human reason. In the "visible future," Simon has written, "the range of problems" which machines

<hr>

[22] *Ibid.*, concluding paragraph, p. 561.

can handle "will be coextensive with the range to which the human mind has been applied." This development will "force man to consider his role in a world in which his intellectual power and speed are outstripped by the intelligence of machines." Simon refers to the advent of the computers as the "new revolution" and expresses the hope that man will learn enough about the workings of his own mind to stay ahead of the machines.[23] Assuming that this hope can be fulfilled, its fulfillment would leave man as little more than a superbly trained mental technician, substantive rationality having been sacrificed to instrumental rationality on the altar of "scientific progress." Man, extolled by the psalmist as "little lower than the angels" is proclaimed by the behavioralist avant-garde as little higher than the machine. Here, indeed, we have the "hollow men" who inhabit the wasteland of T. S. Eliot.

The manipulatory attitude which one finds in Simon's writings is much more pronounced in the works of Harold Lasswell who, in some passages of his works, seems clearly to call for a marriage of behavioralism and a nearly full-blown political messianism. With Lasswell the caution that induces many like-minded behavioralists to refrain from blatant and explicit propagandizing on behalf of a brave new Comtean world is thrown to the winds, and we find his compositions shot through with programmatic declarations on how to achieve a new world peopled by new men.

In recent years, however, Lasswell's tendency to indulge in messianic propagandizing has been subjected to severe scrutiny by nonbehavioralist political scientists. In particular, the essays by Bernard Crick,[24] and Robert Horwitz[25] deserve mention.

Lasswell's objective has been to establish a scientific political

[23] Herbert A. Simon and Allen Newell, "Heuristic Problem-Solving: The Next Advance in Operations Research," *Operations Research* (January-February, 1958), pp. 8-10. I am in no sense advocating an obscurantist revolt against computers. They are here to stay. There have been impressive refinements in them over the past decade. Computers can perform many valuable technical functions with enormous efficiency. I object to the science-fiction aspects of some of the writing about computers, writing which utterly ignores the distinction between instrumental and substantive rationality, for example.

[24] Bernard Crick, "The Conceptual Behavior of Harold Lasswell," in *The American Science of Politics* (Berkeley, University of California Press, 1959), pp. 176-209.

[25] Robert Horwitz, "Scientific Propaganda: Harold Lasswell," in Storing, *Essays on the Scientific Study of Politics, op. cit.,* pp. 227-304.

theory which is sharply distinguished from and disadvantageously compared with traditional political philosophy. This scientific political theory will proceed from the "description" to the "prediction" and, ultimately to the "control" of human behavior. If one asks, control on behalf of what and by whom, the answer given by Lasswell is on behalf of a world-wide democracy or "free man's commonwealth" by an elite of social scientists. As a proponent of the positivist separation of fact and value, Lasswell can supply no objective basis for his commitment to the free man's commonwealth. However, as with Simon, there are repeated implications that this value commitment is quite consistent with, if not in fact derived from, the findings of science itself. The commitment is certainly presented as much more than an arbitrary and subjective opinion. In truth, it is a normative theory smuggled in under the guise of science.

Lasswell has been assiduous in his borrowings, and one finds strong traces of the influence of Comte, Marx, and Freud. Basically the intellectual atmosphere is similar to that of Skinner's *Walden Two*: to read Lasswell is definitely to enter the brave new world of scientism. To Lasswell, the social scientist is no mere detached observer, but, as the possessor of a comprehensive science of behavior, the potential archmanipulator of the human condition. As with Skinner, Lasswell does not conceive that the new knowledge will be put to any but benevolent purposes; his irrepressible optimism appears to be the only foundation for this confidence. *Savoir pour prévoir* is Lasswell's motto as well as Comte's. He is full of praise for the "emphasis on 'unity of theory and practice' in pragmatism and the traditional literature of Marxism."[26]

Lasswell's ultimate objective is very similar to that of Marx and other utopian writers: the elimination of conflict, anxiety, violence, war, "illusion," alienation, and "exploitation." Unlike Marx, however, he has rejected violence as the midwife of the new society in favor of propaganda. By skillful propaganda, a propaganda cognizant of the decisive role which economic and unconscious psychological factors play in shaping the beliefs and responses of people, the masses of mankind can be won over to a "free" and "enlightened" world. But the propagandists have to be instructed by the social scientists, who, as Horwitz suggests, are really "master propagandists." A basic problem is how to get the populace to render them the necessary deference

[26] Cited in *Ibid.*, p. 229.

204 POLITICAL THEORY AND THE OPEN SOCIETY

and respect to make their advice authoritative, but then this pre-sumably can also be accomplished by propaganda.

There is both a gentle and a hard side to Lasswell's teaching. Some of what he has to say sounds like extreme cynicism, and considerable effort is required to square it with the utopian sentimentalism of other passages. It is doubtful that there are two Lasswells, however, and he himself presumably would not recognize or admit any inconsistency. It is primarily a matter of shift in tone or emphasis. Throughout, Lasswell's objective is to secure for the greatest possible number of people the maximizing of indulgences and the minimizing of deprivations. Politics, he affirmed in the title of one of his best-known books, is the study of who gets what, when, and how. The Lasswellian message is essentially a counsel of enlightened self-interest. Man, a creature who seeks "safety, income, and deference," must be convinced that he can in fact achieve these values to the fullest possible extent only by cooperating with others in a polity which insures the successful organized exploitation of the natural environment. Within this context the adumbrated values will be widely shared.

The new social science will by the skillful use of propaganda, "education,"[27] and psychoanalysis, produce a new democratic man to inhabit the new scientistic world. The traits of the "democratic character" are described rather vaguely by Lasswell in a passage which seems to regard openness as a contentless form of sentimental (self-indulgent?) fellow-feeling:

> the democratic attitude toward other human beings is warm rather than frigid, inclusive and expanding rather than exclusive and constricting . . . such a person transcends most of the cultural categories that divide human beings from one another, and senses the common humanity across class and even caste lines within the culture, and in the world beyond the local culture. [The democratic character is] multi-valued, rather than single-valued, and . . . disposed to share rather than to hoard or monopolize.[28]

[27] "A legitimate aim of education," Lasswell has written, "is . . . to reduce the number of moral mavericks who do not share the democratic preferences." Quoted in Crick, op. cit., p. 196.

[28] Quoted by Horwitz in Storing, op. cit., p. 294. This statement, in a sense unexceptionable, is insufficiently grounded on a theory of love. It is possibly open to the objection raised by Max Scheler as to the cult of Humanity (see p. 106).

If the free man's commonwealth can be realized, power will wither away and coercion will be "neither threatened, applied, nor desired." The aim of what Lasswell has called "preventive politics" is thus clearly the prevention *of* politics. Although he speaks of the free man's commonwealth as a "developmental construct," Lasswell, like B. F. Skinner, puts forward a program for a messianic eternity within time. It would be a world without conflict, anxiety, tension, hostility, want, deprivation, or injustice and, one is tempted to add, without *man*.

Even assuming that the promised land could be achieved short of imposing some kind of totalitarian straitjacket, the point to recognize and of which political theory needs to convince thoughtful people, by persuasion rather than propaganda, is that it would not be worth realizing it. The Lasswellian future of mankind would almost certainly be a future of virtually unrelieved tedium, uniformity, and spiritual vacuity. Although man would gain in comfort, he would lose in dignity. This despite the fact that Lasswell—no doubt with complete sincerity, but on what metaphysical or ethical basis we know not—stoutly maintains his faith in the "dignity of man." Floyd W. Matson appears to have judged correctly in observing that for Lasswell the dignity of man is an unexamined assumption. This dignity is not "an inherent attribute of humanity" for Lasswell "but a strategic objective to be achieved in some rational future."[29] Certainly this idea of the dignity of man is very far from the dignity of the person affirmed by the theocentric humanist tradition in political theory. The dignity of the person prevents the manipulation of human beings in terms of any strategic objective.

Lasswell's democratic man would appear to be a shallow being who aims to please at the price of truth, to adjust at the price of integrity. Lasswell's dream of a free man's commonwealth is in fact more akin to a nightmare in which all the antihuman potentialities in modern culture assert themselves in total victory over the human spirit. It is depressing that such facts as the ambiguity of modern "progress," and the unrelieved spiritual torpor of a perfectly hygienic, "rational" (i.e., psychoanalyzed), secular, materialistic, uniform world civilization have to be pointed out to some of the most able and prominent intellectuals of our time, men whose influence might be employed to counter such tendencies rather than to glorify and enhance them.

[29] Matson, *op. cit.*, p. 110.

In his most recent book, *The Future of Political Science*,[30] Lasswell seems eager to enter the world of science fiction. He speaks of the necessity for a new declaration of rights for machines—the supercomputers, which (who?) have taken on virtually all the properties of human intelligence, even excelling that intelligence in certain respects. It seems that one of the urgent problems of political science in the future will be to devise ways to prevent the exploitation of "humanoids" (the supermachines) by man. Like other major problems of political science, this one is to be solved through team research in vast centers of advanced study. One wonders whether political science will have a future, if Lasswell's prognosis were to come about.

Floyd W. Matson has fittingly summarized the nature of the threat posed by extreme behavioralism of the Lasswell type to the freedom of the human spirit:

> The "science of democracy" depends for its initial plausibility upon the prior assumption of what might be called the democracy of science: that is to say, the assumption that the methods of natural science carried over rigorously and faithfully to the study of man move unmistakably toward an affirmation of human dignity and personal freedom. But we have already seen that in the hands of its most devoted missionaries, the natural scientists of behavior, this faith in social and political physics has produced with impressive regularity the vision of a techno-scientific future from which all contest and contingency have been removed; and with it a corresponding image of man—manipulated and managed, conditioned and controlled—from whom the intolerable burden of freedom has been lifted.[31]

The "Scientific Revolution" of Eugene J. Meehan

That a consistent commitment to logical positivism and behavioralism often goes hand-in-hand with a metaphysic—or, better, a

---

[30] Harold Lasswell, *The Future of Political Science* (New York, Atherton, 1965). Lasswell's concern for the humanoids dates back at least to his Presidential Address "The Political Science of Science," *American Political Science Review* (December, 1956), 976-997. He wondered when the new "supermachines" would be "entitled to the policies expressed" in the UN Declaration of Human Rights and feared that they might constitute a "biological elite capable of treating us in the manner in which imperial powers have so often treated the weak."

[31] Matson, *op. cit.*, pp. 114-115.

countermetaphysic—opposed to the open society is evident even among those writers who do not share the exuberant optimism and utopianism of Lasswell. Eugene J. Meehan, in a recent work on political analysis and the twentieth-century "scientific revolution," is considerably more cautious and skeptical about the possibilities of eventually eliminating all tension, conflict, and political controversy than are the other writers discussed in this chapter. He reminds one of some of the advocates of linguistic philosophy who, while excepting the basic premises of logical positivism, are conservative by inclination and refuse to opt for the brave new world of the benevolent conditioners. Unlike the conservative linguistic analysts, however, who assume that philosophy is a limited and technical activity and that all other areas of life, including that of religion, remain essentially unaffected by one's commitment to logical positivism, Meehan has the candor to state that of course these other areas *are* affected and that if one takes these scientific views seriously he will need to re-fashion his ethics and metaphysics. Meehan's world is no less bleak and unidimensional than that of Lasswell, however; the difference is that he does not indulge in Comtean-like, scientistic phantasies in a fallacious attempt to endow it with meaning.

Like Simon and Lasswell, Meehan rejects traditional political science—by which is meant virtually all serious writing about politics that occurred prior to the revelation of the truth of logical positivism in the midst of the Vienna Circle and much that has been written since that revelation—root and branch. Even today, he writes, it is very often the case that the student of politics works with "a set of assumptions and a *modus operandi* that differ only in detail from those employed by Hobbes and Locke, or even Plato and Aristotle."[32] This is unfortunate because "the tools that science and philosophy have developed in this century have made mincemeat of many of the older presuppositions of political science, and produced standards and techniques of very high quality that can be employed in their stead." The "edifice" of traditional political science "is, in part, beyond repair and worthy only of destruction. These conditions, among others, have made it difficult to attract first-rate minds to the field; it has been a very long time, for example, since a really good mathematician turned his attention to political problems. In sum, political

[32] Eugene J. Meehan, *The Theory and Method of Political Analysis* (Homewood, Ill., Dorsey, 1965), p. 5.

science can quite reasonably be held to lie in a shocking state of disrepair."[33]

Fortunately for political science, Meehan tells us, it need not remain indefinitely the preserve of second-rate minds. The discipline can be reconstructed in terms of new discoveries in epistemology and the philosophy of science. Around the beginning of the twentieth century an intellectual revolution took place:

> New techniques for acquiring knowledge, new criteria for judging the validity of claims to the possession of knowledge, and new analytic tools for refining the meaning of terms and raising the level of precision of logical inference were introduced more or less concurrently. Most of the early work was carried out by men intimately connected with science, logic, and mathematics: Bertrand Russell, Ernest Mach, Pierre Duhem, C. S. Peirce, Moritz Schlick, for example; or, somewhat later, Ludwig Wittgenstein, Rudolf Carnap, Morris Cohen, Ernest Nagel, A. J. Ayer, and C. G. Hempel.[34]

Natural science benefited enormously from these developments, and "a sustained attack on traditional philosophy, particularly ontology and metaphysics, reduced a surprising number of problems hitherto considered of the first order to piles of meaningless rubble."[35]

Although primarily a twentieth-century phenomenon, the "new philosophy" also "had roots in the past, particularly in the writings of Comte and his followers, in the works of Darwin and his interpreters, and above all in the work of David Hume."[36] In this intellectual revolution, "a number of disparate strands were combined in a single movement—empiricism, mathematical logic, linguistic analysis, skepticism, naturalism, and even 'scientism.' "[37] Despite certain differences between them, the various representatives were in agreement on their basic position, including the discovery that "empiricism" is "the only epistemic base for human knowledge."[38] The

[33] *Ibid.*, p. 6.

[34] *Ibid.*, p. 10.

[35] *Ibid.*, p. 11.

[36] *Ibid.*

[37] *Ibid.*, pp. 11-12.

[38] *Ibid.*, p. 12.

immediate consequences of the application of this new conception of philosophizing were most gratifying. Immense piles of philosophic rubbish, accumulated from over two millennia of speculation, were speedily dissolved by its cauterizing touch. Traditional philosophy was subjected to ruthless attack and forced to defend its own first principles for perhaps the first time since the speculative genius of the Greeks ran dry.[39]

Now it is unthinkable, according to Meehan, that "future generations of political scientists will not be profoundly influenced" by these salutary intellectual developments.

In the near future, if the signs of the present can be interpreted correctly, we can expect the political scientist to frame his goals, conduct his inquiries, and evaluate his findings using the framework molded by analytical philosophy and the philosophy of science, at least in those cases where the goal is explanation of empirical phenomena. In fact, it is a major defect of contemporary political science that it has thus far failed to absorb the intellectual standards available in philosophy of science as rapidly as it might.[40]

In the concluding portion of his book, Meehan turns his attention to the problem of bringing the value-system of the West more into alignment with the pace-setting occurrences in the philosophy of science. For at present two "fundamentally incompatible" schools of contemporary Western thought stand opposed to each other. Hitherto, the "clash of the two systems of thought—the one older, theologically-oriented, and 'traditional' and the other modern, scientific, empirical, logical, and antimetaphysical—was avoided for the most part, by the use of a crude but highly effective device; that is, the conflict was simply ignored."[41]

Meehan proposes an end to this compartmentalism, this separation of the canons of science and the standards of "social, political, and ethical discourse":

We often deplore the fact that politics is still carried on in terms adapted from the needs of the seventeenth century; how much more significant is the use of standards of normative judgment

[39] Ibid., p. 13.
[40] Ibid., pp. 14-15.
[41] Ibid., p. 237.

that date to the very inception of western civilization. The scientific outlook is a powerful force in the modern classroom, laboratory, or business, but it is usually left behind with the other paraphernalia of the vocation when the individual returns home to family and society and sets about enculturating his children.

This dualism needs to be abandoned. The separation on which it depends is highly artificial. Its consequences are wholly undesirable. Vocational, personal, and social judgments do not relate to three separate and distinct aspects of human life. They are generated by the same substructure of assumptions and beliefs about man, society, and the universe as any other intellectual construction. If the accumulated wisdom of science is a necessary guide and limit in one sphere of human thought, as it seems to be, then it should perform the same function in all others. Thinking that is qualitatively superior in science is also qualitatively superior in other areas of human thought.[42]

What Meehan proposes is a simple operation: the exorcism of Greek philosophy, Judaism, and Christianity from the consciousness of Western man. In the name of "science," he is striking at the basis of political science as it had been conceived. His honesty about what he proposes to do hardly compensates for the gargantuan ignorance regarding the contribution of classical and Christian *epistēmē politikē* which he exhibits on virtually every page of his book. Along with Lasswell and Simon, Meehan would destroy the possibility of the open society by severing our connection with the sources of our knowledge concerning the principles of right order in the psyche and in society.

Meehan's view of the history of Western political theory is a curious one, but its main point—hostility to the Greco-Judaic-Christian tradition—is clear:

> Unfortunately . . . it was not the lucid and critical thought of Greek science and empirical philosophy that survived, but the Platonic aberration. The supremacy of Christianity in the fifth century spelled the supremacy of Plato over Aristotle and the Hellenistics, of Orphism over skeptical rationalism. It was an intellectual catastrophe of unparalleled dimensions. The philosophy to which we are heir is rooted in the history of the early Hebrews and the mystic idealism of the divine Plato. It is an

42 *Ibid.*, pp. 238-239.

odd heritage indeed for a scientific-minded community. Fundamentally, it is oriental, mystical, idealistic, opposed to empiricism,
observation, individualism, and skepticism alike.[43]

"Even in the field of ethics," we are told, Christianity "was an
absolute loss."

It will be the task of the new "scientific political philosophy"
to rectify two millennia of error and superstition. Scientific political
philosophy "will be empirical and rational, in broad terms, and not
metaphysical. In practice, this amounts to a denial of the supernatural
and the extraperceptive until such time as perceptive evidence justifies
their acceptance."[44] It will not be necessary for political theorists of
the future to "postulate a universe without order, but we must understand that the order is imposed by man and not intrinsic in the
structure."[45] The anthropology of the new scientific political theory
will cut man down to size, for

> there is no reason to suppose that man himself occupies any
> special status except in his own value schema. In relation to
> what is already known, man is trivial and may not even be unique,
> for it is statistically likely that conditions similar to those on
> earth recur many times in the whole universe. Man lives on a
> minor planet, orbiting around a very ordinary main-sequence star,
> located rather stodgily in the middle regions of a moderately large
> galaxy that is only one of millions already identified through
> optical telescopes. The life span of mankind, taken collectively,
> is finite and trivial. The star that provides the energy that makes
> life possible is doomed by its own processes; eventually it will
> lose the capacity to generate energy from its own contents and
> leave earth either burned to a crisp or floating in space—barren,
> cold, and lifeless. The earth is a death trap and the possibility of
> escape . . . seems slight. Measured against the known universe,
> man is a puny thing indeed.[46]

---

[43] *Ibid.*, p. 241.

[44] *Ibid.*, pp. 246-247. Here it is proclaimed with breathtaking dogmatism that
sense experience has a monopoly of reality. The experience of the *ens realissimum* beyond the world of the senses is simply declared to be an illusion.

[45] *Ibid.*, p. 247.

[46] *Ibid.*, pp. 247-248.

"Man," we are told, "the most complex of all living things, thus emerges as the outcome of random associations and chance variations, interacting with an environment determined by natural processes."[47] As for those reactionary political scientists who benightedly persist in viewing man as a creature of nobility whose distinctiveness consists in his capacity to participate in the world-transcendent *logos*, Meehan has plans for them:

> Many of the techniques and methods, the points of view, and even the personnel employed in political science have passed their prime and are no longer useful. Past performance, whether by a concept or a person, is no guarantee of current usefulness, as every baseball manager knows and the editor of every learned journal ought to know but often does not. The need to eliminate what is no longer useful and what may be an impediment, is often as great as the need to add new things.
>
> The elimination of the mystical, the metaphysical, the meaningless, and the maximization of the use of empirical data in political theory is well within the range of possibility. Homo mensura, man is the measure of all things—so said Protagoras some 2500 years ago—and so it still remains.[48]

But what kind of man? A man emptied of all content, of all height and depth, of all grandeur and misery, as "barren, cold, and lifeless" as the planet he inhabits is ultimately destined to become. It this the kind of man who should be the measure?

Concluding Remarks

In the confrontation of Eric Voegelin and Harold Lasswell we can see clearly what is at stake in this seemingly academic battle between leading figures of two different wings of the political science profession. The issue involves nothing less than the quality and style of existence man leads on this planet: it is the issue of the open versus the closed society, of existence in the uncertain truth of the psyche open toward Being, and existence in the certain untruth of the psyche attuned only to immanent comfort and maximal self-indulgence. What is at stake in the revival of political theory is the survival and rediscovery, as opposed to the eclipse, of this very crea-

[47] *Ibid.*, p. 250.

[48] *Ibid.*, p. 260.

ture, man, "made in the image of God" and "nourished by one divine law." Without openness toward the experience of transcendence how is man to survive in anything more than the physical sense? However well-intentioned, the "humanism" of Lasswellian scientism is in fact the antihumanism of an immanentist, reductionist ideology.

It is undeniable that most of the champions of a new world civilization based on the values of scientism and immanentist activism intend their proposals to benefit humanity. In fact, with them, as earlier for Comte, humanity takes the place of the Judaeo-Christian God in their affections and their loyalty. The difficulties with this attempted substitution have been cogently analyzed by the French Jesuit Henri de Lubac in a work which, while technically falling within the sphere of theology, is actually in the deepest sense a work of political theory.[49] "The first step" in indicating these difficulties, according to Fr. de Lubac, is

> to show those who have realized that no end short of humanity itself deserves absolutely to be loved and sought—and there are many such men in many different camps, even in those which are most opposed to one another—that they are obliged to look higher than the earth in the pursuit of their quest. For a transcendent destiny which presupposes the existence of a transcendent God is essential to the realization of a destiny that is truly collective, that is, to the constitution of this humanity in the concrete. Otherwise it is not really for humanity that the sacrifice is made; it is still, despite assertion to the contrary, for other individuals, who in their transitory outward form contain nothing that is absolute and do not stand for any essentially higher value than those who are sacrificed to them; in the last resort it is all for one generation of humanity—the last—which is yet no greater than the others, and which will pass away like the others.[50]

Lubac reiterates what is central to the entire tradition of classical and Christian political theory: that it is theocentric humanism that most clearly illumines the principles of right order in society and so points the way to a truly human world. We cannot legitimately demand self-sacrifices from people on behalf of a God called "future society." Social humanism, in contrast to theocentric humanism, if sys-

[49] Fr. de Lubac, *Catholicism: A Study of Dogma in Relation to the Corporate Destiny of Mankind* (London, Barns, Oates, and Washbourne, 1950).

[50] *Ibid.*, p. 195.

tematically adopted, cannot point the way to a truly human world. "In a non-transcendent society, the reduction of man to his 'social relationships' will work inevitably to the prejudice of his personal interiority, and will beget a tyranny of some kind, however novel."[51] The "absolute temporalism" of a doctrine such as Marxism,

> not only indulges chimerical hopes and is untenable in itself; it is also something which cannot possibly be desired by mankind. It is the vision of an entirely monotonous world. It would be a most incomprehensible retrogression if men were satisfied with it, and the most frightful torment if they were not. Marx's social, historical man has only two dimensions, but the sense of the Eternal . . . will repair his loss.[52]

The behavioralism of Skinner, Lasswell, Simon, and others differs from Marxism in its rejection of violent means to achieve the new world as well as with respect to certain features of that world. Insofar as it is messianic, this behavioralism is a form of "soft" rather than "hard" messianism. But it has in common with Marxism the rejection of human existence in openness toward the world-transcendent ground. It also is in revolt against Greek philosophy, Judaism, and Christianity as the sources of experiential openness for Western man. The closed society is the premise—sometimes latent but always present—of the extreme behavioralist world-view.

TEN: POLITICAL THEORY AND THE OPEN SOCIETY

In the preceding chapters we have considered the nature of authentic political theory, sketched the broad outlines of its development as a tradition of inquiry, described the character of the movements which have been and continue to be opposed to the theoretical enterprise, and discussed the revival of political theory in our time with reference both to its contemporary representatives and

[51] *Ibid.*, p. 200.

[52] *Ibid.*, p. 201.

its immediate precursors. Other names than those of Voegelin, Strauss, Jouvenel, Oakeshott, and Arendt could be added to the list of leading figures who have contributed and/or are contributing to the revival of political theory. One thinks of C. J. Friedrich, J. H. Hallowell, Hans Morgenthau, and Yves Simon among professional political scientists, Karl Jaspers, Nicolas Berdyaev, and Jacques Maritain among philosophers, and Reinhold Niebuhr, Karl Barth, and Urs von Balthasar among theologians—to make only a beginning.

There is every reason to expect that political theory *will* have a future. It will not wither away or be superseded by a completely positivized political and social science. Of course the strength of countertheoretical movements of the positivist type remains massive, but there are encouraging signs that the attraction of a simplistic, reductionist positivism or behavioralism of the Lasswellian type is on the wane. Many social scientists who have been intrigued by the possibilities of achieving a "science of man" on the model of the natural sciences are beginning to recognize that these very natural sciences which serve as their model have themselves changed drastically. There is a new breed of social scientists who are far more cautious about the possibility of making exact predictions regarding human behavior than are many behavioralists. They reject the idea that by external, sensory observation one can learn all that is most relevant and significant about man, and they call for imaginative introspection as having a vital complementary role in the science of man.[1] We can expect a certain loosening up of rigidities among social scientists and a gradual subsiding of the obsession with quantification ("What we can't count doesn't count"). This does not mean that the whole social science profession or even a majority thereof will be doing political theory in the full sense. But it does mean that an intellectual atmosphere relatively conducive to the continuation and strengthening of the revival of political theory begun in our time may prevail in the universities. This augurs well for the future of political theory which, more than in the past, will depend upon the universities for its leading representatives. For the great institutions of higher learning continue to be, at least in part, bastions of resist-

[1] Floyd W. Matson's *The Broken Image* (New York, Braziller, 1964) is an unusually perceptive analysis of these developments. A very important book stressing the limitations of behavioralism in the social sciences is Michael Polanyi, *Personal Knowledge* (London, 1958).

ance to the supremacy of the practical-productive attitude so widely prevalent in other areas of society (hence the scorn for ivory tower professors sometimes encountered in popular discourse). This, despite the fact that in many institutions defenders of the liberal arts must resist strong pressures from those who advocate a practical-productive or almost exclusively vocational orientation to higher education.

Political Theory: Tasks for the Future

What will be the task of political theory in the coming decades? Obviously it will not be to elaborate a detailed political *program*, although individual political theorists may indeed offer as participating members of their communities specific suggestions for governmental policy, probably disagreeing with each other on matters of timing, means, and prudential judgments. When one speaks of the revival of political theory he does not mean that political theorists have formed themselves into a *party* with a cause. Political theories by their very nature do not organize themselves into any movement, and arch-positivist enemies of the revival of political theory need fear no sinister plot on the part of theorists to take over the power structure and consign their opponents to dungeons or exile. The theorists of the world will not unite to overthrow the nontheoretical establishment. Perhaps it is slightly ridiculous to forswear such nefarious schemes on behalf of the new political theory, but considering some of the misunderstandings that have arisen with regard to political theorists and the theoretical enterprise in recent years it seems necessary.

The role of tomorrow's political theorist will be essentially the same as that of his counterpart of today and yesterday. He will strive to exhibit in his life, work, and thought those qualities of openness, love of wisdom, concern with the perennial problems of human existence, realism, critical detachment, and intellectual integrity which were found to be the hallmarks of political theory in every age.[2]

As an inevitable by-product of his activity, orientation, and concern, the political theorist of the future will constitute an influence on behalf of the open society and in opposition to the closed society. By virtue of its very survival and existence, political theory contributes

[2] See Chapter 2, pp. 37-44.

indirectly to the fostering and maintenance of the open society. The open society, however, is not a political program. One can say of the open society, grounded as it is upon the freedom of the spirit, what Archibald MacLeish has eloquently asserted about freedom:

> To be free is not perhaps a political program in the modern sense, but . . . it may be something even better. The weakness of political programs—Five Year Plans and the like—is that they can be achieved. But human freedom can never be achieved because human freedom is a continuously evolving condition. It is infinite in its possibilities—as infinite as the human soul which it enfranchises.[3]

The possibilities are considerable that in the coming decades the United States will be the society most profoundly affected by the revival of political theory. It may well contribute substantially to the enrichment of the theoretical tradition. This would be a striking and novel development, to say the least, for hitherto America has been noted for its *lack* of political theory. As Daniel Boorstin, Bernard Crick, Louis Hartz, and others have pointed out, American political thought in the main has been publicistic and derivative, tending to an unquestioning acceptance of the basic premises of Lockean liberalism. One searches the American past in vain for evidence of a political philosophy which critically examines the basic assumptions of the American polity. Only in recent years has such a philosophy begun to develop, with intellectuals such as Walter Lippmann, Hans Morgenthau, and Reinhold Niebuhr obtaining a wide hearing for their critiques of basic American assumptions especially in the realm of foreign policy.

When one studies the contemporary revival of political theory, he is impressed by the fact that almost all of its leading figures either now live in and are citizens of the United States or have lived, taught, and worked there for long periods of their lives. Many political theorists found in America a refuge from Nazi totalitarianism. The American environment has proved congenial to the development of theory, and in no other country have the works of Voegelin, Strauss, Arendt, and others received so much attention. These and other European scholars have also made a profound impact on American

[3] Quoted in Kenneth W. Thompson, *American Diplomacy and Emergent Patterns* (New York, New York University Press, 1962), p. 31.

society through prolonged periods of teaching; many of their students now occupy important positions in the universities.

American society can in the future be expected to produce larger numbers of able political theorists and, perhaps, become the world center of political theory. This will not only be due to the nourishment and stimulus of leading scholars of European origin and intellectual formation. Basically, it will be attributed to the fact that America will be experiencing the full impact of the crisis of modernity. Indeed, it seems probable that the primary reason for the sympathetic reception in the United States of the theorists of the European exodus is that America has, so to speak, become ripe for theory.

Not ripe in the sense of readiness for decay, however. The relative absence of political philosophy in the America of the past has been explained by the youth of the society. Hegel's meditation that philosophy is like the "owl of Minerva that flies only when dusk is falling" is put forward as something akin to an historical law. According to this line of thinking, only at the close of a civilization (as, for example, with Plato and Aristotle in fourth-century Athens), only when a society has grown old does it begin to turn inward on itself and become reflective about its ends and purposes. If the philosophy of politics continues to take root and flourish on American soil, it will not be because that soil has become rich with decay. The United States is still young; what has grown old is not America, but modernity. It so happens that because of its technological advances and existential power the United States is at the forefront of modernity. As America and the wider Western civilization of which it is a part move from the modern to the postmodern age, they will be challenged to reflect upon the portent of this transition.

This will mean that all the basic questions of political theory will have to be considered afresh. What is a "developed society" and a "developed life"? Development for and toward what? What are the characteristics of the open society and open existence? Toward what does the human person open himself and with what does he attune his inner being when he is most fully a person? What is the life of reason and what is the basis of the claim that it is the highest life for man? What, indeed, is the foundation for the concept of the dignity of the human person as such? For the answer to these questions, or at least for their right consideration, one needs to understand political theory in the authentic meaning of the term.

Political Theory and a New Liberalism

American liberalism, and that of the West generally, must enter into a new phase in its development if it is to meet creatively and successfully the challenge and promise of the crisis of modernity and the advent of the postmodern age. The inherited doctrine of Lockean individualism, even as refurbished, softened, and adapted by the programs of the welfare state, is deficient and inadequate in coping with at least two major subcrises of the overarching crisis of modernity: the crisis of equality and the crisis of quality.

The crisis of equality is widely recognized to be the most pressing and urgent problem confronting American society. It also happens to be a fundamental human problem which is pressing and urgent precisely because it has been for so long unconscionably ignored. The traditional Lockean principles as expressed in the Declaration of Independence are inadequate to meet this problem because they rest on a defective theoretical base. The statement "all men are created equal" is absurd if taken in the literal sense and is the product of corrupt Enlightenment psychologizing assuming the mind as *tabula rasa* and all empirical differences among men as attributable to environment. Empirically we know that men differ widely in intellectual ability, leadership capacity, influence, energy, and talent. In sum, individual human beings are empirically unequal, although these inequalities are between individual members of the one human race and not between races. (The idea of the congenital inferiority of nonwhite peoples to whites is one of the pernicious pieces of science fiction of nineteenth-century racist ideology. De Tocqueville was acute enough to recognize it as such at the time when he acidly rejected Gobineau's views on "race-mixing" as the cause of the decline of societies.) This undeniable fact has led to the realistic reinterpretation of the statement in the Declaration of Independence to read, in effect, "all men should have equal opportunity to make the most of their capacities."[4] But it is well known that the liberal idea of equality

---

[4] As T. B. Bottomore has pointed out, frequently this expression is used in a narrow materialistic vein to mean "the opportunity to rise to a higher level" in society. *Elites and Society* (London, Pelican Books, 1966), p. 148. This highly competitive streak in liberalism, which views life as a race between atomistic individuals, somehow needs to be corrected in favor of the idea of a competition with oneself to rise above mediocrity to excellence. Excessive emphasis on competition with others can cripple and destroy the spirit.

of opportunity has meant relatively little to the millions of nonwhites in American society whose color has denied them equal opportunity in fact even when they have been guaranteed it in law. Equal opportunity is not much more than a phrase to the inhabitants of Watts, in which community the smoldering resentment and feeling of isolation of many Negro citizens burst out in rioting and violence in 1965.

To achieve effective and substantial equality of opportunity, the remaining indignities to nonwhite citizens must be rectified. But these remaining indignities tend to be in the private realm, the realm which hitherto liberalism has been reluctant to invade. A law against discrimination in the sale and rental of housing which is enforced will be strongly resisted by many on the grounds that it interferes with the right of association. And yet true equality of opportunity for the great majority of American Negroes and other nonwhites can prevail only after the humiliating enforced housing ghettoes in the large urban centers are broken up. These indignities in the social sphere impose an incalculable psychological burden upon those subjected to them. A similar breaking up of discriminatory patterns in employment will have to be accomplished. The supreme indignity of laws against interracial marriages, which are still on the statute books of numerous states, must be removed.[5]

Even if further legislation complementing the civil-rights statutes of recent years is enacted and effectively enforced, this will be merely a beginning of a mature confrontation with the crisis of equality. Legislation must be accompanied by a moral revolution, a *metanoia* on the part of the white majority. Every effort must be exerted to persuade the persons who compose the white majority to recognize in the interior core of their being the full, complete, essential equality of men as men. Without interior conversions of attitude, all the legislation covering exterior arrangements will be grossly insufficient.

While it would be utopian to expect that the myth of white racial superiority will die at once and while past experience gives every indication that many men will continue to place similarity in physique and skin color first in forming their social ties, there is no objective reason why impressive strides cannot quickly be made in the direction of a society which will be open horizontally to the inclusion of all, in full membership, regardless of color. This is a

[5] By its decision of June 12, 1967, handed down after this book was already in galleys, the Supreme Court had put an end to these pernicious "laws."

human and not a partisan issue. Political theory can do much to explicate the experiential basis of the equality of man as man. It is perfectly clear why racism must be combatted at once as a *practical* matter. Negro citizens have in increasing numbers lost patience with and faith in the society of which de jure if not de facto they are a part. A morally alive and sensitive political science has the task of pointing out the evils of racism *on principle*, regardless of the admittedly grave and serious pressures of the moment and the dangers of mounting violence.

What this means is that the political, cultural, moral, and intellectual leadership in America must take the initiative in providing the white majority an education in virtue, by example, by exhortation, through total commitment to the reality of man's essential equality. The onus of responsibility, the obligation to take and keep for decades the initiative in reaching out to the nonwhite world rests with the American white majority. Traditionally, liberalism has tended to separate politics and ethics, law and morality. There were certain historically valid reasons for this attempt and certain practical advantages have been derived from it. But in the area of the fundamental, essential equality and dignity of man, the area which is called "civil rights" but which really should be called "human rights," the distinction does not hold.[6]

A new and open liberalism would be at once blind to color and appreciative of racial diversity as an enriching and joyous fact of life. A multiracial society in a multiracial world must be seen as a glorious opportunity for the enrichment of all men, hardly as a source of difficulty and embarrassment. The new liberalism must reach out to embrace all men as brothers, all men as essentially equal. In other words, it must go beyond providing real and effective equality of opportunity for self-fulfillment to establishing a moral climate in which equality of essence is recognized and affirmed.

In Chapter Two, I wrote of the possible emergence in the postmodern age of a new type of liberalism. I called it "theocentric

---

[6] The hold which blatantly racist attitudes have had on even the liberal political mind in the U.S. until the very recent past is emphasized in Thomas F. Gossett's highly significant book, *Race: The History of an Idea in America* (New York, Schocken Books, 1965). A reading of Gossett's book will indicate the extreme urgency and necessity of contrition and *metanoia* on the part of the American white majority.

liberalism."[7] The revival of political theory can contribute much to the development of such a liberalism by pointing out the need for a reinfusion of liberal doctrine with the truth expressed in the theocentric humanist tradition. The source of modern, "secular" liberalism's belief in the dignity of man rests ultimately on his being experienced as existing out of the transcendental ground. To employ the Stoic formulation, all men are brothers because they have a common father. Man, as such, has dignity because through his own individual reason, *logos*, he participates in a unique way in the divine *logos*. This is the ultimate philosophical and experiential source of the faith of liberalism in the dignity of man and the essential equality of all men. Even those political theorists who cannot bring themselves explicitly to confirm the transcendent source of man's dignity—and who therefore fall short of a full-fledged theocentric humanism— nonetheless, by their very activity as theorists, contribute to establishing an atmosphere of experiential openness in which a theocentric liberalism can develop.

When one speaks of the new liberalism as a theocentric liberalism, it is not meant that all supporters of the new liberalism would be explicitly theocentric in their intellectual orientation. As to political style and the ultimate direction of policy, however, the theocentric perspective, rediscovered and reexpressed, is of essential importance. Considerable agreement can be reached on immediate practical objectives between theocentric and secular liberals. However, without the leavening influence of a theocentric humanism refashioned in response to contemporary intellectual developments and moral dilemmas, the new liberalism will not be fully adequate to deal with the challenges it faces. The need for the new liberalism to draw sustenance from a theocentric core, already apparent with reference to the crisis of equality, is particularly evident in the discussion which follows.

There is another and even more profound crisis, which ultimately includes the crisis of equality, and that is the crisis of *quality*. No one denies that the achievements of modernity are impressive in the external and quantitative sense, but no perceptive observer would make the same judgment concerning the interior quality of men's lives.

The equivocal nature of the modern legacy becomes clear when one considers that material progress can be bought at the price of moral retrogression and that technology or know-how can come to

---

[7] See Chapter 2, p. 36.

replace wisdom or knowledge respecting the ends of human life. The modern period is one of steadily increasing control over the natural environment, of improved health standards, increased longevity, decreased illiteracy, and improved techniques of transportation and communication. But it is also the period of totalitarianism, world wars, the threat of nuclear extermination, and increasing divorce, suicide, and crime rates.

The task of postmodern civilization will be to conserve—and to expand, far more successfully than has been done so far, to the non- or partially-industrialized societies comprising the vast majority of mankind—the quantitative, technological advances of modernity while correcting and reversing trends toward the squandering and misuse of these advances through spiritual and qualitative deterioration. With the increase in man's power over the phenomenal world there must be a heightened awareness of the need for moral restraint in the use of this power.

The postmodern age in America, and the West generally, promises to be one of unprecedented affluence and leisure. With the much-heralded but little prepared for advent of automation, shorter working days, and earlier retirement, the problem of leisure bids fair to become the central preoccupation of the age. It will become progressively more difficult for work to serve as an escape, a deliverance from contemplation and the life of reason, a balm for an otherwise nihilistic existence. The search for salvation in work, as described in the following passage by Emile Zola, will be available to fewer and fewer men:

> I had only one faith, one source of strength: work. I was held up only by that immense task I had laid on myself. . . . The work of which I speak is regular work, a lesson, a duty which I have assigned my self to make some progress in every day, even if only one step forward. . . . Work! Consider gentlemen: work forms the only law of the world. Life has no other Purpose, there is no other reason for existence, we all come into being only in order to do our share of the work, and then vanish.[8]

In any event, work is capable of providing only a temporary forgetfulness from confronting the ultimate and inescapable questions about the meaning and end of human life. Immersion in work for

[8] Quoted in Karl Loewith, *From Hegel to Nietzsche* (New York, Holt, Rinehart and Winston, 1964), p. 288.

its own sake is a reaction of desperation and despair and can scarcely offer lasting fulfillment.

As Aristotle explained long ago, work is not an end but a means to leisure. But leisure is not inactivity nor is it the same thing as recreation. Recreation itself is a means to work—to recuperation in order that one may do more work. Leisure is creative activity; it is preoccupation with other than necessary, productive tasks. It is the condition in which man, having acquired the requisites of life, can proceed to live well, to enter into the *bios theorētikos*.

All too often, for untold millions of people, the leisure afforded by modern industrial society is the occasion not for the good life, not for the life of reason, but for trivial, inane, and mindless diversions. The question posed to a new liberalism will be, therefore: what kind of an environment is it that will assist all those who choose to take advantage of their leisure to live well, not merely in the quantitative but also in the qualitative sense? How can men be assisted in heightening the quality of their lives, in employing their newly gained leisure to the development of the highest that is in them?

The open liberalism of the future will have to involve itself far more immediately and directly than ever before with providing richer cultural opportunities to increasing numbers of people. Again, earlier liberalism balks at such suggestions: leisure and culture are supposedly in the private realm and cannot be invaded by public authorities. Inevitably there are real dangers of censorship and/or indoctrination, for example, if government begins to lay down stricter guidelines for television programming, to sponsor programs of adult education, and to encourage through grants and subsidies music and the fine arts. Basically, however, an attitude of fearfulness toward greater governmental activity in these spheres is a hangover from the period of laissez-faire liberalism which views government as the inevitable enemy of human freedom, and which regards the amount of freedom in a society as coextensive with the size of the private realm. Thus, according to this line of thinking, the smaller the public realm and the larger the private realm, the greater the freedom in a given society.

The theoretical foundation for liberalism's advancement from the negative to a positive concept of freedom—freedom understood above all as spiritual development and growth—was laid as long ago as 1881 by T. H. Green in his signal essay on "Liberal Legislation and Freedom of Contract":

> We shall probably all agree that freedom, rightly understood, is
> the greatest of blessings; that its attainment is the true end of
> all our effort as citizens. But when we thus speak of freedom,
> we should consider carefully what we mean by it. We do not
> mean merely freedom from restraint or compulsion. We do not
> mean merely freedom to do as we like irrespectively of what it
> is that we like. We do not mean a freedom that can be enjoyed
> by one man or one set of men at the cost of a loss of freedom
> for others. When we speak of freedom as something to be so
> highly prized, we mean a positive power or capacity of doing or
> enjoying something worth doing or enjoying, and that too, some-
> thing that we do or enjoy in common with others. . . .

The "ideal of true freedom" wrote Green, is "the maximum of
power for all members of human society alike to make the best of
themselves"; seen in that light, the "freedom to do what one will
with one's own" is a means to a higher end: "freedom in the positive sense: in other words, the liberation of the powers of all men
equally for contribution to a common good."[9]

Welfare state liberalism, from the New Deal onwards, has done
much to correct such a negative view of freedom in the United States.
It has affirmed that government may and should legitimately undertake a policy designed to secure a certain minimal *material* condition
for all its citizens. What will be needed in the coming decades is an
awareness, similar to that professed by Green, that society also has a
responsibility to provide the human person with an environment
which encourages rather than represses the growth of the life of the
spirit in man. To paraphrase Richard Hooker, the aim of the body
politic is more than to "fat up men like hogs." Government is not
an abstract something removed from society, but a body of living
men. If the governmental elite has internalized a commitment to the
dignity of the person and the interior freedom of the spirit, then
the activity of government need scarcely be repressive of that freedom.
Freedom of the spirit, the capacity of the person to exist in openness
toward transcendence, can be repressed as easily by extragovernmental,
or social as by governmental, or political forces. Indeed, what is the

[9] Reprinted in J. R. Rodman's excellent selection of Green's writings, *The
Political Theory of T. H. Green* (New York, Appleton-Century-Crofts, 1964),
pp. 43-73 at pp. 51, 53. Cf. also Rodman's important introductory essay,
"Green as a Political Theorist," pp. 1-40.

diet of violence, banality, trivia, tastelessness, and utter mindlessness which prevails in so much of contemporary mass culture except a potent pressure against the development of freedom of the spirit? What is the quality of existence enjoyed by men who occupy their leisure time almost exclusively with these distractions? Of course it would be out of character for the new liberalism, which after all remains a form of liberalism, to advocate the censorship or suppression of these diversions.

Freedom of the spirit is not enhanced by suppression, but by providing alternatives for those who choose to take advantage of them. The test of any concrete program should be whether it serves, enhances, promotes, and is consistent with the dignity of the human person. If government were to use its vast resources (complementing the efforts of private philanthropy) to increase the number and variety of opportunities available for the creative employment of leisure time (for example by establishing a network of noncommercial, educational television stations, divorcing sponsorship from control of programming on commercial television, financing a nationwide program of adult education, subsidizing local opera groups, etc.), who would call this censorship and an invasion of freedom so long as the policy were carried out with common sense and responsible self-restraint? Power may ennoble as well as corrupt men. And there are other forms of power than that exercised by the governmental elite. Is not the excessive influence on American television of commercial sponsors who pander to the lowest common denominator of mass taste an exercise of power inimical to freedom of the spirit? Is it not rather censorship in reverse for that portion of the population which would respond if it could to programming designed to help them become aware of the rich legacy in the arts, letters, philosophy, theology, and science which was bequeathed them by the civilization of which they are part, not to have the opportunity so to respond?

Liberalism, the most undogmatic, flexible, and adequate of the political doctrines of the modern age, is capable of a new phase in its development. Liberalism would appear to be receptive to the leavening influence of political theory. One of the exciting possibilities of the postmodern period is that out of a dialogue between the new political theory and liberal doctrine there will emerge a new liberalism of the open society. Political theory will play an indirect role in this development, for the elaboration of doctrine will be the work of philosophically minded publicists.

The new liberalism, if it comes into being, will be based on a demythologizing of symbols that in turn rests on or goes hand in hand with the critical work of authentic political theory. Myths and abstractions regarding popular sovereignty, inevitable progress, atomistic individualism, and negative freedom (freedom as freedom *from*) will be replaced in the vocabulary of the new liberalism by symbols more adequate to reality. Like the political theory that nourishes it, the new liberalism will aspire to be "beyond ideology." It will focus upon the reality of the existing human person in openness toward the transcendental ground. It will recommend specific programs on the concrete basis of whether they contributed to the creation and maintenance of the open society, of a society dedicated to assisting in the full development of the distinctively human qualities in the men who comprise it.

While preserving the institutional achievements of the anthropocentric liberalism of Locke and Mill, a new, open, and at least implicitly theocentric liberalism will give more content and direction to the goal of individual self-realization on the basis of the articulated experience of openness toward transcendence and will discard rigid and unworkable dichotomies between the public and private sphere by citing the dignity of the human person, who develops himself within, through, and beyond, but not apart from society, as the alpha and omega of organized political action.

Regardless of whether the critical activity of the theorist in the liberal democratic West has the effect of impelling liberal doctrine into a new and creative phase in its long history, the work of the theorist proceeds because theoretical activity is pursued for its own sake and the prospects of success or failure at the practical level do not determine the magnitude of the theoretical revival or the ardor with which it is undertaken. The fact is that we live today in an intellectual climate which, despite the existence of strong counterpressures, augurs well for the continuation of the revival of political theory begun over the past two decades.

Political Theory and the Demythologizing of the Political Vocabulary

A cardinal task which political theory is always called upon to perform is the demythologizing of the political vocabulary. Symbols employed in the practical idiom are ordinarily in need of critical clarification before they are adequate for the description of reality. The deficiency of symbols at the practical level for contributing to the understanding of reality has been especially marked during the period of isms and ideologies, i.e., from around 1750 until the end of World War II. One of the exciting possibilities of our age is that the new liberalism (a political doctrine) could move closer to the kind of critical awareness one finds in authentic political theory. The revival of political theory can have a leavening effect upon an open liberalism of the postideological age. Thus, the demythologizing and deideologizing of the political vocabulary accomplished by the new political theory would also be reflected in the language of the new liberalism whose newness would consist in nothing so much as in the discarding of ideological blindfolds to reality and an acceptance of the realities of the human person in his total existential situation.

One front on which the battle for demythologizing must be waged has to do with the "progress rhetoric." In the context of the progress rhetoric, the problem of the good life for man and society is shelved and the goal of human social action is found by the simple operation of extrapolating present trends in the exterior life of modern industrial societies. The idea of the developed society (if indeed it may be called an idea in view of the rather thoughtless way it has been injected into the current political vocabulary) is utterly inadequate as a symbol for articulating the end toward which human societies should presumably aspire.

As one author has aptly expressed the matter, the idea of a developed state is a copy or approximation of American and western European democracies, other states being viewed as pathological in relation to this model.[10] Such an approach is parochial and ethnocentric and carries with it an only thinly concealed arrogance. It is based on an uncritical exaltation of modern western industrialized societies as model societies, thereby betraying ignorance of or insensitivity to certain pathological features of those societies themselves as well as the immense cultural achievements of a so-called underdeveloped society like India. These pathological features of modern Western

[10] Ann Ruth Willner, "The Underdeveloped Study of Political Development," in World Politics, XVI (April, 1964), 468-482 at 471-472. She warns of a "latent ethnocentricism" in the current literature. This essay deserves to be read carefully; it is an acute and trenchant analysis of the defectiveness of so much of the current literature regarding political development.

societies include high divorce, crime, and suicide rates, mass loneliness, anomie, the debasement of cultural standards, egoism, the idolatrous worship of physical comfort, the loss of joy and meaning in work, spiritual vacuity, and the crowding out of the picture of contemplative and aesthetic activities in favor of productive, technocratic activity. While there are aspects of the modern achievement that contribute to enhancing the dignity and nobility of the human person, modernity without restraint would destroy that dignity and establish a closed society.

Not infrequently those scholars who employ the "underdeveloped" or "developing" and "developed" terminology also use the terms "traditional," "transitional," and "modern" in an identical way.[11] Such a vocabulary is scarcely adequate for political analysis. Tradition cannot be regarded as something utterly to be scrapped because all societies, including so-called modern societies, have a substratum of tradition, a network of ways of behaving inherited from the past which is vital to their existence. A society entirely without tradition would be a society without memory, without a history, a wasteland of the spirit. It would be the kind of society envisaged by Antonio Gramsci, the Italian Communist intellectual, about whom Aldo Garosci has observed: "His ideal was truly a country without 'superstructure,' with the minimum possible inheritance from the past and characterized by concentration on the problem of production —that is, material production of 'objects,' of 'goods,' not of services."[12] Similarly every society is "transitional" in the sense that it is in the process of changing from what it is to something that is different in many respects. No society is entirely static. Every society is in a measure traditional and transitional at once.

Throughout this volume the thesis has been argued that the open society, not the modern society, is the valid goal for human beings to seek in their collective efforts. To formulate the matter in this way means to concentrate upon substance rather than form and interior depth rather than external "greatness." The open society is a paradigm to be approximated but never fully attained. It is not a static entity that can be realized once and for all. There are many

[11] Cf. for example Joseph P. La Palombara, *Interest Groups in Italian Politics* (Princeton, Princeton University Press, 1964).

[12] From the essay "Totalitarismo e storicismo nel pensiero di A. Gramsci," in Aldo Garosci, *Pensiero politico e storiographia moderna* (Pisa, 1954).

conceivable varieties of the open society, not all of which need necessarily be "democratic" precisely in the modern western signification of this term. Furthermore, should a given society achieve for a time the maximal possible degree of openness there is always the danger of retrogression and decline from these heights of intellectual and spiritual renaissance because of inimical external pressures or the failure of succeeding generations to preserve the gains so arduously won.

In this context, a correction of the Platonic teaching as expounded in the *Republic* regarding open existence and the open society needs to be indicated. Plato appears to have corrected the defect himself in the *Laws*, but the point needs to be made with particular emphasis and explicitness. In the *Republic*, men are divided into three types in accordance with the "myth of the metals." The philosophers have gold mixed with their natures, while the soldiers are constituted of silver, and the workers of iron and brass. Here the danger of derailing into the idea of distinct (closed and open) human natures presents itself. In the *Laws*, on the other hand, human nature as such—all men in general—are seen as puppets subject to the pulls of different cords, i.e., the golden cord of reason and the iron cord of appetite. The myth of man as puppet, expressed in the *Laws*, is the necessary corrective to the myth of the metals found in the *Republic*.

In the *Republic*, the philosophic character types are put forward as a separate class of men, and the best regime is sketched as a static entity. This is an oversimplification of existential reality. At one level, we can and must speak of an individual or a society as characteristically possessing the tendency toward openness; indeed, this tendency is what we mean by "character" or *ethos*. But in an equally basic sense it is true to say that openness is a condition, whether for societies or men, only fleetingly attained, then lost, then possibly recovered. Openness is a moment of metaphysical insight. Wherever there are men and societies the possibility of achieving openness at a crucial moment of reflection or decision is present—as is the possibility of decline into the defensive, routine, anomic, antagonistic, or other types of reaction of the closed mentality. The capacity for openness and its loss is a quality of man as man. There are, then, in one sense, no philosophic character types and no societies oriented to the truth of philosophy, but in every life and in every society there are—even if inadequately recognized, explored, or developed—philosophical moments.

The fact of the fleeting character of openness is at once a source of despair and of hope: despair that the gain can so easily be lost, the ascent to the spiritual heights so briefly maintained; hope because even in the seemingly most closed and repressed existential situation the possibility of renewal and a decisively new beginning exists. It is for the latter reason that one dares to affirm, as a realistic proposition, that human existence, as such, cannot and will never be perpetually enslaved within the cave of purely one-dimensional activity, that fissures will inexorably appear in the walls of even the most totalitarian societies. On the other hand, the same realistic awareness warns against regarding the open society as an achievement which, once realized to any significant degree, can be frozen in time. As Arendt has written, every generation is a new beginning. It must, we would add, determine for itself the quality of its existence and the degree to which it avails of the source of strength available to lift it from every fall, the source apprehensible through revelation, philosophy, and the untutored consciousness of simple men of good will.

The substance of a body politic inheres in the experiences of order which motivates its citizenry and above all its ruling strata. This means concretely that the political education of the ruling strata is a matter of the greatest theoretical and practical significance. Political education is understood here in the broad sense to include both formal education in political science and related subjects and the cultural traditions assimilated from earliest childhood through the family, the religious community, and the school. Because the higher religions transmit the experience of right order in its most fully differentiated form throughout a society, the question of the vitality of the religious traditions of a society and their continued relevance for the political and societal elites must be matters of basic concern for political science as a study of right order.

Political education would also be a central preoccupation of the new liberalism. While legislation can do much to create the conditions for a relatively open society, the quality of a society's intellectual and spiritual atmosphere is ultimately dependent on the activity, vision, and influence of nongovernmental intellectual, moral, and cultural elites. In an open society the political education of the citizenry (in the widest sense) can hardly be the monopoly of government, nor can it be directed by the government elite. But it ought to be the concern and preoccupation of all those who are politically interested and active, and its importance can be constantly underscored by the spokesmen of the new liberalism. Furthermore, governmental leaders can take a far greater role than they have done on the whole in helping to create a moral climate conducive to the open society by learning to speak again, by learning to do for contemporary society what Pericles was once able to do for Athenian society. As Michael Oakeshott has said, politics is three-quarters talk, and our leaders must learn again the art of inspiring men with evocative and moving verbal images, images that are true to the human condition.

The entire democratic rhetoric is in need of overhauling in order to bring to light once again the inevitable importance of elites and the fact that the democratic machinery does not automatically insure the existence of a community in ordered freedom. Democratic machinery—such as, periodic elections, representative institutions, the free competition of political parties, the rule of law, and procedural guarantees—like any machinery is not an end in itself but a means to an end. The defense of democracy should rest on the quite tenable, empirical proposition that such institutions and procedures as those described above are the most adequate structural means for promoting and preserving conditions conducive to the open society that have thus far been devised for industrialized societies with a high rate of literacy and social mobility.

Recognition of the fact that elites rule in all societies, including those which may plausibly be labelled democracies, is open to the objection that such recognition in itself may encourage insolent domination or even repression and exploitation by the elites themselves. And indeed there is always the danger of debasement and misunderstanding of elite theory to justify unmerited privilege. Any elite theory properly conceived, however, will carry with it certain counterweights to such a development, the most important being the recognition of fundamental human equality. At the risk of being repetitious, it must again be emphasized that men are essentially equal but empirically unequal. They are equal as persons with inviolable dignity. They are unequal in skill, intelligence, industry, prudence, common sense, motivation, capacity for literate expression, and ability for leadership. Those who find themselves in positions where even in a minor way they can influence the course of affairs in a society need to recognize that for their position to be justified they must act responsibly, respecting the essential dignity of those affected by their actions. Elites, whether in government, society, or the world of culture must see themselves as representatives, as persons who act and speak on behalf of the whole community of persons of which they are a part. And they are only a part; they are not the whole.

One absolutely fundamental requirement for an adequate theory of politics as well as for a new, demythologized liberalism is the total eradication of any vestiges of racist thinking that may remain in the intellectual and spiritual atmosphere. Racism must be exposed as a vicious poison. If the person, as such, is the carrier of inviolable dignity, there can be no justification on principle for erecting any barriers whatsoever between men on the supremely irrelevant ground of color or ethnic origin. In an open society based on the dignity of the person, every effort must be made to encourage racial diversification of elites, assuming the multiracial composition of its people, even if this should mean, for example, a conscious policy of favoring for a time the entrance of nonwhite persons into elite positions as against equally well-qualified whites. As has previously been said regarding the racial crisis in America, the brutal fact of racism and racist thinking, even if of the "genteel" variety, must be squarely recognized and confronted, and the predominant initiative and effort must come from the white sector. The white sector must willingly assume the task of redressing generations of injustice inflicted on nonwhites who have been hurt and inwardly wounded by exclusion on grounds of race more deeply than most members of white majorities have so far given any evidence of comprehending. In this effort of opening the elite horizontally to widen the racial base, all attitudes of paternalism and condescension must be discarded. This effort must be a movement of equal human beings to other equal human beings who, because of cruel accidents of history and not by any realities of nature, have been wounded and hurt in their inner being.

Conclusion: The Open Society and the Future

It is often said, implied, or assumed by the proponents of behavioralism and scientism that theocentrically oriented writers are dogmatic, intolerant, reactionary, and repressive, and that their objective is to impose a uniform ideological straitjacket on the world.

However, if the argument of the last chapter has any merit, it could much more plausibly be argued that these qualities of mind are actually exhibited by the extreme behavioralists themselves. For what the latter advocate is an ultramodern world; a universal civilization closed to the freedom of the spirit, to the experience of transcendence, to activities above and beyond the productive, the utilitarian, and the functional. It will be an efficient, bureaucratized, uniform, secularized, rationalized world in which men behave and manipulate rather than act and live.

Theocentric liberalism would reject such a world—and any uniform world—on principle. For the influence of theocentric liberalism would be on behalf of a postmodern, as distinct from the ultramodern, world (or the clean, well-lighted habitat of the behavioralists). The postmodern epoch would be a period full of possibilities and fresh attempts to reapply the discoveries of the great intellectual and spiritual *virtuosi*—both of East and West—to the problems of contemporary man. Although one could predict the basic patterns of an ultramodern "civilization"—which will be all too deadening and uniform—the postmodern world would abound in variety. The latter would be a world open to the unexpected. This is not to say that routine, mechanization, and spiritual vacuity would have disappeared. Human existence would remain human existence, which means that in the future as in the past there would be prolonged periods of spiritual aridity for individuals and even societies. The open society would remain as a paradigm and a possibility, however, always there to be achieved at least in part and at least for a time.

Thus, a new liberalism, a postmodern liberalism, would be critical rather than assertive; it would adopt a listening, interrogative attitude. It would listen to the past and the present. It would understand again the sources of its own openness in Greek philosophy, Judaism, and Christianity. It would be appreciative of the different types of openness in the great nonwestern civilizations with which it would delight in having increasing communication. It would recognize that there is a variety of ways in which the open society may be approximated and that other civilizations have much to teach in this regard.

Were such a new liberalism to take root and flourish in the United States it would mean a new style and direction respecting American influence around the globe. The influence of America, of course, would remain great—inevitably as a result of its existential power. But it would be exercised in a new way. The greatest care would be taken by a new, critical, open liberalism to avoid imposing elsewhere replicas of institutional forms and ideas happily rooted in America and the West but which are not, without significant alteration and adaptation, transferrable to societies with different political and cultural traditions. While recognizing the vital importance of the balance of power in maintaining the peace, it would not overextend and place too much reliance upon its own military power in an attempt to prevent inevitable and unperilous adjustments of that balance in a world in which even the Communist states are moving toward multipolarity. It would recognize that men in Communist systems are also men, and would follow the advice of Pope John in distinguishing between "error and the person who errs."[13] If they are men they can be reached in time, for they share potentialities for openness and freedom of the spirit with all men. They share a common human nature and they possess inviolable dignity. With patience, the monolith can be expected to soften further and the process of demessianizing the Communist ideology to continue. While the open society must receive minimal protection by power, it—or better the many varieties of it—can truly advance only at the level of spirit and through the leavening of the spirit.

The open society would, of course, exist in this world, which means it will exist in a political world, a world of power. Its leaders will need to be skilled in the pragmatic exercise of power. But power is not enough: it is not the *summum bonum*. Future historians should

[13] Despite certain quasiutopian passages, John XXIII's encyclical *Pacem in Terris* remains perhaps the most eloquent, moving, and effective anticipation of the new theocentric liberalism in the entirety of contemporary political thought. His teaching regarding the centrality and dignity of the person is unexceptionable. Mention should also be made of another significant encyclical, *Populorum Progressio* (On the Development of Peoples) by Paul VI. Paul's letter, in addition to explicating further the principles of theocentric humanism as they bear on contemporary problems of political development in the world, frankly discusses the enormous dangers inherent in the grave economic imbalance prevailing between the wealthy minority and the poorer majority of mankind. His remarks on the debasement of raw material prices in the world market and the dangers of unregulated international economic competition between stronger and weaker powers in particular demand careful consideration. Cf. *The New York Times*, March 29, 1967, for the complete text of the encyclical.

be able to say of American society what Werner Jaeger observed about fifth-century Athens: that it is a society in which "spirit and power are balanced in marvelous equipoise." Whether America is to approximate more closely the Athens or the Sparta of the postmodern period now hangs in the balance.

The struggle vis-à-vis Communism will take a different turn if guided by the principles of a new liberalism of the type described in this chapter. The struggle will only incidentally be against Communism: it will be for the open society. Marxist-Leninist ideology will inevitably fall into unflattering relief when seen in the light of the new liberalism, for Marxism-Leninism is not a liberating or progressive but a reactionary force. The closed society advocated by Marxist-Leninist ideology is emphatically not the inevitable wave of the future. There is every reason to hope, indeed to expect, in view of recent changes within the Communist world itself, that the age of closed ideologies will come to an end in good time also in that third of the world officially committed to it.

The new liberalism would not be a counterideology, however. It would not be capable of reduction to a simplistic catechism. There will be no Liberal Manifesto. It would not even be a minimal civil theology as Plato understood the term. It would rather be a doctrine, flexible, imaginative, and inventive, growing out of a new attitude toward existence and reflecting a new style of existence which also would have in it something reminiscent of an attitude and a style that is very old: the *metanoia* presupposed in classical philosophy, Judaism, and Christianity. An open society founded on the new liberalism would not defeat or repress its intellectual opponents—the champions of ideological and messianic modes of political thinking whether within or without the society—but would seek to win them over gradually, by example, by the force of a supremely liberating idea grounded on the reality of the existing human person in all the richness of his experience.

The new liberalism, like the political theory nourishing it, would be neither left-wing nor right-wing, nor would it be a doctrine of the center. These categories have little bearing on reality and are hangovers of the age of ideology. It is time that they be excluded from serious political analysis. The new liberalism would be new precisely in that it could not be contained within the old categories. If any adjective were to describe it, it could be "radical," in the sense of *radix*, the root, i.e., going to the roots. The new liberalism would exhibit the spirit of a theoretical radicalism, which is at the same time the highest form of realism. Thus we can say that for both the political theory and the liberal doctrine of the open society, radicalism is the true realism and realism the true radicalism.

The frequent use of the conditional tense is an indication that the advent of a theocentric liberalism of the type described in America and elsewhere in the West is hardly an inevitable development. History does not deal in inevitabilities, but is the outcome of action by responsible human persons who may or may not seize initiatives and possibilities. T. S. Eliot once wrote that a Catholic is a man who has absolute ideals and moderate expectations. This observation might be cast in the form of a recommendation as the proper attitude for all men who grapple with the problems and mysteries of human social existence. The political theorist and the realistic publicist will know that between the paradigm and its actualization, a great gulf is fixed. In the realm of the spirit the future may be characterized by mediocrity rather than excellence, by vacuity rather than richness, by triviality rather than nobility, by routinization rather than creativity, by egoism rather than compassion, by greed rather than charity. But it need not be so. If we are to see the advent of at least a partial realization of the open society in our time, the *sine qua non* thereof is vision, for "where there is no vision the people perish." The major task of political theory is to illumine the sources of that vision, to elaborate a paradigm of the open society. The vision of the open society would serve as the foundation of a new liberalism. The achievement of the open society in our time rests partly on the circumstances of the world power struggle and partly on the success of the revival of political theory and the new liberalism it hopefully will inspire.

APPENDIX ❧ Bibliographical Notes

One of the signs that political theory is far from dead in our time is the appearance of a number of excellent general works on the history of political thought which show a keen awareness of the nature of philosophical inquiry and the inadequacy of interpreting all political thought as ideological or publicistic in character. We include here as particularly worthy of mention John H. Hallowell, *Main Currents in Modern Political Thought* (New York, Holt, Rinehart and Winston, 1950); Lee Cameron McDonald, *Western Political Theory: The Modern Age* (New York, Harcourt, Brace & World, 1962); Leo Strauss and Joseph Cropsey, eds., *History of Political Philosophy* (Chicago, Rand McNally, 1964); and Sheldon S. Wolin, *Politics and Vision* (Boston, Little, Brown, 1960). Indispensable for the Judaic heritage and Greek philosophy is Eric Voegelin, *Order and History*, 3 vols., (Baton Rouge, University of Louisiana Press, 1956, 1957), and for medieval political thought Alois Dempf, *Sacrum Imperium. Geschichts-und Staatsphilosophie des Mittelalters und der politischen Renaissance*, 2nd ed. (Darmstadt, Wissenschaftliche Buchgemeinschaft, 1954). George H. Sabine, *A History of Political Theory*, 3rd ed. (New York, Holt, Rinehart and Winston, 1961) remains a classic which, in a negative way, is a defense of political theory against ideological thinking. Sabine is a skeptic in the genuine sense.

The positivization of political science (especially American political science) is brilliantly treated in Arnold Brecht, *Political Theory: The Foundations of Twentieth-Century Political Thought* (Princeton, Princeton University Press, 1959), and Bernard Crick, *The American Science of Politics* (Berkeley, University of California Press, 1959). Roland Young, ed., *Approaches to the Study of Politics* (Evanston, Ill., Northwestern University Press, 1958), is a good indicator that despite the rather sweeping claims of Richard Snyder in his essay on the "decision-making" approach, behavioralism has not carried the day. The discipline has entered a period of reexamination and questioning of its goals and methods.

On ideology and political messianism, Norman Cohn, *The Pursuit of the Millennium* (Fairlawn, N.J., Essential Books, 1957) is a detailed account of chiliastic speculation in the high middle ages. It is in truth essential background reading for nineteenth-century developments. J. L. Talmon's two volumes, *The Origins of Totalitarian Democracy* and *Political Messianism: The Romantic Phase* (London, Secker and Warburg, 1952 and 1960), despite some controversial pages on Rousseau, is a rich mine of source material on messianic ideology from the French Revolution to the middle of the nineteenth century. Especially valuable for unearthing the roots of Nazi racist ideology is Hannah Arendt, *The Origins of Totalitarianism*, 2nd enlarged ed. (Cleveland, World Publishing, 1964), which also contains her masterful essay "Ideology and Terror: A Novel Form of Government." Albert Camus, *The Rebel* (New York, Vintage Books, 1956), is unrivaled as an exposition of the perils of ideological thinking. With this work, Camus established himself as one of the major political theorists of our time. Also important, on Dostoevski, Comte, Nietzsche, and Feuerbach, is Henri de Lubac, *Le Drame de l'Humanisme Athée* (Paris, Editions Spes, 1959). The best interpretive account of Tracy and Marx on ideology is Hans Barth, *Wahrheit und Ideologie* (Zurich, 1945). Two general works of interest on the subject of ideology are Arne Naess, *Democracy, Ideology, and Objectivity* (Oslo, 1956), and Judith N. Shklar, ed., *Political Theory and Ideology* (New York, Macmillan, 1966).

The reductionism and rigidity of logical positivism in its most extreme and consistent form may be found in Rudolf Carnap, *The Unity of Science* (London, Routledge, 1934) and *Philosophy and Logical Syntax* (London, Routledge, 1935), as well as in A. J. Ayer's well-known tract, *Language, Truth & Logic*, 2nd ed. (London, Gollancz, 1958). This work has had a very wide circulation since its first publication in 1936 and has acquired the status of a basic text. Barbara Wooten's *Testament for Social Science* (New York, 1951) is a militant apologia for the behavioralist viewpoint. More moderate and open examples of the behavioralist outlook—and, again, let it be noted that what we can call behavioralist social and political science runs a gamut between messianic scientism and near-eclectic empiricism in the broader sense—are Heinz Eulau, *The Behavioral Persuasion in Politics* (New York, Random House, 1964), and Vernon Van Dyke, *Political Science: A Philosophical Analysis* (London, Stevens & Sons, 1960). The latter describes himself as a proponent of "common-sense positivism." See also Avery Leiserson, "Problems of Methodology in Political Research," *Political Science Quarterly* LXVIII: 558–584 (1953) for an indication of how even a relatively moderate brand of positivism narrows and shrinks the field of inquiry regarded as the proper business of the political scientist qua political scientist.

Floyd W. Matson's *The Broken Image* (New York, Braziller, 1964) is a clearly written and perceptive account of how reductionist behavioralism is meeting with resistance in the disciplines of psychology, sociology, and anthropology. See also in this connection Peter L. Berger, *Invitation to Sociology: A Humanistic Perspective* (London, Pelican Books, 1966).

T. D. Weldon has made the most sustained and interesting attempt thus far to apply the techniques of linguistic analysis to politics. See his *The Vocabulary of Politics* (London, Penguin Books, 1953) as well as his essay "Political Principles" in P. Laslett, ed., *Philosophy, Politics, Society* (Oxford, Blackwell, 1956). Another example of this orientation is Margaret MacDonald, "The Language of Political Theory" in Anthony Flew, ed., *Logic and Language*, first series (Oxford, Blackwell, 1952), pp. 167–186. Despite the withering attack to which it was subjected by the champions of linguistic philosophy in Great Britain, I regard Ernest Gellner's *Words and Things* (London, Gollancz, 1959) as the most perceptive account published so far of the limitations and inadequacies of linguistic philosophy. The storm aroused by the book is wittily described in Chapter One of Ved Mehta's *Fly and the Fly-Bottle* (London, Pelican Books, 1965).

The book by I. M. Bochenski, *Europäische Philosophie der Gegenwart*, 2nd ed. (Munich and Bern, Francke Verlag, 1951) is a classic which deserves to be read by every serious student of recent and contemporary philosophy. After an introductory chapter characterizing the temper of twentieth-century philosophizing in juxtaposition to that of the nineteenth (the century of system-building par excellence), Bochenski proceeds to analyze neopositivism, Crocean idealism, the neo-Kantians, Bergson, Husserl, Scheler, Heidegger, Sartre, Marcel, Jaspers, Hartmann, Whitehead, and neo-Thomism.

James Meisel's *The Myth of the Ruling Class* (Ann Arbor, University of Michigan Press, 1958) despite its unfortunate title, is a first-rate treatment of Mosca's political teaching. It also deals briefly with Dorso's revision of Mosca. A useful chapter on Mosca, Pareto, and Michels may be found in Stuart Hughes, *Consciousness and Society* (New York, Knopf, 1953). T. B. Bottomore's *Elites and Society* (London, Penguin Books, 1966), repays reading for the way it grapples with the problem of the equality of man and the indispensability of elites.

Michael Oakeshott has collected a number of his essays written in the now defunct *Cambridge Journal* and elsewhere over the past two decades in *Rationalism in Politics* (New York, Basic Books, 1962). It is to be hoped that he will decide to publish a new edition of *Experience and Its Modes* (Cambridge, Cambridge University Press, 1933), now virtually unobtainable. A little known essay by Oakeshott on the meaning of representative democracy may be found in Albert Hunold, ed., *Masse and Demokratie* (Zurich and Stuttgart, Eugen Rentsch Verlag, 1957). Then there is Guy Griffith and Michael Oakeshott, *A New Guide to the Derby* (London, Faber, 1947). "Contemporary British Politics," *Cambridge Journal*, I: 474–490 (1947–1948), does not show Oakeshott at his best as a political theorist and confirms Masao Marayuma's remarks about the difficulty of unfailing abstinence from mere polemics discussed in Chapter One.

Hannah Arendt's principal works are *The Origins of Totalitarianism* (mentioned earlier); *The Human Condition* (Garden City, N.Y., Doubleday, 1963); *Between Past and Future: Six Exercises in Political Thought* (New York, Meridian Books, 1963); *Eichmann in Jerusalem* (New York, Viking, 1962); and *On Revolution* (New York, Viking, 1963).

In addition to *Power: The Natural History of Its Growth* (London, Hutchinson, 1947), and *Sovereignty: An Inquiry into the Political Good* (Cambridge, Cambridge University Press, 1957), Bertrand de Jouvenel's writings include the *Pure Theory of Politics* (New Haven, Yale University Press, 1963); "The Idea of Welfare," *Cambridge Journal*, V: 647–661 (August, 1952); "A Discussion of Freedom," *Cambridge Journal*, VI: 707–724 (September, 1953); and "Essai sur la politique de Rousseau" in his edition of *Du Contrat Social de Jean-Jacques Rousseau* (Geneva Editions du Cheval Oilé, 1947), pp. 3–140.

For Leo Strauss, see, inter alia, *Philosophie und Gesetz: Beiträge zum Verständnis Maimunis und seiner Vorläufer* (Berlin, Schocken Verlag, 1935), which reveals deep concern over the problem of the tension between revelation and reason, orthodoxy and "enlightenment" in Jewish philosophy; *The Political Philosophy of Hobbes*, Elsa M. Sinclair, trans. (New York, Oxford University Press, 1936); "The Literary Character of the Guide for the Perplexed," in Salo Wittmayer Baron, ed., *Essays on Maimonides* (New York, Columbia University Press, 1941), pp. 37–92; "On a New Interpretation of Plato's Political Philosophy," *Social Research*, XIII (1946); *On Tyranny—An Interpretation of Xenophon's Hiero* (New York, Free Press, 1948); *Persecution and the Art of Writing* (New York, Free Press, 1952); *Philosophical Essays by Isaac Husik*, edited with Milton C. Nahm (Oxford, Blackwell, 1952); *Natural Right and History*

(Chicago, Chicago University Press, 1953); *Thoughts on Machiavelli* (New York, Free Press, 1958); *The City and Man* (Chicago, Rand McNally, 1964); and the intellectual autobiography contained in the reissue and translation of his work on Spinoza, *Spinoza's Critique of Religion* (New York, Schocken, 1965). Then there is Strauss's Epilogue to Herbert Storing, ed., *Essays on the Scientific Study of Politics* (New York, Holt, Rinehart and Winston, 1962).

A bibliography of Eric Voegelin's extensive writings may be found in Hannah Arendt and Alois Dempf, eds., *Politische Ordnung und Menschliche Existenz: Festgabe für Eric Voegelin* (Munich, 1962). If only one of Voegelin's major writings is consulted, it should be *Order and History*, 3 vols. (Baton Rouge, Louisiana State University Press, 1956, 1957), rather than the brief and perhaps excessively schematic *New Science of Politics* (Chicago, Chicago University Press, 1952). The fourth and final volume of *Order and History*, which will be organized around topics of political science, when it appears, will be of major significance.

Voegelin's most recent book is a collection of essays in German entitled *Anamnesis: Zur Theorie der Geschichte und Politik* (Munich, Piper Verlag, 1966). The volume is divided into three parts: "Recollection," "Experience and History," and "The Order of the Consciousness." Some of the material included in this volume dates back to 1943, but most of the essays, and in particular the lengthier ones, were written over the last three years. Part I contains a moving tribute to the late Alfred Schütz, a critique of Husserl's phenomenological philosophy expressed in the form of a lengthy letter to Schütz, a significant essay indicating the difficulties facing and the necessity for a radically new philosophy of consciousness (or epistemology) and some "anamnetic experiments" of Voegelin, in which he recalls certain early and basic experiences which have a bearing on his theory of consciousness. Part II includes his article "Historiogenesis" (originally published in 1960) which challenges the conventional interpretations of Babylonian and Egyptian conceptions of history as cyclical, essays on Aristotle's conception of the Right by Nature and on the concept of nature, an article on the Mongol Orders of Submission as a document for the history of order, essays on Bakunin and Mill, and an important contribution to the philosophy of history entitled "Eternal Being in Time." Part III, a lengthy analysis bearing the title "What Is Political Reality," and which is an expansion of a lecture given to the 1965 annual convention of the German Political Science Association, draws together the themes discussed in the preceding sections and affords an excellent indication of how Voegelin conceives the task of contemporary political theory. Particularly noteworthy for our concerns in this volume is the section encompassing pp. 328–333; there Voegelin comes to grips in characteristically radical (in the proper sense of this word) fashion with the current intellectual situation and the extraordinary difficulty and yet live possibility of achieving a breakthrough beyond ideology and "secondary ideologies." Secondary ideologies are political movements which are burdened by their reaction against the primary ideologies (Nazism, Fascism, and Communism) so that they have been unable to perceive the need for a radically fresh attempt to articulate a theory of right order in human existence on the basis of man's openness toward world-transcendent Being. Voegelin is also preparing a lengthy work *Hitler und die Deutschen* which should be a major contribution to the understanding of Nazi totalitarianism.

Other writers who should be cited here as contributing significantly to the revival of political theory today are Albert Camus, Karl Barth, Carl J. Friedrich, Etienne Gilson, John H. Hallowell, Karl Jaspers, Jacques Maritain, Hans J. Morgenthau, Reinhold Niebuhr, Yves Simon, Hans Urs von Balthasar, and Eric Weil. Friedrich's major work, *Man and His Government: An Empirical Theory of Politics* (New York, McGraw-Hill, 1963), deserves special mention because of its truly exceptional grasp of recent and traditional political theory and its creative reinterpretation of this vast literature. Hans J. Morgenthau's paper "The Purpose of Political Science," in James C. Charlesworth, ed., *A Design for Political Science: Scope, Objectives, and Methods* (Philadelphia, Annals of the American Academy of Political and Social Science, December, 1966), 63–79, is a trenchant indictment of a political science that either overconforms to the existing order and its premises or preoccupies itself with trivial and irrelevant problems to the neglect of fundamental ones. A critical political science must tread the narrow path between iconoclasm (opposition for its own sake) and complacent conformity. Morgenthau may in this paper veer too closely to iconoclasm (although his discussion on pp. 133–139 qualifies some of his harsher statements), but there is no question but that he has done political theory in our time a signal service by writing this essay. Morgenthau properly takes Socrates as a model for the genuinely critical political scientist—the man who seeks truth above all else. For Eric Weil, see his *Philosophie Politique* (Paris, J. Vrin, 1956), and Pierre Hassner, "La philosophie politique de M. Eric Weil," *Revue française de Science politique*, VIII: 423–431 (June, 1958). For a discussion of recent Christian political thought see Kenneth W. Thompson, "Beyond National Interest: A Critical Evaluation of Reinhold Niebuhr's Theory of International Politics," *The Review of Politics*, XVII (April, 1955), 167–188—the most able brief summary of Niebuhr's political teaching—and Dante

Germino, "Two Types of Recent Christian Political Thought," *The Journal of Politics*, XXI: 455–486 (August, 1959).

Nicolas Berdyaev's works, although uneven in quality, contain moments of profound theoretical insight. See especially his posthumously published *Truth and Revelation* (New York, Collier Books, 1962) which can be profitably read along with Voegelin's *Order and History*. Berdyaev, along with other writers in the existentialist camp, normally attacks Aristotle and Aquinas for supposedly objectifying man and looking at reality in terms of an untenable subject-object relationship. Berdyaev eschews subjectivism, however, and calls for philosophy to press on beyond the subject-object dichotomy. It is difficult to see how a Thomist could oppose such a call, given the analogical character Thomism sees in all symbolization. So long as the crucial fact of man's existence in openness toward the world-transcendent God is recognized, there are many possible ways of expressing philosophically the mystery of man's participation in Being.

One of the principal tasks of Western political theory in the coming decades is to benefit from the insights and perspectives of the other great civilizations, especially in the Oriental world. Highly significant in this regard are the many books of Mircea Eliade. In particular, see *Cosmos and History: The Myth of the Eternal Return* (New York, Harper & Row, 1959); *Images and Symbols* (New York, Sheed and Ward, 1961); and *Myths, Dreams and Mysteries. The Encounter between Contemporary Faiths and Archaic Realities* (New York, Harper & Row, 1960). Eliade's disciplined analysis brings out the richness of mythical as distinct from philosophical ("Socratic") thought and subjects the contempt for mythical thought in nineteenth century positivism to telling criticism.

INDEX

Acton, Lord, 37
Ainslie, Douglas, on Croce, 161
Allegory of the cave, 8, 19, 22, 28, 47
Anthropocentric humanism, 18, 28–31, 35, 43
Anthropology, of Aristotle, 23
of Plato, 19, 174
of Voegelin, 168–174
Aquinas, Thomas, on chiliasm, 25
misunderstood by behavioralists, 2
on natural law, 23–24
theory, 14, 36, 41
Arendt, Hannah, in America, 217
on behaviorism, 140
contributions to revival of political
theory, 14, 139–144, 215, 231
on dangers in modern society, 143
discussed bibliographically, 242
and Jouvenel, 146, 148–149
in resistance, 183
Aris, Reinhold, 10n.
Aristotle, anthropology of, 23
applied to Bentham, 39
elite theory, 110
empiricist, 192
on leisure, 223–224
Meehan on, 207
misunderstood by behavioralists, 2,
3, 207
on origin of philosophy, 80
spoudaios, 23
Strauss on, 150, 153, 156
as transcendent theorist, 7–9, 42
Arnold, Matthew, on criticism, 9, 9n.,
136
Augustine, on chiliasm, 14, 41
focus on perennial issues, 25, 44
on incarnation, 25
Averroism, and Leo Strauss, 160
Ayer, A. J., Meehan on, 208
not a political conservative, 78

on value judgments, 76n.
on verification, 74, 75

Bacon, Francis, 7
Bakunin, M. A., precursor of totali-
tarianism, 32
Balthasar, Urs von, on Barth, 142
contributor to revival of theory,
166, 215, 244
Barnes, Harry E., 4
Barrés, A. M., 104
Barth, Hans, on de Tracy, 49n., 50
Barth, Karl, 142, 215
Behavioralism, Arendt on, 140
Bentley, 3
and the closed society, 187–214
passim, 233–234
diversity in, 190–191
and empiricism, 192–193
Froman on, 3
issues involved, 212–214
Lasswell, 190, 202–206
Lundberg, 194
Meehan, 206–212
opposing classical theory, 1–4
origins in Watson, 193–194
Simon, 190, 198–202
Skinner, 195–198
Strauss on, 156–161
Benda, Julien, prophecy for society,
187–188
resistance to positivism, 102–104
on role of the intellectual, 102–104
Bentham, Jeremy, as publicist, 16n.,
39
Bentley, Arthur F., 3
Berdyaev, Nicolas, 215
discussed bibliographically, 245
Bergson, Henri, as democrat, 101
inconsistency in, 99
metaphysics, 89–90, 97–98

Bergson (*Continued*)
"open society," 96–101
theoretical perspective, 89–90
Voegelin on, 167
Blitzer, Charles, 40
Bluhm, William T., 68n.
Bobbio, Norberto, on elite theory, 113–114, 129n.
Bochenski, I. M., on nineteenth- and twentieth-century political thought, 94n., 241
on Scheler, 105n.
Bodin, Jean, classification of, 14, 49
idea of the state, 95n.
Boorstin, Daniel, 217
Botero, Giovanni, 14
Bottomore, T. B., on equality and elites, 219, 241
Bradley, F. H., 139
Brecht, Arnold, on positivization of the social sciences, 68–69, 76n., 82, 105n., 239
Burke, Edmund, as publicist, 39–40
Burzio, Filippo, 111, 113

Campanella, Thomas, 42
Camus, Albert, on messianism, 31
as political thinker, 240
Cantril, Hadley, 190
Carnap, Rudolf, as logical positivist, 72–73, 208
Chiliasm, 14, 41, 47, 240
Cicero, 8
Civil theology, 29
Cobban, Alfred, on decline of political theory, 1, 1n., 4–5, 16, 16n.
on separation of political science and theory, 82
on theorist as partisan, 9, 35
Cohen, Carl, 15n.
Cohn, Norman, on messianic humanism and chiliasm, 47, 240
Collingwood, R. G., political wisdom of, 80, 108
Comte, Auguste, deification of humanity, 213
historical stages, 52–53

ideologist, 28, 51–56
influence on Lasswell, 203
and Meehan, 208
messianism of, 31, 43, 51
positivism of, 51–56, 67
similarity with Marx, 55
Condillac, Etienne B. de, 49
Condorcet, Marquis de, 14
Confucius, 3
Corradini, Enrico, 94
Crick, Bernard, on American political science, 68, 217
on Lasswell, 202, 204n.
on Oakeshott, 132n.
Croce, Benedetto, anti-Fascist, 93
on Aristotle, 91
influence of, 90–91
as radical immanentist, 92–95
resistance to positivism, 90–96
on transcendence, 91, 95, 139
Cushman, Robert, on Plato, 11n.

Dahl, Robert A., 1, 113
D'Annunzio, Gabriele, 103
Dante, 39
Darwin, Charles, 208
Dempf, Alois, as contemporary theorist, 166, 169
on Hegel, 30
on Voegelin, 162n.
Descartes, René, originator of term "system," 166
rejected by de Tracy, 49–50
Dorso, Guido, achievements of, 128–129
analytical concepts, 127
biography, 115
divisions in society, 119–120
"fission" in ruling classes, 121–122
parties, 122–127
political teaching of, 114–116
terminology, 116–118
Drucker, Peter, 16n.
Duverger, Maurice, 110

Easton, David, on decline of theory, 1, 1n., 4–5

Easton (*Continued*)
on fact and value, 71
Eichmann, Adolph, Arendt on, 140
Eliade, Mircea, discussed bibliographically, 245
Eliot, T. S., 237
Elite theory, Aristotle, 110
Bobbio, 113–114, 129n.
Dahl, 113
Dorso, 109–129
Duverger, 110
Friedrich, 113
Michels, 109–113
Mills, 118
Mosca, 109–113
Pareto, 109–113
Elites, importance of, 232
Elliott, W. Y., 101
Empiricism, in history of political theory, 192, 208
Engels, Friedrich, 65
Epicureanism, 24
Epistēmē politikē, challenged by positivism, 70
defined, 7
Meehan's ignorance of, 210
Plato and Aristotle on, 9
and reality, 38
Strauss, 154
Voegelin, 163, 167–182
Equality, crisis of, 219–220
Eulau, Heinz, 190–191n.

Feigl, Herbert, 72
Feuerbach, Ludwig, 45, 62–63
Filmer, Robert, 14
Fourier, Charles, 31
Freud, influenced Lasswell, 203
Friedrich, C. J., contributor to revival of theory, 215
on elites, 113, 244
Froman, Lewis W., Jr., behavioralist concept of theory, 3, 3n.
on verification, 75–76
Fromm, Erich, misinterpretation of Marx, 57

on transcendence, 185n.
utopianism, 183

Garosci, Aldo, on Gramsci, 229
Gelasius I, on Two Realms, 25
Gellner, Ernest, on linguistic philosophy, 78, 241
on logical positivism, 73, 241
Gentile, Giovanni, apologist for Mussolini, 93
Giles of Rome, 14
Gnosticism, discussed by Voegelin, 181–182
history of, 181n.
Gobetti, Piero, 111
Gobineau, on "race-mixing," 219
Goethe, J. W. von, 9
Gossett, Thomas F., history of racism, 221n.
Gramsci, Antonio, as communist intellectual, 114–115, 229
Grant, G. P., on pragmatism and Protestantism, 188–189
Green, T. H., on positive freedom, 224–225
as theorist, 14, 108
Guardini, Romano, on modern theory, 5, 169

Hadas, Moses, attack on Voegelin and Jaspers, 171n.
Hallowell, J. H., contributor to revival of theory, 215, 244
on goodness and being, 83n.
Harrington, James, as publicist, 39–40
Hartmann, Nicolai, and metaphysics, 89, 107
Hartz, Louis, 217
Hauriou, Maurice, 16n.
Hegel, G. W. F., on goals of philosophy, 34–36
order in, 29
separation of church and state, 30
as theorist, 2, 4, 24, 28, 43
Voegelin on, 177–178
Heidegger, Martin, 9, 104

Helvetius, C. A., 49
Heraclitus, precursor of Plato, 18, 168, 174
  on theory, 6
Hobbes, Thomas, in anthropocentric subtradition, 42–43
  dilution of the paradigm, 41–42
  not messianist, 33–34
  Strauss on, 149, 153
  as theorist, 14, 28–29, 41–43, 65, 207, 218
Hooker, Richard, intellectual honesty of, 44, 185
  theocentric humanism, 26–27, 27n.
  as theorist, 1, 14
Horwitz, Robert, on Lasswell, 202–203
Hughes, Stuart, 241
Hume, David, 208
Husserl, Edmund, phenomenology of, 10, 104–105

Ideological reductionism, see Reductionism
Idéologues, political program, 50–51
  relation to Marx, 57
Ideology, challenge to theory, 45–66 passim
  in Comte, 51–56
  contrasted with theory, 46, 66–67
  defined, 51
  in Marx, 56–66
  messianic implications of, 52
  in de Tracy, 48–51
Immanence, defined, 27
Incarnation, discussed by Augustine, 25
  by Voegelin, 181

Jaeger, Werner, on Athens, 235
Jaspers, Karl, contribution to revival of theory, 89, 215
  Hadas on, 171n.
Jemolo, A. C., on Croce, 90n.
Joachim of Flora, 178
John XXIII, 235
Jouvenel, Bertrand de, contribution to

revival of theory, 14, 183, 215, 242
  on Marsilius, 39, 39n.

Kaplan, Abraham, 2, 2n.
Kelsen, Hans, 72
Kierkegaärd, Soren, 89
Kraft, Victor, 72

Laski, Harold, 16n., 137
LaPalombara, Joseph P., 229n.
Laslett, Peter, 1, 1n.
Lasswell, Harold D., and behavioralism and the closed society, 190–191, 194, 202–206
  contrasted with Voegelin, 213
  Eulau on, 190n.
  on fact and value, 3, 203
  goals of, 204–206
  influences on, 203
  logical positivism, 71
  misinterpretation of theory, 2, 2n., 3, 4
  as political messianist, 202–206
  scientism, 203
Leap in being, in Voegelin, 171n., 180
Lenin, V. I., 62, 65
Leone, Enrico, 101
Lewis, C. S., 56, 143
Liberalism, new, 226–228
  See also Theocentric liberalism.
Libido dominandi, ideologists and, 31, 38, 46
  in Marx, 60
  in Skinner, 197–198
Linguistic philosophy, 72, 76–81, 241
Lippmann, Walter, 217
Locke, John, anthropocentric liberalism, 227
  inadequacy of, 219
  Meehan on, 207
  Strauss on, 153
  as theorist, 14
Loewith, Karl, 223n.
Logical positivism, conservatism in, 77–78

Logical positivism (*Continued*)
  discussed bibliographically, 240–241
  Gellner's description of, 73
  orientation of, 73
  on verification, 74–76
  in Vienna Circle, 72–73
Lubac, Henri de, 213, 240
Lundberg, George A., 194

McGovern, William, 101
Machiavelli, Niccolò, and civil religion, 29
  dilution of the paradigm, 33, 41–44
  and elites, 110
  empiricist, 192
  Strauss on, 149, 152, 152n.
  as theorist, 2, 3, 14, 28, 114, 156
McKenzie, Robert, study of British parties, 126
MacLeish, Archibald, on freedom, 217
Maistre, Joseph de, as publicist, 14, 39–40
Mannheim, Karl, 151
Marayuma, Masao, 12, 12n.
Marcus Aurelius, 24, 96
Maritain, Jacques, contribution to revival of theory, 14, 175, 183, 215
  on philosophy, 11, 11n.
  on theocentric and anthropocentric humanism, 17
Marsilius of Padua, 39
Marx, Karl, on Hegel, 65
  ideological reductionism of, 56–67
  as ideologist, 28–29, 45–47, 177–178
  and idéologues, 57
  influence on Lasswell, 203
  messianic humanism of, 43
  on philosophy, 59
  on Plato, 65
  on "reality," 57–61
  on science, 60
  similarity to Comte, 55

temporalism of, 214
  on theocentric humanism, 58–59
  on theory, 7
  totalitarianism, 66
Matson, Floyd W., 6n., 205, 215n., 241
Maurras, Charles, 93–94, 102
Mazzini, Giuseppe, 32
Meehan, Eugene J., hopes for future, 209–212
  on Plato, 210–211
  rejection of traditional political science, 207–208
  "scientific revolution" of behavioralism, 206–212
Meisel, James, on Mosca, 241
Messianic humanism, 30–32, 43–44, 46
Messianism, consequences of, 190
  in Lasswell, 202
  in Skinner, 197
  Talmon on, 240
Metanoia, 31, 220, 236
Metastasis, 31
Michels, Roberto, 109–113, 117n., 119
Mill, John Stuart, 3, 39, 54, 227
Mills, C. Wright, 118
Modernity, crisis of, 189, 218–219
Montaigne, Michel de, 149
Montesquieu, Baron de, 14, 156
Moore, G. E., 78
Morgenthau, Hans, discussed bibliographically, 215, 217, 244
Mosca, Gaetano, elite theory, 108, 112
  empiricist, 192
  inadequacy of, 90
  opponent of Fascism, 110

Neopositivism, defined, 68n.
  influence on contemporary political science, 75–76, 187–214 *passim*
Neurath, Otto von, 72, 77
Niebuhr, Reinhold, 14, 21, 215, 217
Niess, Robert J., on Benda, 104n.

Nietzsche, F. W., 104, 174n.
Nous, in Stoicism, 24
  in Voegelin, 164

Oakeshott, Michael, Collingwood's
  influence on, 108
  contributions to revival of theory,
    14, 131–139, 149, 232
  discussed bibliographically, 241–242
  on experience, 133–134
  on ideology, 137–138
  on political philosophy, 136
Open society, 214–237 passim
Oppenheim, Felix, 71
Order, science of, 16n., 66, 163, 231
Owen, Robert, 42

Pacem in terris, 235n.
Paradigm, dilution of, 32–34, 42–43,
    176
  ideologists attack on, 46
  Machiavelli on, 33
  of the open society, 229
  Plato on, 37–39
  Rousseau on, 33, 43
  as useful model, 174–176
Pareto, Vilfredo, 92, 109
Parmenides, 18
Pericles, 232
Phaleas of Chalcedon, 14
Philip of Opus, 21n.
Plato, and allegory of cave, 8, 19,
    22, 28
  anthropology of, 19, 174
  attacked by Meehan, 207, 210–211
  behavioralists on, 2, 3
  on best regime, 20–21
  character types of, 19–20
  Cushman on, 11n.
  on elites, 110
  Hegel on, 218
  on open society, 230–231
  as political realist, 20–21
  Strauss on, 150, 153
  theocentric humanism of, 18
  on theory, 7–9
  on transcendence, 28

Polanyi, Michael, 74, 74n., 215n.
Political theory, approaches to, 5–6
  of Arendt, 139–144
  attacks on, 45–67, 67–87
  contemporary revival of, 131–161,
    228
  decline of, 1–17, 67–68
  and demythologizing of vocabulary,
    227–233
  of Dorso, 114–129
  ideological reductionists on, 45–67
  of Jouvenel, 144–149
  marks of authentic, 37–44
  meaning of, 5–13
  and new liberalism, 219
  of Oakeshott, 132–139, 144
  and open society, 214–237 passim
  and political education, 231–233
  positivists on, 67–87
  and racism, 220–221
  and religion, 231
  Strauss on, 149–161
  survival among elitists, 108–130
  tasks of, 17n., 32, 216–218, 237
  and theocentric liberalism, 221–222
  as tradition of inquiry, 17–44
    passim
  of Voegelin, 161–185
Polybius, 33
Popper, Karl, 72, 100–101
Positivism, axiological, 81–84
  Brecht on, 68–69
  conceived by Comte, 52–56
  diversity in, 69
  of Easton, 81
  in elitists, 111
  in linguistic philosophy, 76–81
  logical, 72–76
  resistance to, 89–109 passim
  in social sciences, 67–68, 239
  of Waldo, 81–82
  in Weber, 84–87
Praxis, in Marxism, 62–66
Protagoras, 18, 46
Proudhon, P. J., 32

Quality, crisis of, 219, 222–227

Racism, 219, 221n., 233
Radbruch, Gustav, on values, 71
Reductionism of Comte, Tracy, and Marx, 45–67
   opposed by Croce, 92
Reichenbach, Hans, 76n.
Revelation, in Judaism and Christianity, 24–25
Revival of political theory, *see* Political theory
Riemer, Neal, 1n.
Rodman, John R., on Green, 225n.
Rousseau, Jean Jacques, 2, 3, 14, 16n., 28–30, 33, 38, 42–43

Saint-Simon, Henri Comte de, 31, 56
Salvatorelli, Luigi, on Croce and Maurras, 93–94
Sartori, Giovanni, on elites, 129n.
Scheler, Max, on metaphysics and theology, 106
   and phenomenological school, 6, 89, 104–106
Schlick, Moritz, as positivist, 72, 77, 208
Schmidt, Richard, on positivism, 70
Schmoelz, Franz-Martin, on Weber, 85n.
Schuetz, Alfred, 10
Scientism, *see* Behavioralism; Comte; Lasswell
Simon, Herbert, and behavioralism, 4, 71, 190, 194, 198–199
   on fact and value, 71, 198–199
   tension in thought of, 200, 200n.
Simon, Yves, 215
Skinner, B. F., behavioralist utopianism, 190, 195–198, 203, 205
Sociology, as conceived by Comte, 52–56
Socrates, 19, 22, 37
Spengler, Oswald, 179
Spoudaios, 70, 160, 169–174, 177, 183
Stoicism, 23–25
Storing, Herbert J., on Simon, 198–199

Strauss, Leo, on Aristotle, 154–155
   on behavioralism, 155–157
   contribution to revival of political theory, 149–161, 183, 215
   discussed bibliographically, 242–243
   on Machiavelli, 152
   methods, 151–152
   on positivism, 75, 108
   reception in America, 217
Summum bonum, in anthropocentric humanism, 27
   Christian view of, 26
   in gnosticism, 182
   Strauss on, 160, 191n., 197, 235

Talmon, J. L., on messianism, 57, 240
Theocentric humanism, of Aristotle, 23
   in Christianity, 26
   discussed by Lubac, 213
   in Hooker, 26–27, 43
   in modern theory, 28–31
   in Plato, 18
   sources of, 24
Theocentric liberalism, of John XXIII, 235n.
   need for, 221–222
   and open society, 234–237
Theoria, defined, 8n.
   impossibility of in Marx, 61–62
   in Plato and Aristotle, 8
   in Voegelin, 163
   See also Political theory
Thompson, J. A. K., 23
Thompson, Kenneth W., 217n., 244
Thucydides, 153
Tocqueville, Alexis de, on Gobineau, 219
Totalitarianism, in Marx, 66
Toynbee, Arnold, 179
Tracy, Destutt de, ideology of, 48–51
Transcendence, defined, 27
   in Fromm, 185n.
   in Hegel, 35
   in Plato, 28
   in Voegelin, 164–165, 185n.

Treitschke, Heinrich von, 103

Utopianism, Campanella, 42
Fromm, 185n.
Owen, 42
political theory distinguished from,
41-42
Skinner, 195-198
Voegelin rejects, 175

Vienna Circle, 54, 68n., 74, 207
See also Logical positivism
Voegelin, Eric, in America, 217
contrasted with Lasswell, 213
contributions to revival of political theory, 14, 161-185 passim,
215
discussed bibliographically, 243-
244
epistēmē politikē of, 163, 167-182
on good society, 174-177
on limits of knowledge, 107
on metastasis and messianic humanism, 31, 47
metaphysics of, 166-167
on order and history, 177-182
philosophical anthropology of, 168-
174

on value, 82-83

Waldo, Dwight, 4n., 7-8
Watkins, Frederick, 33
Watson, John B., founder of behavioralism, 193
Weber, Max, on fact and value, 85
limitations of theory, 87
as representative of best positivism,
69
on value-free social science, 13n.,
84, 172, 201
Weldon, T. D., on purpose of philosophy, 78-79, 241
Whitehead, Alfred North, 89, 107-
108
Willner, A. R., on ethnocentricism,
228n.
Wittgenstein, Ludwig, influence on
linguistic philosophy, 72, 76-77
208
Wren, Matthew, 40

Xenophanes, 18

Zeno, 23
Zola, Emile, 223